Gender in Georgia

Gender in Georgia
*Feminist Perspectives on Culture, Nation,
and History in the South Caucasus*

Edited by
Maia Barkaia and Alisse Waterston

berghahn
NEW YORK • OXFORD
www.berghahnbooks.com

First published in 2018 by
Berghahn Books
www.berghahnbooks.com

© 2018, 2021 Maia Barkaia and Alisse Waterston
First paperback edition published in 2021

All rights reserved. Except for the quotation of short passages for the purposes of criticism and review, no part of this book may be reproduced in any form or by any means, electronic or mechanical, including photocopying, recording, or any information storage and retrieval system now known or to be invented, without written permission of the publisher.

Library of Congress Cataloging-in-Publication Data

Names: Barkaia, Maia, editor. | Waterston, Alisse, 1951– editor.
Title: Gender in Georgia : feminist perspectives on culture, nation, and history in the South Caucasus / edited by Maia Barkaia & Alisse Waterston.
Description: 1st Edition. | New York : Berghahn Books, [2017] | Includes bibliographical references and index.
Identifiers: LCCN 2017037765 | ISBN 9781785336751 (hardback : alk. paper) | ISBN 9781785336768 (ebook)
Subjects: LCSH: Women—Georgia (Republic)—Social conditions. | Sex role—Georgia (Republic) | Women's rights—Georgia (Republic) | Abused women—Georgia (Republic) | Women—Georgia (Republic)—Political activity—History.
Classification: LCC HQ1726.64 .G46 2017 | DDC 305.4094758—dc23
LC record available at https://lccn.loc.gov/2017037765

British Library Cataloguing in Publication Data

A catalogue record for this book is available from the British Library

ISBN 978-1-78533-675-1 hardback
ISBN 978-1-80073-220-9 paperback
ISBN 978-1-78533-676-8 ebook

In solidarity with the women of Georgia, past and present, engaged in struggle, knowledge production, and activism toward the goal of social justice transformation for the benefit of all.

Contents

List of Figures ix

Acknowledgements xi

Introduction
Contextualizing Gender in Georgia: Nation, Culture, Power,
and Politics 1
Alisse Waterston

Part I. Power and Politics

Chapter 1
Pioneer Women: "Herstories" of Feminist Movements in Georgia 21
Lela Gaprindashvili

Chapter 2
"The Country of the Happiest Women"? Ideology and Gender in
Soviet Georgia 33
Maia Barkaia

Chapter 3
"The West" and Georgian "Difference": Discursive Politics of Gender
and Sexuality in Georgia 47
Tamar Tskhadadze

Chapter 4
Overcoming the "Delay" Paradigm: New Approaches to Socialist
Women's Activism in Georgia and Poland 61
Magdalena Grabowska

Chapter 5
Women's Political Representation in Post-Soviet Georgia 78
Ketevan Chkheidze

Part II. Violence

Chapter 6
The Domestic Violence Challenge to Soviet Women's
Empowerment Policies   95
Tamar Sabedashvili

Chapter 7
Domestic Violence in Georgia: State and Community Responses,
2006–2015   110
Nino Javakhishvili and Nino Butsashvili

Chapter 8
Remembering the Past: Narratives of Displaced Women
from Abkhazia   125
Nargiza Arjevanidze

Chapter 9
Displacement, State Violence, and Gender Roles: The Case of
Internally Displaced and Violence-Affected Georgian Women   138
Joanna Regulska, Beth Mitchneck, and Peter Kabachnik

Part III. Identities, Representations, and Resistance

Chapter 10
Images of "The New Woman" in Soviet Georgian Silent Films   155
Salome Tsopurashvili

Chapter 11
Gender Equality: Still a Disputed Value in Georgian Society   172
Nana Sumbadze

Chapter 12
Georgian Women Migrants: Experiences Abroad and at Home   181
Tamar Zurabishvili, Maia Mestvirishvili, and Tinatin Zurabishvili

Chapter 13
Being Transgender in Georgia   194
Natia Gvianishvili

Chapter 14
Tracing the LGBT Movement in the Republic of Georgia: Stories
of Activists   205
Anna Rekhviashvili

Afterword   223
Elizabeth Cullen Dunn

Index   234

Figures

Figure 0.1	Tin Roofs of Tbilisi	1
Figure 10.1–10.6	*Prison Cell 79*, directed by Zakaria Berishvili, 1929	159–161
Figures 10.7–10.9	*Eliso,* directed by Nikoloz Shengelaia, 1928	164
Figures 10.10–10.18	*Saba,* directed by Mikheil Chiaureli, 1929	168–169

Figures

Acknowledgments

There are few scholarly works published in gender studies from post-Soviet countries, particularly those in Central Asia and the South Caucasus. This volume helps fill that gap, offering voices from feminist academics and activists that are all too often ignored or silenced, locally and internationally. *Gender in Georgia* announces that this state of affairs will be no more. We are deeply grateful to the contributors to this volume, the majority of whom are Georgian scholars specializing in gender studies who helped establish the discipline at Tbilisi State University. Their chapters are complemented by contributions from international feminist scholars who have worked in Georgia. Altogether, this collaborative endeavor is a project of knowledge production and dissemination that affirms the value of gender studies as a significant area of engaged scholarship. The editors' royalties from this book will go to the Gender Studies Programme, Tbilisi State University, as a tribute to the extraordinary effort of the Georgian scholars who established it.

We extend our deepest thanks to Marion Berghahn and Vivian Berghahn for believing in this project, and to those who offered thoughtful reviews of the manuscript. We greatly appreciate Burke Gerstenschlager's shepherding of the peer review and editorial processes, Caroline Kuhtz's careful attention to the production process, and Nigel Smith's sharp copyediting eye. Our gratitude extends to contributor Salome Tsopurashvili, whose powerful photograph graces the cover of the book.

Maia Barkaia expresses her deep sense of gratitude to Alisse Waterston, co-editor and collaborator, who stimulated the idea for and nurtured this edited volume. I would have not ventured on this path but for Alisse's encouragement and brilliance; she set high standards and fostered excitement. Both this book and I have been enriched by Alisse's insights, accessibility, and sheer human kindness. My gratitude extends to all the contributors to *Gender in Georgia,* who believe the volume needs to exist.

Thanks are due to the colleagues and students of the Gender Studies Programme. I am much obliged to my friends and comrades for their intellectual and personal friendship, and for discussions that always helped. And finally my thanks to my mother, who has been the source of the deepest sustenance.

Alisse Waterston gives special thanks to Maia Barkaia, colleague and collaborator on this project. Maia's insights are always spot-on, she is a pleasure to work with, and I am grateful for her warm friendship and collegiality. I offer special thanks to all the contributors to *Gender in Georgia* for their belief in the volume, their work, and their efforts to keep on track and on schedule. It is my honor to be a part of *Gender in Georgia,* and my good fortune to work with brilliant scholars, activists, and friends in Tbilisi.

My gratitude extends to the Open Society Institute Europe Foundation of the Open Society Foundations for naming me International Scholar, which was administered by the International Higher Education Support Program. As International Scholar, I was afforded the opportunity to travel and work in Georgia over a three-year period (2012–2015). *Gender in Georgia* is a direct outgrowth of this program. Among many friends and colleagues in Georgia, I extend many thanks to Tinatin Bregvadze, Marine Chitashvili, Ketevan Khutsishvili, Lela Kiria, Diana Lezhava, Gender Studies Programme Chair Tamar Sabedashvili, and Joseph Salukvadze. With special affection, I thank *deda, mama,* Khatuna and Tamar Tskhadadze, past-chair of the Gender Studies Programme.

For their love and sustenance, I thank Leah Horowitz, Adrienne Waterston, David Waterston, and Matthew and Beth Zuckerman. None of my work would be possible without Howard Horowitz, my husband and intellectual partner. I thank him for the constancy of his love and support.

Introduction

Contextualizing Gender in Georgia
Nation, Culture, Power, and Politics

Alisse Waterston

Figure 0.1 Tin Roofs of Tbilisi. Photo by the author

Viewpoints

I introduce this volume on *Gender in Georgia* with my first impressions of a remarkable place that has been undergoing enormous transformation for over two decades since the Georgian Parliament declared independence from the Soviet Union on 9 April 1991. My travels from New York to Tbilisi go by way of Istanbul, where "East and West combine gracefully," and by means of the International Scholars Program of the Open Society Institute (Smith 2006). As an international scholar, I am formally assigned to students and scholars working to establish and grow the Gender Studies Programme for undergraduate and graduate students at Tbilisi State University (TSU). Over the course of three years (2013–15), I come to know and appreciate the women, the constraints under which they operate, their projects, the contradictions of their efforts and of my participation in them. This book project emerges from that collective labor.

My first trip to Georgia brings unexpected adventure. My plane arrives early on a Friday in late March (2013) and I am brought by taxi to the university where I meet my new colleagues—they include Tamar Tskhadadze, Tamar Sabedashvili, Anna Rekhviashvili, Diana Lezhava, Nargiza Arjevanidze, Salome Tsopurashvili, and Lela Kiria. We make social plans for the weekend and work plans for the week. I soon find my way to my lodgings, a modest boutique hotel up a steep hill that reminds me of the streets of San Francisco. The hotel is within a set of eclectic buildings, many of which are in various stages of repair, disrepair and dilapidation. The hotel accommodations are comfortable and sparse, and I have a lovely view from my room. I see mountains in the distance and the tin roofs of Tbilisi directly below. The streets are windy and narrow, and the 1-2-3 story buildings that look like residences are a jumble of styles, sizes, and materials—wood, cement, stone, and tin. I wonder how these dwellings fit into the history of this old city, and look forward to learning more from my new friends in the coming days.

Morning comes and Lela gives me a six-hour walking tour of old and new Tbilisi, making stops at several Georgian Orthodox churches, including the seventh-century Sioni Cathedral, the sixth-century Anchiskhati Basilica and the thirteenth-century Metekhi Church with the tomb of St. Shushanik, a fifth-century martyr who, legend has it, was imprisoned for refusing to give up her Christian faith. The pungent smell of incense stays with me as we move from icon to icon, service to service, and chant to chant. We stroll along the wide boulevard of Rustaveli Street and spy the architectural curiosity that is the hyper-illuminated Bridge of Peace. Each time we cross any of the streets of Tbilisi, Lela takes my hand protectively.

That would be the last day for months I would be able to take such a walk. On Sunday, Tamar Tskhadadze, then chair of the Gender Studies Programme, picks me up by car for a drive to the Mtskheta region and the Jvari Church, a revered, holy Georgian site and favorite tourist attraction atop Mt. Armazi. We pass through remnants marking fifteen hundred years of regional Christian piety and power, catch a vista of the Caucasus Mountains and watch the confluence of the Aragvi and the polluted Mtkvari rivers below. Wending our way home, I ask about the plastic bags tied into bows that adorn the trees alongside the curving road. Suddenly the grill of a luxury Mercedes sports utility vehicle (SUV) accelerates toward us, its 18-year-old male driver crashing head on into Tamar's small vehicle. There are injuries (acute, but not life threatening), delays (after hours, we are brought to a hospital in the city from a countryside clinic), and absurdities, including the sudden appearance of two non-uniformed US Marines, one on either side of me as I sit in stunned confusion alongside the destroyed vehicle, unsure of the extent of my injuries.

Amidst the crisis of the accident, Tamar, her family, my new colleagues at Tbilisi State University and I form a hard and fast bond. The silver lining of the experience is the relationships that we forge. We quickly dispense with formalities, find common ground, and despite the distraction of the injuries and hospitalization, I receive a crash course in the challenges facing Gender Studies at TSU, and of gender in Georgia more generally.

Illuminations

With this brief "impressionistic autoethnography" (Skinner 2003; 2012), I intimate a series of issues and themes that are central to this volume, and which I highlight in this introduction. Embedding myself in this initial narrative suggests that social and geopolitical locations—those of my Georgian colleagues and of mine—are relevant to the framing of gender in the contemporary Georgian context, not least the role of the Open Society Institute that created the infrastructure to make our interactions possible. As an anthropologist, I consider it important to depict place not as abstraction but as physical space that offers clues to influences, power structures, and prevailing narratives—all of which figure in the topics discussed by contributors to this volume. These aspects constitute conditions under which the contributors conduct research and engage activism; they write in and of this place.

Elements of my narrative are suggestive of larger meanings, deeper contexts, and longer histories. For example, anthropologist Paul Manning's

"City of Balconies" (2009; see also Van Assche and Salukvadze 2012) offers tidbits of a history that helps explain the striking clutter of architectural forms and construction materials that greeted me on my first day in town, which I liberally excerpt below:

> The coup of 1992 [that ousted the first post-socialist government of Zviad Gamsakhurdia] was not the first time Tbilisi had experienced a violent transformation of its architectural space. In fact, for a city that is sometimes claimed to be one of the oldest continuously inhabited urban areas on the face of the earth (more than 6 thousand years according to Bolkvadze 2003: 28), very little in the way of architecture remains that predates the 19th century aside from the famous baths and a few churches. This is because the city was razed almost entirely prior to Russian occupation by the Persian invasion of the late 18th century ... Unlike many Oriental cities that underwent European colonization ... the opposition between Oriental and European architecture that developed in Tbilisi under Russian rule was not entirely an opposition between the old and the new, but rather, the two architectural streams developed almost simultaneously. Even though the construction process was nearly simultaneous, by mid century Tbilisi already presented an image of continuous opposition of Old Oriental and New European elements ... Tbilisians love the architecture of the old city [although] seemingly no one actually wants to live in such buildings ... [Their] distinctly 'non-romantic' view of Old Tbilisi [is of] a place defined by poor infrastructure (narrow streets) as well as the uncomfortable proximity to neighbors because of the proximity of balconies (the 'second storey' of the narrow streets). (Manning 2009: 90–92)

Signs of post-Soviet political economy abound in new architecture, the highlighted tourism spots and the active sounds and smells that emanate from the Orthodox churches. Mikheil Saakashvili, credited with leading the Rose Revolution in 2003 and who subsequently served as Georgia's "pro-Western" president (2004–2013), ushered in the era of democratic reform (e.g., addressing police corruption, revising school curriculum) and neoliberal development, with new building construction a central focus (Van Assche and Salukvadze 2012: 10). With Saakashvili at the helm, Georgia's "modernization" project included the construction of the amusing Bridge of Peace, designed by an Italian architect and illuminated with twelve hundred LEDs. What anthropologist Martin Demant Frederiksen describes for Batumi, Georgia's second largest city, is true also for Tbilisi: "It is not surprising that 'lights' became such a common mechanism for symbolizing change following the [Rose] Revolution: lack of electricity had dominated much of the 1990s in Georgia (Devlin 2004) and a relatively stable supply of electricity was an accomplished goal of Saakashvili's government" (Frederiksen 2013: 37). Architecture, lights and the development of Georgia's tourism industry come together in "officially chosen illuminated sites" (ibid.: 36–37). These sites include centuries-old churches, newly built government buildings and the renovated balconied structures of Old Tbilisi that some consider a "Ye Olde" form of facadism and "slapdash commercialism over historical authenticity" (Levine 2013).

Behind the illuminated facades are layers of the hidden, unspoken or lost, that which and those whom Frederiksen says are "condemned to a life in the shadows, unwanted" (2013: 37). Land use planner Kristof Van Assche and human geographer Joseph Salukvadze argue that "untempered, neoliberal enthusiasm" has left Tbilisi and its residents without systematic urban planning, and with limited public sector housing, homelessness (a new phenomenon) alongside gated communities (also a new phenomenon), environmental problems, poor quality construction, and a transportation system in crisis (Van Assche and Salukvadze 2012: 1, 14, 17–18). On the ruinous impact of new construction, Manning observes it is a particularly threatening form of destruction "because it is wrought by the wheels of commerce, visible everywhere, the aggregate irrational and destructive product of the individually rational and creative actions of newly liberated liberal subjects" (Manning 2009: 93; see also Gordillo 2014).

The wheels of commerce include, literally, the rise in the number of private automobiles across Georgia but especially in the metro Tbilisi area, a mix of very old (generally compact sized and in poor condition) and very new (generally large SUV) vehicles (UNEP-EEA 2007; Adeishvili et al. 2011; Pkhaladze 2015). According to an NGO-supported environmental assessment report endorsed by Tbilisi City Hall, during the Soviet period, urban transportation in the city was "well developed and diverse"; in contrast, during the post-Soviet period, "this smoothly operating system almost collapsed and eventually the number of private cars increased dramatically" (Adeishvili et al. 2011: 2). In describing the ever-intensifying "colonization" by cars of the sidewalks of Tbilisi, anthropologist Perry Sherouse recalls his experience crossing its busy streets. As Sherouse and his colleague Paul Manning "scurried across a hazardous intersection," the latter "likened crossing Tbilisi streets to a real-life enactment of the arcade game *Frogger*," the goal of which is to survive a deadly game of traffic (Sherouse 2016: 2). Thus I came to learn why Lela took my hand each time we crossed the street, and to understand that the car "accident" had resulted from a set of circumstances set in motion by that very "untempered, neoliberal enthusiasm," its harmful effects too often hidden and unspoken.

The Georgian Orthodox Church is neither hidden nor silent in my impressionistic autoethnography, or in Georgia more widely. Churches figure prominently in my short story and first visit. Over a twenty-four-hour period, I stepped into or passed by at least half a dozen of them; indeed my fateful accident occurred on my way from the most holy of Georgian sites. In Georgia too, the church figures prominently, having undergone an enormous rise to power and prominence during the post-Soviet period in stark contrast to its "dilapidated state" in the Georgian Soviet Socialist Republic (Rapp 2010: 152). The 1995 Constitution of Georgia privileged the role of the church in the nationalist narrative and provided an infrastructure on which the church could expand its reach even as it institutionalized the separation of church and state in Georgia: "The state shall declare complete freedom of belief and religion, as well as recognize the special role of the Apostle Autocephalous Orthodox Church of Georgia in the history of Georgia, and its independence from the state" (Parliament of Georgia 1995: 3). In 2002, an agreement was signed between the church and state (the Concordat), which affirmed the Orthodox religion "as a marker of national identity, its pivotal role legally recognized" (Bertelsmann Stiftung 2016: 7). Then, in a controversial move, Saakashvili's administration began granting many millions of dollars to the Georgian Orthodox Patriarchate, and gave each of the ten archbishops a luxury SUV (Corso 2009; BBC News 2013).

The contradictions that pervade this seemingly cozy relationship between the twin icons of "modernity" (the state) and "tradition" (the church) suggest the need for a deeper exploration of post-Soviet political economy in relation to competing forms of nationalism and nationalist identity. Scholars making headway on these concerns include the philosopher Giga Zedania, whose article "The Rise of Religious Nationalism in Georgia" identifies key paradoxes in the dynamics of ethnic, civic, revolutionary, and religious nationalism in post-Soviet Georgia (Zedania 2011). Zedania observes that the religious renaissance in post-Soviet Georgia, which "took a stronger and more vital form than in the other countries of the region … gained popularity after the revolution of 2003, that is, after the modernization project had been explicitly endorsed by the political elite with its strong revolutionary-nationalistic sentiments" (ibid.: 123–24). Likewise, historian Konstantine Ladaria's article, "Georgian Orthodox Church and Political Project of Modernization," explores the "cohabitation of religion and liberalism in contemporary Georgia," and the irony that "the Church emerged as the primary advocate of anti-Western sentiments in society; paradoxically, it is one of the institutions that incurred greatest losses during the Soviet totalitarian regime" (Ladaria 2012: 110–11). In succinct terms, Ladaria captures the ideological tension between the state and the church (although scholars have yet to fully draw the power and resource connections that make for these strange bedfellows):

> The government-led modernization project in Georgia proposes close ties with the West, integration into NATO and EU structures, and participation in global

politico-cultural and economic affairs as a solution to the country's problems. This is a classical Western project of modernization, which suggests that Western cultural program of modernity and its major administrative institutions will eventually spread throughout the modern world. The Georgian Orthodox Church, on the other hand, presents Western "soulless" humanistic culture as the main menace for Georgia. (Ladaria 2012: 112)

Contextualizing Gender in Georgia

Ladaria's summation gives context for understanding the dynamics of gender in Georgia. As a post-Soviet state, Georgia is at once its own nation and its struggles are in some ways emblematic of those of other post-Soviet states (Banović 2016). The country is at a critical juncture, still in process of reinventing itself as a nation-state in what is a long post-Soviet "transition." The ongoing transformation is gendered; "gender," broadly speaking, is the lightning rod issue in Georgia around which controversy swirls and contradictions are revealed. Georgian women writing in this volume are maneuvering to cope with and accommodate the new (neoliberal) economic, social, and political order. They do so as self-proclaimed feminist scholars and/or activists demanding social and political change and policies to transform discourses and women's lives. Many are supported by international (mostly Western) nongovernmental organizations (INGOs) and foundations, even as they investigate, document and theorize gender in Georgia on their own terms. Several have been at the forefront of the struggle to institutionalize and professionalize Gender Studies at Tbilisi State University, the country's oldest university.

Gender in Georgia is groundbreaking work, not least because there are few scholarly works published in Gender Studies by Georgian scholars. This volume offers a corrective on a number of fronts. As the first edited volume that brings together an international group of feminist scholars to explore the political, economic, social, and cultural conditions that have shaped gender dynamics in Georgia from the late nineteenth century to the present, it provides an important opportunity for dialogue between Georgian scholars and scholars in the international English language academy. The project enables the volume's contributors to share with scholars their important work in deconstructing and challenging the grand narratives on gender in Georgia that have been or continue to be nurtured by proponents of deeply entrenched, sometimes unyielding, ideologies. It also provides information and insight on the instrumentality and complexity of gender roles in a nation that historically has been embedded in "East–West," "metropole–periphery," and "Soviet–post-Soviet" tensions.

In the context of Georgia's strategic geopolitical location at the intersection of Europe and Asia, and with its contested northern border with Russia, knowing how gender fits in the country's turbulent history and how gender is performed, reinforced, and interpreted has broad implications for understanding larger global processes and dynamics.

This project is itself an instance of decolonizing post-Soviet gender research and an alternative to androcentric knowledge production. As co-editor of the volume, my socio-political location and professional position as a tenured professor in the United States with knowledge and experience in scholarly publishing has enabled me to facilitate access to resources. I have multiple motivations for engaging this project. For one, it is a response to the call by my discipline of anthropology to recognize one's own location in multiple fields of power and to act accordingly in a responsible and ethical way. At least since the mid-1980s with the publication of the widely referenced *Writing Culture,* anthropologists have reflected deeply on the politics and poetics of representation, questioning the right, ability, and reasons for speaking on behalf of others (Clifford and Marcus 1986). Many anthropologists have come to understand, as Gupta and Ferguson put it, that all participants in any project are situated within a field of power relations and are products of shared historical processes that operate in a world of culturally, socially, and economically interconnected and interdependent spaces (Gupta and Ferguson 1992: 14–17; see also Harrison 1997). With this understanding, and appreciating that I both represent and seek to resist Western global hegemony, in this project I adopt Paul Farmer's "Partners In Health" credo to shift resources from where there are too many to where there are too few, and to use my privilege where I have it to support others seeking their own flourishing.

I am well aware of the contradictions of my position and my effort, starting with my status as International Scholar of the Open Society Institute, an INGO that has had a presence in Georgia since 1994 "to help the country pursue the development of a democratic and open society after [it] gained independence from the Soviet Union in 1991, [using] donor funding, partnerships, and training to help [its] transition process move forward and to meet the economic, political, and social challenges it ... faced" (Open Society Georgia Foundation). That the Soros Foundation "actively assisted the opposition" leading up to and after the Rose Revolution, means the organization is a vested stakeholder and operator in the unfolding of Georgia's political economy (Wheatley 2005: 189; Esadze 2007: 112; Machavariani 2007: 45). The organization's interests are not necessarily aligned with the interests and motivations of actors on the ground, who receive support from the Open Society Foundations or from one of the hundreds of NGOs operating in Georgia (Ritvo et al. 2013: 14; Dunn 2012, 2014). Nevertheless, they are a significant force in fashioning the contours of a field of action that make some things possible and other things impossible for local actors operating on that constructed and structured field. In the Georgian case, the contemporary field of action is shaped in large part by that Western project of modernization, with its newly made liberal subjects and neoliberal capitalist political economy.

The above discussion offers another layer of context to reading this volume. *Gender in Georgia* is created almost entirely by Georgian women—scholars and activists who live, work, think, act, and write within the field of action delineated by the forces and factors outlined above. Nearly all contributors have been supported by INGOs operating in Georgia, including the Open Society Georgia Foundation and UN Women, which provide career opportunities and stable employment in a place with a decidedly unstable labor market (Sulaberidze 1999; World Bank 2013; Frederiksen 2013). At play in the Georgian setting are the kinds of tensions identified by Kristen Ghodsee resulting from "the hegemony of Western cultural feminism" delivered via women's NGOs, including the potential pitfalls of a "gender first paradigm" that can occlude identifying and challenging the very socio-political-economic relations that ensure the flourishing of patriarchy (Ghodsee 2004a: 727–28, 733; see also Roth 2008).

Feminist Perspectives on Culture, Nation, and History in the South Caucasus

At its core, the volume provides the first-ever, woman-centered collection of research and analysis on Georgia. It offers a feminist critique of power in its many manifestations, is itself an assessment of women's political agency in Georgia, and reclaims a history that is in the process of being written. Contemporary debates in Georgia about women's rights, gender relations and sexuality—which in some situations have led to violent confrontation—must be understood in terms of contingent history, a past that is worth recounting because it informs the present. Indeed, the volume traces developments relevant to women's rights and gender relations in Georgia, beginning in the second half of the nineteenth century when Georgia was a province of the Russian Empire, then briefly an independent country (1918–1921), and extends to the Soviet period (1921–1991) and the post-Soviet period (1991–present). This volume treats gender as social construct, personal and social experience, political focal point and analytic category in relation to the social forces of class, religion, and local and global political economy. Taken as a whole, this work demonstrates the value of foregrounding gender in this way in order to gain a deeper understanding of the dynamics of Georgian culture, nation, and history.

Part I on "Power and Politics" provides important historical perspective and theoretical grounding essential for assessing the arguments, data, and issues raised by contributors throughout the volume. The five chapters that comprise "Power and Politics" are in conversation with each other in terms of questions of historiography, and of the meanings and make-up of "modernity," revealed in the details of Georgian women's lives and their gendered personal and political struggles across a complex history. The chapters are also in conversation with one another in terms of Georgia's relation to the Russian Empire, the Soviet Union, the West, and Orthodox Christianity in the past and present—a complex of relations and dynamics that have too often been collapsed into simplistic, dualistic ideological constructs that tend to erase substantive history. On this point, the combined chapters in Part I are especially illuminating.

The volume leads with "Pioneer Women: 'Herstories' of Feminist Movements in Georgia" (Chapter 1) by activist-scholar Lela Gaprindashvili who is professor of philosophy and, for nearly twenty years, chair of the Women's Initiative for Equality, an NGO located in Tbilisi. She provides an overview of women's activism in Georgia, starting in the late nineteenth century by depicting three women activists and their political biographies: Barbare Eristavi-Jorjadze, Ekaterine Tarkhnishvili-Gabashvili and Kato Mikeladze. Gaprindashvili challenges what she considers the prevailing perspective that feminist activity has been newly brought to Georgia by the West, a process that some argue began with the collapse of the Soviet Union. In her revisionist history, she demonstrates early linkages between nineteenth-century Georgian "feminists" and those in the United States and parts of Europe, and the establishment in pre-Bolshevik Georgia of a particular form of feminist activism. In recounting the three "herstories," Gaprindashvili details a form of women's advocacy centered on emancipation through writing and education, activities directly linked to Georgia's nationalist struggle. It was no accident that their form of activism centered on writing in Georgian and on other forms of resisting Russification, as well as advocating access to education for girls.

Whereas Gaprindashvili sees Georgian women's activism as "interrupted by the Russian imperia and later by the Soviets," Gender Studies scholar Maia Barkaia, author of "'The Country of the Happiest Women'?: Ideology and Gender in Soviet Georgia" (Chapter 2), explores the project of women's emancipation in Soviet Georgia, with a focus on the 1920s ("the era of ideological radicalism") and the 1930s ("the era of conservatism"). Both Gaprindashvili and Barkaia reference writings as key indicators of emancipatory projects in Georgia. In Gaprindashvili's case, these were the writings of bourgeois feminists for literate audiences. In Barkaia's study, writing was tied to an official women's publication (*Chveni Gza* [Our Way], later *Mshromeli Kali* [Woman Worker]), authorized by the Soviet authorities as a tool for consciousness raising and political organizing, and targeting proletariat and peasant women listener-readers (the magazine was used also in literacy campaigns).

Grounding Soviet practice in classical Marxism, and tracing the theoretical bedrock from which the Bolsheviks drew their agenda (including that of Lenin and Kollontai), Barkaia explains the Marxist premise that "women's participation in the labor force was a key challenge to the gender division of labor, and a necessary condition of the proletarian revolution and of women's subsequent emancipation." Through the lens of decolonial feminism, Barkaia's brilliant exploration of Georgian women's emancipation as it unfolded in peripheral Soviet Georgia reveals Soviet conceptions of modernity vis-à-vis its Georgian subjects. She demonstrates the ways in which the notion of "the East" was invoked in different localized contexts reflecting this modernity project, which led to a set of inconsistent depictions of proletarian women (as backward, as progressive, as downtrodden, as emancipators). In all, Barkaia explains how the discordance between the ideal and the real was played out in actual policy and practice, first under Leninism and then Stalinism. In this way, she identifies how motherhood, family, domestic labor, and gender "came to occupy a central place in the discourses of the new socialist state."

In "'The West' and Georgian 'Difference': Discursive Politics of Gender and Sexuality in Georgia" (Chapter 3), philosopher and Gender Studies scholar Tamar Tskhadadze offers a challenge in relation to a central theoretical and political concern of this volume: how to resolve the contradictions inherent in Georgia's condition as an independent nation-state that has historically been, and continues to be, situated at the crossroads of competing empires and imperialisms. The discursive politics at the center of Tskhadadze's chapter reflects the difficulty of coming to terms with the immediate problems faced by people in Georgia today (material needs, physical dangers, ideological threats) and their "choice" of solutions, which come with unwanted consequences (must Georgia keep the dirty bathwater in order to keep the baby?). Operating in the world as it exists rather than as how people may want it be, Tskhadadze asserts that Georgians must come to terms with its history and positionality—"how colonial thought works on us," and "how the normative idea of the West functions in post-Soviet Georgia, which may not necessarily be to our benefit."

Tskhadadze offers a rich, multi-dimensional interrogation of the role of "the West" as the norm in the Georgian political imaginary and in relation to contemporary debates on women's emancipation and the status of sexual minorities in Georgia. She argues that the discursive politics during Georgia's post-Soviet moment have been linked to the idea of the West (the US and/or the EU) as the standard, the source of modernity, progress, human rights, and economic prosperity, and at the center of various claims for gender equality by those who are concerned with such issues, and by feminist and LGBTQ rights advocates. This stands in contrast to conservative nationalists and religious leaders who openly challenge and critique the West as a vector that imposes ideas about gender equality from the outside and against so-called local tradition. Like Barkaia, Tskhadadze unpacks a series of simplistic, essentialist binaries operating here, and inquires about the contexts within which the idea of the West is conceived in opposition to that which is "Georgian, Eastern, Soviet, Russian, or even anti-Western." Thus, Tskhadadze offers a corrective to—or at least a caution about—those histories, including feminist histories that rest on shaky assumptions about Georgian Europeanness and Georgian non-Europeanness, of which the transition narrative is a symptom (see also Gal and Kligman 2000: 10–12). At the center of Tskhadadze's critique is an instruction on reading history and the contemporary moment: we must see continuities in history where they exist (not only the ruptures), and we must see the oppressive, regressive, and reactionary elements inherent to neoliberal modernity (ibid.: 12–13).

If Tskhadadze regrets the lack of nuanced history, Magdalena Grabowska seeks to reclaim it in "Overcoming the 'Delay' Paradigm: New Approaches to Socialist Women's Activism in Georgia and Poland" (Chapter 4). Grabowska, a Gender Studies scholar who works in Poland, offers a comparative history of the two post-Soviet states noted in her title. Grabowska brings readers into the homes and histories of an aging cohort of women who lived, worked, and engaged in political activity during the Soviet period. Their words are telling. Halina, for example, feels attacked by those contemporary feminists and others who dismiss women's activism and agency of the communist period as irrelevant, and their recollections as distorted memory or mere nostalgia (Pine 2002; Ghodsee 2004b; Todorova and Gille 2012). In keeping with Tskhadadze's instruction, Grabowska provides a more complete genealogy of women's movements by including socialist women's activism and socialist state feminism as significant in efforts to advance gender equality.

Part I closes with "Women's Political Representation in Post-Soviet Georgia," (Chapter 5) by Ketevan Chkheidze, who is a Gender Studies scholar and consultant on gender issues for the Asian Development Bank. Focusing on the post–Rose Revolution period between 2003 and 2012, Chkheidze identifies specific factors that have led to dashed hopes for a gender-sensitive multiparty and inclusive political system in Georgia. On the basis of empirical data, she concludes that in Georgia, men hold the key leadership positions in political parties and in the Georgian Parliament, suggesting that the promises of democracy and of progress, prosperity, and equality have not been fulfilled. Considered in the context of the previous four chapters, Chkheidze's findings are not surprising. Indeed, sociologist Silke Roth, writing on gender politics in the expanding European Union, notes that EU directives for post-socialist states (such as Georgia) looking to join it, have prioritized "social and economic reforms based on neoliberal principles that are characterized by an implicit anti-equality bias"; the mechanisms to ensure effective implementation of gender equality directives are weak (Roth 2008: 6). This point gives further context to Chkheidze's assessment of party level characteristics and features of the Georgian electoral system that shape women's low representation in the Parliament.

The four chapters that comprise Part II focus on "Violence," with two chapters devoted to the social problem of domestic violence and two to the violence of displacement, dispossession, and war. Tamar Sabedashvili, who chairs the Gender Studies Programme at Tbilisi State University and is program specialist for UN Women, offers a historical consideration of domestic violence in the Soviet period. In "The Domestic Violence Challenge to Soviet Women's Empowerment Policies" (Chapter 6), Sabedashvili provides a review of the historical trajectory and legacies of identifying domestic violence as a social problem. She seeks to document trouble on the Soviet family front, identifying the key ideological and political factors in official acknowledgement and/or disregard of the existence of domestic violence. Sabedashvili concludes that for the Soviets to recognize domestic violence would be to admit state failure in achieving women's liberation. She also suggests that recognizing domestic violence would directly challenge the Soviet "grand narrative" that gender equity was achieved. Turning to the post-Soviet period, in "Domestic Violence in Georgia: State and Community Responses, 2006–2015" (Chapter 7), psychologists Nino Javakhishvili and Nino Butsashvili critically analyze state and community responses to gender-based domestic violence. They describe the domestic violence problem in Georgia, document its prevalence based on available evidence, and explore perceptions of the domestic violence problem by various stakeholders. Their analysis reveals an interplay of factors that constitute obstacles in efforts to combat domestic violence, including structural gender inequality, patriarchal attitudes and beliefs among a significant swath of the population, and a lack of cooperation and coordination among local actors and those responsible for implementing policies to combat domestic violence. Taken together, the two chapters on domestic violence raise a series of additional questions. Does the presence and prevalence of domestic violence suggest that an indictment of the state is in order? Put another way, is the state delegitimized by its failure to address domestic violence? Also, if the Soviet state under-acknowledged the presence and prevalence of domestic violence, as Sabedashvili asserts, is there hyper-attention to the issue now? If so, what accounts for that attention? Does denoting this form of violence as a domestic crime obscure the magnitude of a deep social malaise (Manz 2009: 154)? Finally, does the focus on visible interpersonal violence in the domestic sphere in effect divert attention from larger-scale, more invisible structural violence?

The two subsequent chapters on displaced women's experiences in pre- and postwar Georgia provide insight into the "dynamic discrepancies between discourses, institutional practices and subjectivities" (Gal and Kligman 2000: 12). In "Remembering the Past: Narratives of Displaced Women from Abkhazia" (Chapter 8), Nargiza Arjevanidze, a doctoral student and recipient of an Open Society Foundations academic fellowship, gives readers a glimpse into descriptions, memories, and assessments by those who lived through a history marked by calm and turbulence, work and leisure, stability and precarity. A work in progress, Arjevanidze's intimate ethnography captures women's voices as they construct their past prior to armed conflict, and how they link these constructions to their current circumstances—their lives in protracted displacement. By invoking women's own stories and the words they use to tell it, Arjevanidze moves from the abstract to the experiential, providing a moving portrait of past and present joys, struggles, adaptations, and resiliency for a heterogeneous group of Georgian women. Moving to a larger sample of internally displaced persons (IDPs) from Abkhazia and South Ossetia as a result of separatist conflicts and the 2008 war between Russia and Georgia, Gender Studies scholar Joanna Regulska and her US-based co-authors, geographers Beth Mitchneck and Peter Kabachnik, examine how the upheaval has impacted on how Georgian women claim identity and agency. In "Displacement, State Violence, and Gender Roles: The Case of Internally Displaced and Violence-Affected Georgian Women" (Chapter 9), the authors acknowledge that conflict, displacement, state violence, and the post-Soviet "transition" have significantly influenced gender practices, discourses, and identities. The authors find that these conditions have led to the expansion of women's role as the household breadwinner and as caregiver to their families, leading them to conclude that, "[f]or some Georgian women, the return to 'tradition' may be the very enactment of their agency." The data and interpretations offered by Arjevanidze and Regulska et al. suggest the need to flesh out subjective meanings and analytic treatments of what constitutes the "traditional" when it comes to gender attitudes, beliefs, roles, duties, norms, and behavior.

The five contributions in Part III on "Identities, Representations, and Resistance" can be seen as an effort to question "tradition" from a number of vantage points. Tsopurashvili has a doctorate in gender studies from TSU and was recipient of an Open Society Foundations academic fellowship. Her contribution, "Images of 'The New Woman' in Soviet Georgian Silent Films" (Chapter 10), offers an intriguing deconstruction of 1920s representations of women in film. In a close reading of three representative films, Tsopurashvili finds the not-so-subtle inversion of male–female essentialisms: "[T]he [female] characters achieve full agency at the expense of traditional feminine attributes such as maternity, affection, love, sexuality, and beauty ... [here] femininity is not redefined as something positive and powerful; instead women acquire agency by adopting normative masculinity." In "Gender Equality: Still a Disputed Value in Georgian Society" (Chapter 11), psychologist Nana Sumbadze does not so much problematize the notion of traditional gender beliefs, roles, and behaviors as assert its prevalence in the contemporary Georgian context. In the following chapter, sociologist Tamar Zurabishvili and her co-authors psychologist Maia Mestvirishvili and sociologist Tinatin Zurabishvili take us in a different direction with "Georgian Women Migrants: Experiences Abroad and At Home" (Chapter 12), highlighting the transformative experiences for these women who are part and parcel of "the feminization of emigration" phenomenon. On the basis of interviews they conducted with migrant women, the authors discover that the women themselves attribute the experience of "going away" to a new awakening and a newfound ability to critically assess "tradition."

The final two chapters directly call tradition into question. Natia Gvianishvili, a self-proclaimed lesbian feminist activist and researcher, traces the relatively recent emergence of transgender persons in Georgian public space. In "Being Transgender in Georgia" (Chapter 13), Gvianishvili describes the difficult life conditions in Georgia for transgender persons, including their vulnerability to physical violence, public humiliation, and demonization by powerful social actors and ordinary citizens. Likewise, in "Tracing the LGBT Movement in the Republic of Georgia: Stories of Activists" (Chapter 14), Anna Rekhviashvili (a doctoral student in Canada and recipient of an Open Society Foundations academic fellowship) reconstructs the LGBT rights movement in Georgia. She recounts the spring day of 17 May 2013 when a small group of activists gathered for a peaceful rally to celebrate the "International Day against Homophobia and Transphobia" on Rustaveli Avenue, the main street of Georgia's capital city, Tbilisi. The peace was short lived: it became a day of unprecedented violence. As a scholar-activist involved in the movement, Rekhviashvili analyzes the events of the day and the movement itself in relation to the political and social scene in contemporary Georgia, revealing how gender is indeed the lightening rod political issue involving the Georgian Orthodox Church, homophobia, rights, nationalism, and public opinion. The narratives provided by Gvianishvili and Rekhviashvili are particularly relevant to the significance of this volume. As with other geopolitical locations across the globe, the social, cultural, political, and economic dimensions of gender in Georgia are an indicator of lived reality, ideological manipulation and contestation, cultural meaning, and the constancy of social change.

Alisse Waterston is Presidential Scholar and Professor of Anthropology at John Jay College, City University of New York. She is the author most recently of *Light in Dark Times: The Human Search for Meaning*, illustrated by Charlotte Corden (University of Toronto Press, 2020). She is past-President of the American Anthropological Association (2015-2017), and Editor of the *Intimate Ethnography* series (Berghahn Books).

References

Adeishvili, M., M. Adeishvili, T. Chachua, T. Gugushvili, Z. Jincharadze, E. Kakabadze, and M. Sharabidze. 2011. "GEO Cities—Tbilisi: An Integrated Environmental Assessment of State and Trends for Georgia's Capital City." December. Retrieved 7 July 2016 from http://www.unep.org/geo/pdfs/GEO-Cities_Tbilisi_Full-report.pdf.
Banović, B. 2016. *The Montenegrin Warrior Tradition*. New York: Palgrave Macmillan.
BBC News. 2013. "Georgia's Mighty Orthodox Church." 2 July. Retrieved 7 July 2016 from http://www.bbc.com/news/world-europe-23103853.
Bertelsmann Stiftung. 2016. "Georgia Country Report BTI 2016."
Clifford, J., and G.E. Marcus. 1986. *Writing Culture: The Poetics and Politics of Ethnography*. A School of American Research Advanced Seminar. Berkeley, Los Angeles and London: University of California Press.
Corso, M. 2009. "Georgia: Church–State Separation Becomes an Issue Amid Government Financial Support for Georgian Orthodox Church." 5 April. Retrieved 7 July 2016 from http://www.eurasianet.org/departments/insightb/articles/eav040609b.shtml.
Dunn, E.C. 2012. "The Chaos of Humanitarian Aid: Adhocracy in the Republic of Georgia." *Humanity: An International Journal of Human Rights, Humanitarianism, and Development* 3(1): 1–23.
———. 2014. "Humanitarianism, Displacement, and the Politics of Nothing in Postwar Georgia." *Slavic Review* 73(2): 287–306.
Esadze, L. 2007. "Georgia's Rose Revolution: People's Anti-corruption Revolution?". In *Organized Crime and Corruption in Georgia*, ed. L. Shelley, E.R. Scott, and A. Latta, 111–20. London: Routledge.

Frederiksen, M.D. 2013. *Young Men, Time, and Boredom in the Republic of Georgia.* Philadelphia, PA: Temple University Press.
Gal, S., and G. Kligman. 2000. *The Politics of Gender after Socialism: A Comparative-Historical Essay.* Princeton, NJ: Princeton University Press.
Ghodsee, K. 2004a. "Feminism by Design: Emerging Capitalisms, Cultural Feminism, and Women's Nongovernmental Organizations in Postsocialist Eastern Europe." *Signs* 29(3): 727–53.
———. 2004b. "Red Nostalgia? Communism, Women's Emancipation, and Economic Transformation in Bulgaria." *L'Homme Z. F. G.* 15(1): 23–36.
Gordillo, G.R. 2014. *Rubble: The Afterlife of Destruction.* Durham, NC: Duke University Press.
Gupta, A., and J. Ferguson. 1992. "Beyond 'culture': Space, Identity, and the Politics of Difference." *Cultural Anthropology* 7(1): 6–23.
Harrison, F.V. (1991) 1997. *Decolonizing Anthropology Moving Further Toward an Anthropology for Liberation.* Arlington, VA: American Anthropological Association.
Ladaria, K. 2012. "Georgian Orthodox Church and Political Project of Modernization." *Identity Studies in the Caucasus and the Black Sea Region* 4: 107–117.
Levine, J. 2013. "In Tbilisi, Georgia, Bold New Buildings Rise from the Ruins of Dead Empires." *New York Times,* 1 November. Retrieved 7 July 2016 from http://www.nytimes.com/2013/11/01/t-magazine/tbilisi-georgia-architecture.html?_r=0.
Machavariani, S. 2007. "Overcoming Economic Crime in Georgia through Public Service Reform." In *Organized Crime and Corruption in Georgia,* ed. L. Shelley, E.R. Scott, and A. Latta, 37–49. London: Routledge.
Manning, P. 2009. "The City of Balconies: Elite Politics and the Changing Semiotics of the Post-Socialist Cityscape." In *City Culture and City Planning in Tbilisi: Where Europe and Asia Meet,* ed. K. Van Assche, J. Salukvadze, and N. Shavishvili, 71–102. Lewiston, New York: Edwin Mellen Press.
Manz, B. 2009. "The continuum of violence in post-war Guatemala." In *An Anthropology of War: Views from the Frontline,* ed. A. Waterston, 151–65. New York and Oxford: Berghahn Books.
Open Society Georgia Foundation. n.d. "Open Society Foundations." Retrieved 8 July 2016 from https://www.opensocietyfoundations.org/about/offices-foundations/open-society-georgia-foundation.
Parliament of Georgia. 1995. "The Constitution of Georgia." Retrieved 7 July 2016 from http://www.parliament.ge/files/68_1944_951190_CONSTIT_27_12.06.pdf.
Pine, F. 2002. "Retreat to the Household?" In *Postsocialism: Ideals, Ideologies and Practices in Eurasia,* ed. C.M. Hann, 95–113. London and New York: Routledge.
Pkhaladze, I. 2015. "Monitoring Report on the Implementation of City of Tbilisi Sustainable Energy Action Plan." US Agency for International Development (USAID), Georgia. September. Retrieved 7 July 2016 from http://pdf.usaid.gov/pdf_docs/PA00KVWP.pdf.
Rapp Jr, S.H. 2010. "Georgian Christianity." In *The Blackwell Companion to Eastern Christianity,* ed. K. Parry, 137. Malden, MA: Wiley-Blackwell.
Ritvo, R.A., G. Berdzenishvili, N. Khazalia, M. Khidesheli, A. Liqokeli, and S. Samkharadze. 2013. "Public Attitudes toward Non-governmental Organizations (NGOs) in the Republic of Georgia." *International NGO Journal* 8(1): 13–19.
Roth, S. (ed.). 2008. *Gender Politics in the Expanding European Union: Mobilization, Inclusion, Exclusion.* New York and Oxford: Berghahn Books.
Shelley, L., E.R. Scott, and A. Latta (eds). 2007. *Organized Crime and Corruption in Georgia.* London: Routledge.
Sherouse, P. 2016. "Where the Sidewalk Ends: Douchebags Drivers and Eco-urban Activists in Tbilisi, Georgia." Paper presented at the American Ethnological Society conference. Washington, DC.

Skinner, J. 2003. "Montserrat Place and Mons'rat Neaga: An Example of Impressionistic Autoethnography." *The Qualitative Report* 8 (3): 513–529.

———. 2012. "Introduction: Writings on the Dark Side of Travel." In *Writing the Dark Side of Travel*, ed. J. Skinner, 1–28. New York and Oxford: Berghahn Books.

Smith, A. 2006. "Interview with Orhan Pamuk." 12 October. Retrieved 6 July 2016 from http://www.nobelprize.org/nobel_prizes/literature/laureates/2006/pamuk-telephone.html.

Sulaberidze, A. 1999. "Toward Poverty Eradication in Georgia." In *Poverty in Transition and Transition in Poverty: Recent Developments in Hungary, Bulgaria, Romania, Georgia, Russia, Mongolia*, ed. Yohesh Atal, 130–176. New York and Oxford: Berghahn Books; and Paris: UNESCO Publishing.

Todorova, M.N., and Z. Gille (eds). 2012. *Post-Communist Nostalgia*. New York and Oxford: Berghahn Books.

UNEP-EEA. 2007. "Transport." In *Sustainable Consumption and Production in South East Europe and Eastern Europe, Caucasus and Central Asia*. Copenhagen: European Environment Agency. Retrieved 7 July 2016 from www.eea.europa.eu/publications/.../07_Transport.pdf; and http://www.unep.fr/shared/publications/pdf/WEBx0133xPA-Environment4Europe.pdf.

Van Assche, K., and J. Salukvadze. 2012. "Tbilisi Reinvented: Planning, Development and the Unfinished Project of Democracy in Georgia." *Planning Perspectives* 27(1): 1–24.

Wheatley, J. 2005. *Georgia from National Awakening to Rose Revolution*. Aldershot, England and Burlington, VT: Ashgate Publishing.

World Bank. 2013. "The Jobs Challenge in the South Caucasus—Georgia." 12 January. Retrieved 8 July 2016 from http://www.worldbank.org/en/news/feature/2015/01/12/the-jobs-challenge-in-the-south-caucasus---georgia.

Zedania, G. 2011. "The Rise of Religious Nationalism in Georgia." *Identity Studies in the Caucasus and the Black Sea Region* 3: 120–28.

Part I

Power and Politics

Chapter 1

Pioneer Women
"Herstories" of Feminist Movements in Georgia

Lela Gaprindashvili

Introduction

In post-Soviet Georgia, women's civic activity and public discourse on gender equality have been an essential part of the democratic process. Political leaders and members of the general public frequently question the need for "women's emancipation," which they think is unnecessary considering sexual equality is guaranteed by Georgian law and is believed to be the cultural norm. As if to affirm their beliefs, skeptics name eminent women from the ancient Georgian past who are recognized for their the religious and political contributions: Queen Tamar from the twelfth century, Queen Ketevan from the seventeenth century and the monument "Kartlis Deda" (Mother of Georgia), who have come to symbolize Georgian history. From their point of view, recognizing these mythical-historical figures signals respect for the historical and cultural roles of women in Georgian society.

As a feminist researcher and civic activist, I find these discussions useful in raising questions and in inspiring me to look for answers—a search at the center of my professional life. It has led me to study women's pursuits not in the ancient past but in the nineteenth century, when, by means of putting enlightenment ideas into practice, the foundation was laid for building a secular state. It has also led me to bring this history into the contemporary women's movement in Georgia, both as a source of inspiration and as an effective argument in response to those who call Georgia's feminist movement a recent import that is irrelevant to contemporary Georgian society.

Notes for this chapter begin on page 31.

It took many years for me to accomplish my goal of uncovering nineteenth-century women's histories. I found it challenging to obtain reliable information and to gather the data I needed to "reanimate" the women's voices. My exhaustive search took me to books, journals, newspapers, memoirs of famous male writers and public figures, and archives of their descendants. By means of this "intellectual archaeology," I had the good fortune to meet other women like myself who also conduct research on women's roles in Georgian society. Gathering data from scientific research organizations, museums, and archives of the Soviet era, these scholars have published articles and monographs on women who were Georgian public figures in different historical periods.[1]

This chapter focuses on the stories of three important nineteenth-century Georgian women who helped place "women's issues" in the public sphere, and played critical roles in women's liberation. In what follows, I narrate the political biographies of Barbare Eristavi-Jorjadze, Ekaterine Tarkhnishvili-Gabashvili, and Kato Mikeladze. Even as it is true that women's activism has increased in the post-Soviet period, this history contests the commonly held view that women's activism in Georgia was born with the fall of the Soviet Union. Ideas about gender equality, women's rights and the women's movement were not simply recent imports but are linked to Georgian history, traditions, and culture. The "herstories" presented here reveal that Georgian ideas about women's personal, sexual, social, economic, and political freedoms were synchronized early on with the European/Western process; but this was interrupted by the Russian imperia and later by the Soviets, resulting in the marginalization of civil activism and women's movements after 1921.

Out of the Home and into the Community

By the mid nineteenth century, Georgia was already part of the Russian Empire. As the previous century came to a close, Georgia's "northern friend" would violate the 1783 Treaty of Georgievsk, designed to ensure mutual military-political security, which ultimately resulted in the subjugation of the Georgian kingdoms to Russia. In the turbulent period leading up to nineteenth-century Russian rule, some members of the Georgian royal family were deported, some acceded, and the most disobedient Georgians survived by fleeing to Persia and the Ottoman Empire where they made several unsuccessful attempts to organize a rebellion.

Having cleared Georgia of the "rebels," the Russians carried out what Georgians considered to be economic and later cultural enslavement of the population. The Russian *Prikaz* (literally, an "order")—a mortgage loan given by the representatives of the empire to the Georgian nobility—significantly contributed to the impoverishment of the country. In the transition from feudalism to capitalism, debtors were unable to pay back the loans, which left their landed fortunes open to Russian possession.

The Russian effort to culturally assimilate Georgia began in the schools. The primary, two-year education was available only to a very small number of those ranked high in the social order. The masses, girls among them, received education in so-called "home schools," where they were instructed to memorize historical legends, fairy tales and religious texts. There were also private boarding schools for girls from elite households who were taught sewing, embroidery, and how to play the piano, as well provided with instruction in the natural sciences and Russian, French, and Georgian. In these various educational contexts, the Georgian language was relegated to subordinate status. If taught at all, classes in Georgian were scheduled at the end of a long school day and ignorance of one's mother tongue was not a barrier to academic advancement. In the personal archive of Nino Kipiani, a nineteenth-century Georgian public figure, she describes the demonization of Georgian, an essential step in the Russian forced assimilation process:

> The Georgian language was labeled as "a language of dogs," and speaking Georgian was prohibited. If somebody dared to speak Georgian, they would hang a red plate over his neck with an image of a dog's tongue on it. If a student was seen reading a Georgian newspaper, the teacher would snatch it out of his hands and say, "Do not fool yourself with this rubbish" (Kipiani Archive: 6087).[2]

Not everyone acquiesced to the pressure to assimilate. Some people found ways to resist, including through the use of print media. Notwithstanding pervasive censorship, writers helped unify those Georgians who were deeply concerned about the situation facing their country, which many considered a tragic situation. One example was the journal *Tsiskari*, which under the editorship of Ivane Kereselidze (1829–1883) published the poem "The Sad Woman Sitting by the River," introducing Georgian society to 26-year-old Barbare Eristavi-Jorjadze, whose "herstory" I outline here.

Eristavi-Jorjadze was born to Nino Amilakhvari and David Eristavi in 1833. After her mother's death, Eristavi-Jorjadze was raised by her nurse, Dilavardisa, who taught the girl to read and write as well as to sew and embroider, which every girl was obligated to learn. According to Ketevan Iremadze, Dilavardisa would tell the child Barbare stories about prominent historical and religious figures (Iremadze 1945: 66–67). At seven years old, Barbare was fully ready for school, though it seems nobody thought about her education. Her brother Raphiel would study in the Gori district school and then in the Tbilisi gymnasium.

By age twelve (1845), Eristavi-Jorjadze was betrothed to Zakaria Jorjadze, who had been expelled from St. Petersburg Military Academy for physical assault. As recounted by her contemporary, the writer Mariam Ivanishvili-Demuria, Eristavi-Jorjadze describes herself as a child bride:

> Women in those days, as a rule, were married at a very young age, and I too was so young that during the marriage service I thought it was just a game; when the priest was carrying out his service, a bat flew into the church and as soon as I saw it, I told the priest, "Oh, priest, priest, I beg you, please keep silent, I think my nightingale has just flown in and I want to catch it." (Ivanishvili-Demuria 1895)

By the 1860s, Eristavi-Jorjadze and her children (Mikheil, Noshrevan, Manana) had spent years travelling across Georgia with her husband who, unable to pay the *Prikaz* loan, was looking for work. Archival records document Eristavi-Jorjadze's efforts to bring education to those women whom she met in parts of the country far from her native home. Frequently on the move, Eristavi-Jorjadze offered a farewell message to her students on the importance of getting an education in her unpublished article, "Farewell and My Testament":

> Today you see in your schools somebody else instead of me ... For our ancestors have said, "Education is the light, and ignorance is darkness." I think, you too, have heard that said quite often. So strive to learn before it is too late! Now you see clearly how necessary and important education is, don't you? Do not deprive your children of the chance to read and write Georgian! As long as you have time and a good chance, learn yourself, and what is more important, send your children to school. Haven't you heard? Live a century and learn a century! (Jorjadze's Archive: N 9974)

In the 1860s Eristavi-Jorjadze participated in discussions over the modernization of Georgian literature and literary language raised by Lavrenti Ardaziani and Ilia Chavchavadze, who represented a younger generation. They demanded that editors of journals and newspapers stop using certain Old Georgian letters (there were only a few such letters); replace the language of the Bible with "modern," popular language forms, which they argued would be intelligible to readers; refrain from publishing poetry; and translate from foreign languages contemporaneous "realistic" literature rather than classic works or literature deemed sentimental.

Barbare Eristavi-Jorjadze was among the key figures who dared to oppose the reformers. She argued that banning poetry, for example, would serve to prevent writers from fulfilling their creative potential. She contended that it was not necessary to ban the old in order to introduce the new and "modernize" literary forms. Her position was that the old and the new could coexist quite well, and this view is reflected in her two letters in the journal *Tsiskari* (1860, 1861a).

Eristavi-Jorjadze was also an innovative writer who applied her pen to prose and drama. She published stories, novels, and plays on historical and social themes in the journals *Tsiskari, Kvali,* and *Iveria*. Among the gender-related themes in her writings were parental authority and arranged marriages of daughters, patterns of marital infidelity by husbands, preference for and preferential treatment of sons over daughters, and tragic stories centered on themes of romantic love and devotion. Her plays were staged in theaters in Tbilisi, Kutaisi, and Telavi to great acclaim.

An accomplished writer, Eristavi-Jorjadze's portfolio of writings include the 1874 book, *Georgian Cuisine and an Approved Directory of the Domestic Economy,* which affirmed the value of traditional Georgian and Georgian–European dishes. She also authored a textbook titled *Starting to Learn,* a primer on teaching reading and writing. While both books were published, these works were not attributed to the author.[3] In her 1893 essay, "Remarks to Draw the Attention of Young Men," Eristavi-Jorjadze critiques the Georgian system of raising children and restricting women's access to education. For contemporary Georgian women, this essay is a manifesto, a call to social change on behalf of future generations. Eristavi-Jorjadze's words, quoted below, resonate with current concerns:

> Men have been casting aspersions on women since the very beginning. They attribute all the faults to women and they try to belittle and humiliate them. Since early childhood it is drummed into women's ears—the Creator made you a woman and you have to obey these rules: "You must always keep silent; you must not raise your eyes at anybody, you must not go anywhere, you must block your ears, close your eyes, and sit back; education and learning foreign languages to improve your knowledge is none of your business." Men, [on the other hand], full of pride and arrogance, announce: "As I am a man, I will set off, take to my heels to the end of the sky and nothing can stop me; I'll be eloquent, I'll learn, get an education and acquire all the freedom and power of the world." At least now, our gentlemen should give up pride and envy, and give their sisters an opportunity to enjoy equal education and direction, so that they can work side by side with men and be accountable. (Eristavi-Jorjadze 1893)

Eristavi-Jorjadze died in 1895. Her works influenced women from her own time, including the Georgian actress and poet Nino Orbeliani (1838–1919), the actress Mako Safarova-Abashidze (1860–1940), and Elisabed Cherkezishvili who performed in Eristavi-Jorjadze's plays. Eristavi-Jorjadze leaves a legacy that continues to have influence on Georgian women, especially those looking to write, publish, and engage in feminist activism.

Ekaterine Tarkhnishvili-Gabashvili and the Political Mobilization of Women

In 1879, the "Society for the Spreading of Literacy among Georgians" (hereafter, the society) was established to confront the Russian Empire's assimilationist policies. Soon thereafter, it became a powerful educational and "enlightenment" organization. It rallied the intellectuals of the period to build Georgia as a national state. The society provided support to young boys interested in getting a European education, and it introduced European thinkers to Georgian culture. The organization facilitated the translation of foreign literature into Georgian, and helped disseminate this literature by publishing books and articles. Long after the society was established, Ekaterine Tarkhnishvili-Gabashvili emerged to inspire a Georgian women's movement centered on the struggle for access to education.

Tarkhnishvili-Gabashvili was born in 1851 to Revaz Tarkhnishvili and Sopio Bagration-Davitashvili in the city of Gori. She received primary education in "Sharikov's Widow," a domestic school. She went on to study in Madam Favre's boarding school, considered at that time the best school and where Georgian was on the curriculum along with French and natural sciences (mathematics and geography). At age seventeen, Tarkhnishvili-Gabashvili opened her own private school for peasant children. By the age of nineteen, she was married to Aleksandre Gabashvili. Here, Tarkhnishvili-Gabashvili recalls those years:

> I was nineteen years of age when I got married. Soon I became the mother of eleven children. Our family was rather hard up. I was deprived of any kind of freedom. But I did not abide by the general fate of the woman—serfdom and self-sacrifice for hearth and home—for which I had gone through a big struggle. I did possess some strength for the fight ... I made a tiny hole through those narrow walls called housewifery, and kept my ears and eyes wide open to observe the general growth and development of my country. I tried to lay at least a couple of bricks over the sacred groundwork that the best sons of my country laid down during the second half of the nineteenth century. A few bricks on the public altar is not a big deal, but as it is said, "Where there is nothing, even a bit might seem a lot." (Iremadze 1945: 181–82)

Tarkhnishvili-Gabashvili was affected deeply by two works that had been translated into Georgian. One was Harriet Taylor Mill's "Enfranchisement of Women," which may have been co-authored with John Stuart Mill; and the other was Fanny Lewald's "Woman: Pro and Contra [*Für und wider die Frauen*].[4] Both works denounced cultural norms that deprive women of educational opportunities and, consequently, the chance for effective social and political engagement. Under such circumstances, women are economically dependent and subjugated. The two authors were themselves on a search for and in process of demanding protection of their rights. In her essay, Taylor Mill (1869) looks to the "organized agitation" in the United States as a model for British women to demand equal rights in the spheres of employment, education, and political participation.

Tarkhnishvili-Gabashvili recognized that in the Georgian context it was essential to mobilize women and establish their own organization if they were ever to raise women's inferior status. To this end, Tarkhnishvili-Gabashvili established "Women's Circles" in various locations: Tbilisi, Kutaisi, Gori, and Khoni. A central activity of the women's circles was to enable women to publish their own literature and to translate the literature from foreign languages on relevant topics.[5]

It was during this time that Tarkhnishvili-Gabashvili recognized the need for a school dedicated to women's education. After all, the Society for the Spreading of Literacy among Georgians only provided educational opportunities for Georgian boys, and did nothing to encourage the establishment of a school for girls or mixed gender education. In 1897, Tarkhnishvili-Gabashvili opened a women's professional school; its graduates followed suit, establishing schools for girls in various regions of Georgia.

By the end of the nineteenth century, Tarkhnishvili-Gabashvili was a well-established, renowned author and educator. Her short stories and novels follow plot lines that reveal opposition to traditional assumptions and customs regarding girls and women. In her most significant novels, including *Love-Affair in Big Kheva, While Sorting Maize,* and *Orena and Kuche,* the author explores themes of personal freedom and romantic love, ideologies and practices that violated the will of parents and the social norms of the day. Tarkhnishvili-Gabashvili's sympathies in these novels upset the patriarchal foundation of the social order of her time.

Georgia was an independent nation between 1918 and 1921, and Tarkhnishvili-Gabashvili remained an active public figure. Starting in 1922, things changed. Once the Bolshevik regime was established, Tarkhnishvili-Gabashvili's private school was shut down. Her activism began to wane. Twelve years before her death in 1938, she and her fellow women writers regrouped to publish the journal, *Literary Almanac* (1925–26). They were only able to publish two issues, and the pieces in them represent the group's final struggle before they were redesignated as "children's writers and poets," and their social work and activism consigned to oblivion.

Backlash and New Generation of Women

Georgian women's efforts to mobilize on behalf of winning their own space, their freedoms, and their rights did not go unnoticed by prominent and ordinary men alike. A nineteenth-century version of backlash saw public appeals for women to follow tradition and return to the confines of home. For example, the Georgian writer David Kezeli admonishes those women who dare to venture out. His words appear in the 1882 edition of the newspaper, *Shroma*:

> If you want to bear the name of a Georgian woman once celebrated all over the world for her dignity, dispel your dreams about becoming doctors [or] professors, and try to become mothers appropriate to our time. In order to do that, you have to learn the past of your homeland, the history of ancient nations, and in particular the history of Rome. You will find there a lot of dignified ladies deserving fame, and you are obliged today to imitate them! You have nothing in common with American and European women, because '*Quod licet Jovi, non licet bovi*' (What is permitted to Jove [Jupiter] is not permitted to an ox). (Kezeli 1882)

A letter (1894) in the Georgian newspaper, *Iveria*, from Marjory Scott Wardrop, the English translator of Georgian literature, prompted a firestorm of letters to the editor.[6] Two letters—one from a man named Artem Akhnazarov, and the other from Mose Toidze—bemoaned the "ruin" of Georgian women who they blamed for failing to sustain the Georgian language, which they believed was the purview of wives and mothers. Women, they noted, should be of humble character—good housewives who should care about their husbands and children, and educated only enough to enable their husbands to have satisfying conversations with them (Akhnazarov 1894; Toidze 1894). Seven women, including Nino Kipiani, a member of the "Women's Circle," wrote strong letters contesting the logic posed by the men.

The backlash also included claims of women's inherent inferiority. For example, a certain Doctor Ekvtime Vashakidze attempted to use "scientific arguments," invoking "nature" to justify women's lack of economic and political rights. In the newspaper *Moambe*, Vashakidze wrote, "A woman's brain is less developed as it feeds on less blood because of menstruation, because she gets pregnant and bears children" (Vashakidze 1897).

Kato Mikeladze, the subject of the final portrait I provide in this chapter, responded to Vashakidze as follows:

> Whether women's skeletal bones are better linked than are men's, or whether her brains are smaller than men's won't stop the emancipation movement. The emancipation movement emerged from need—the need to earn money for the household. The movement will continue until the root causes [of inequality] are eradicated. Science shows the causes of economic and political inequality do not result from inequality in ability or intelligence. It is the other way around. Because of existing economic and political inequalities there are inequalities in abilities. (Mikeladze 1898)

Mikeladze was a twenty-year-old graduate of the St. Nino School in Kutaisi when she wrote those comments in the Georgian journal *Kvali*. A cosmopolitan, she studied in Moscow (1903) and in Brussels (1906), where she graduated with a degree in the Social and Political Sciences. Between 1910 and 1915 she lived in Paris, where she became acquainted with the history of European women's movements and their contemporaneous expressions. She was particularly interested in the issue of women's political participation and the activities of the National Union of Women's Suffrage Societies, the Women's Social and Political Union, and in the British suffragists involved in them, such as Emmeline Pankhurst.

Upon returning in 1916 to Kutaisi, her native city, Mikeladze established "The Inter-Partial League of Women," the main objective of which was to mobilize women into active political participation. To achieve this goal, Mikeladze founded a newspaper, *The Voice of Georgian Women*, which covered the state of women's legal position in Georgia, Russia, Europe, and the United States. The newspaper printed poems, stories, and articles on social and political issues by like-minded Georgian women, as well as by women from Europe such as Bertha von Suttner and Emmeline Pankhurst's daughter Christabel. Mikeladze's powerful rhetoric is captured in this excerpt from a 1918 article she published in *The Voice of Georgian Women*:

> When we, the women fighting for our rights, demand the national and civic rights and fight against the enemies of women's human rights, we fight not against a human being in the shape of man, but against the traditional injustice that the majority of men have mastered, and which is leading one half of the nation to mental and spiritual emptiness. We do not want to drag on this wretched existence but must get rid of it at any cost. We demand justice and not revenge. In this case we need the understanding and the sympathy of every honest and unprejudiced man, instead of drumming in the idea that suffragette women in Georgia hate men and demand separation from them, as the crowd following the anti-suffragettes profusely talks about. Among the suffragette women, there are plenty of mothers, wives, daughters and sisters of men, and their hearts are full of better feelings and desires for them, but at the same time they remember their human personality and demand adequate rights. (Mikeladze 1918)

Due to Mikeladze's activism, and that of her followers such as Safo Mgeladze, Mariam Tateishvili, Barbare Sulkhanishvili, Barbare Kherkheulidze, Mariam Dadiani, and Aneta Kapanadze, five women were among the 132 members of the first parliament of independent Georgia assembled after the 1919 democratic election. However, three of the five women met untimely ends. Elisabed Nakashidze-Bolkvadze and Ana Sologhashvili were shot and killed in 1937 by the Bolsheviks, and Eleonora Terfarsegova-

Makhviladze was deported, never to be found. Christine Sharashidze and Minadora Toroshelidze survived the Bolshevik terror.

Mikeladze died in extreme poverty and obscurity in 1942. Twenty years earlier, she had been expelled from the Georgian Writers' Union for publicly criticizing several important male writers and public figures as "erotomaniacs." She accused them of depicting women in their writings in essentialist terms as either a mother or a whore, incapable of engaging significant social or political activity ((Mikeladze archive: 8385).

Concluding Remarks

During the Soviet period and the repressions associated with it, the histories of the Georgian political struggle for democracy, Georgian–Western dialogue, and women's activism were effectively erased. In this process, the women who had "translated" and adapted aspects of the European experience in granting women the right to education, and to economic, civic, and political participation were also erased from public consciousness. Since contact with the Western world was regarded as treachery, and since the women activists were associated with the West, women activists in the late nineteenth and early twentieth century were either killed or relegated to obscurity.

It is symbolic that in 1921 when the Bolsheviks invaded the capital of Georgia, Ekaterine Gabashvili's granddaughter, Maro Makashvili, and Barbare Eristavi-Jorjadze's great-grandson, Gabriel Gechtman, died on the battlefield. Maro and Gabriel were buried near the wall of the Military Temple, built by the Russians as a symbol of victory over the mountainous peoples of the Caucasus in 1897. Today their graves are missing, having been destroyed by the Soviets to build the House of Government, the current building of the Georgian Parliament. Like their grandchildren, the women activists and their significance to Georgian history were nearly wiped out. Recent scholarship, including the work on which this chapter is based, has brought their stories back to Georgia and to the world, "herstories" that are part of a global movement for women's emancipation.

Acknowledgements

This research would not have been possible without the support of the Open Society Georgia Foundation (OSGF) and the Heinrich Böll Foundation, the latter of which has helped bring these lost "herstories" back to public consciousness via the Internet (http://www.feminism-boell.org/

en). I would like to express my deep gratitude to Alisse Waterston, whose idea it was to bring this volume and thus these Georgian "herstories" to an international audience.

Lela Gaprindashvili is a professor of philosophy at Tbilisi State University where she has been teaching courses on gender for more than fifteen years. She helped integrate Gender Studies as a field of study into the higher education system in Georgia. Her research focuses on feminist movements in Georgia. She is a women's rights and civil society activist. Since 1997, she has served as chair of the Women's Initiative for Equality, an NGO in Tbilisi.

Notes

1. This includes the distinguished scholars Ketevan Iremadze and Nino Chikhladze, who have researched the contributions of dozens of Georgian women from the nineteenth and twentieth centuries.
2. Translations from Georgian to English in this chapter were provided by Ms. Lela Dumbadze.
3. The writer wrote about this to her brother, Raphiel Eristavi. The book is kept in the Georgian National Center of Manuscripts in the Barbare Jorjadze's Archive, manuscript N 16.
4. Both studies were published in the journal *Mnatobi*. Harriet Taylor Mill's work was originally published in her own name in 1851; subsequently it is sometimes attributed as a joint work with her husband John Stuart Mill. In *Mnatobi*, it was published in 1869 under her husband's name, John Stuart Mill (N 7, 8). Excerpts of Fanny Lewald's book, originally published in 1870, appears in *Mnatobi* in 1871, N 4, 5, 6, 7.
5. In one of those publications, Ekaterine encouraged her friend, Keke Meskhi, to publish an excerpt she had translated of Elizabeth Fries Lummis Ellet's "The Women of the American Revolution," originally published in 1848–50.
6. Wardrop's letter informed the Georgian writer Ilia Chavchavadze that she had translated his poem "The Hermit" into English and she asked his permission to publish it, which became a matter of a lengthy discussion. Wardrop was a Kartvelologist, a popularizer of Georgian culture in Europe. She translated into English various Georgian legends, fairy tales and "The Knight in the Panther's Skin," the twelfth-century epic poem by Shota Rustaveli. Her brother, Sir John Oliver Wardrop, was the United Kingdom's Representative to the South Caucasus and Georgia in the years 1919–21.

References

Akhnazarov, A. 1894. "Cursory." *Iveria* 194: 3.
Eristavi-Jorjadze, B. 1860. "Clarification." *Tsiskari* 1: 119–123.

———. 1861a. "About the Criticism of Ilia Chavchavadze." *Tsiskari* 5: 33–45.
———. 1861b. "Response to Response." *Tsiskari* 5: 87–106.
———. 1893. "Remarks to Draw the Attention of Young Men." *Kvali* 16: 1–2.
———. n.d. "Farewell and my Testament." Giorgi Leonidze Georgian Literary Institute, Barbare Jorjadze's Archive, manuscript no. 9974.
Iremadze, K. 1945. *Literary Medallions.* Tbilisi: Publishing House Sablitgami.
Ivanishvili-Demuria, M. 1895. "The Memoirs about Barbare Jorjadze." *Iveria* 91: 3.
Kezeli, D. 1882. "To Georgian Women." *Shroma* 10: 1–2.
Lewald, F. 1871. "Woman: Pro and Contra." *Mnatobi* 4, 5, 6, 7.
Mikeladze, K. 1898. "Women's Question and the Women's Talant." *Kvali* 11: 103–22.
———. 1918. "Equality of Women and Men in Front of the Law." *The Voice of Georgian Woman* 32: 1.
———. n.d.. "My story." Giorgi Leonidze Georgian Literary Museum, Kato Mikeladze's Archive, manuscript no. 8385: 5.
Mill, J.S. 1869. "Enfranchisement of Women." *Mnatobi* 7, 8: 1–40; 42–75.
Toidze, M. 1894. "To the Young Georgian Women." *Iveria* 231: 3–4.
Vashakidze, E. 1897. "Women's Issue in Modern Science." *Moambe* 11: 65–83.
Wardrop, M.S. 1894. "Letter to Editor." *Iveria* 191: 1.

Chapter 2

"The Country of the Happiest Women"?
Ideology and Gender in Soviet Georgia

Maia Barkaia

Introduction

Early Marxists viewed women's participation in the labor force as a key challenge to the gender division of labor, and a necessary condition of the proletarian revolution and of women's subsequent emancipation. In this chapter, I explore the implications of emancipation for Georgian women and the specific ways it unfolded in peripheral Soviet Georgia. I examine ideologies of gender and the construction of female identity in a thematic analysis of women's magazines published in Soviet Georgia during the era of ideological radicalism of the 1920s, and of conservatism of the 1930s. Specifically, I have selected the only women's magazine in Soviet Georgia, which was first published under the name *Chveni Gza* (Our Way) from 1923 to 1925, and was later renamed *Mshromeli Qali* (Woman Worker) and published from 1926 to 1939. Further, I have sampled articles that overtly or tacitly focused on the "woman's question" and identified themes and concepts in my data. In particular, I have examined these materials for what they reveal about conceptions of domestic labor, motherhood, and labor force participation in Soviet Georgia during the period in question.

In order to bring women into the public domain and engage them in the building of the socialist state, the Soviet authorities adopted a "special approach," which entailed actions such as the establishment of the Zhe-

Notes for this chapter begin on page 44.

notdel, the women's section of the Communist Party, and the publication of *Chveni Gza*, mentioned above (Ckhakaia 1924; Makharadze 1924). The Soviet authorities viewed print media as a powerful tool that could raise awareness among women and break the shackles that kept them confined to the household (Japaridze 1926). The newspaper, in Lenin's view, was not limited merely to the propagation of ideas and agitation, but also served as a collective organizer (S-i 1928: 1). Zhenotdel employed various methods of engagement with women, including using the women's magazine. Firstly, the magazine was disseminated and read out loud, so that the illiterate could hear it. For better results, the Communist Party leaders avowed that they and their contemporaneous writers were talking and writing in "a language alien to the masses," and insisted on the use of clear and simple language that would be easily understood by nearly everyone (Makharadze 1924: 3). Further, the magazine's letters section was a platform where peasant and proletarian women could speak out. In this way, Zhenotdel established networks aimed at recruiting local women and encouraging them to write (ibid.).

These women's magazines divided the world into two unequal parts: the Soviet Union, where women were emancipated, and the capitalist world, where women experienced double oppression as women and as workers (Makharadze 1927a). The Soviet leadership used women's emancipation to showcase its progressiveness. The different expressions of family and women's labor participation have themselves become both products and signifiers of Soviet modernity. I explore how and why family and gender came to occupy a central place in the discourses of the new socialist state.

Gendering the "Backward"

Soviet Georgia was discursively divided between the nexus of the modern/premodern, Soviet/pre-Soviet, secular/religious, literate/illiterate, and progressive/backward dichotomies. Like all regulatory discourses, the idea of a new Soviet order and gender roles needed its civilizational "others." The magazine articles constructed and defined what they sought to displace. The *Woman Worker* featured women as "the main victims of barbarism and backwardness" ("Raze Unda Sweron Qalkorebma" 1927; Anaida 1928; N-a 1928), and the Soviet state as the agent of change that withered away "dark, barbarian and oppressed women" (Zorini 1931: 8). Depictions of proletarian women were equivocal: they were idealized as the bearers of the New Soviet emancipatory politics, but they were also portrayed as victims of old customs that kept them "backward" and downtrodden. Women's oppression was depicted as the remnant of the pre-Soviet past.

The Soviet government targeted "backward," "living in the darkness" proletarian women, who were in need of enlightenment and "awakening" in order to build the socialist state (Makharadze 1924; "Werili Zemo Rachidan" 1926; "Mivardnil Kutxeebis Glexis Qalebic Erkvevian" 1926; Makharadze 1927b: 3).

To describe people, regions, or communities as "culturally backward," "backward," or "uncivilized" implied that these people and places were reluctant to support women's emancipation, and that they held rigid patriarchal norms. The second implication of the use of "backwardness" was "religiousness." Those who still believed in God and trusted in priests were depicted as the ignorant who live in "darkness" (Glekhishvili 1928: 10). Labels such as "backward" and "uncivilized" were especially and consistently invoked to describe minority Muslim women (Gr. 1924; Saqartvelos Musha da Glex-Qalta Shoris Momushave Ganqofileba 1927: 8; Ivanovi 1927; Makharadze 1927b: 3). For example, "backward child of the East" was a specific reference to Muslim women (Gr. 1924).

Early marriages, polygamy, and "all these kinds of patriarchal customs" were assigned to a world of backward customs and were described as *asiatchina* or Asiatic practice (Gaji-Zade 1935). "Asiatic" or "Eastern" signify "backward" and "patriarchal." For the metropole (Moscow), Georgia was "East," but for Georgian readers, Adjara (which is actually in the western part of Georgia) was "Eastern" or read as backward, Muslim, and a place where women were oppressed ("Oqtombris Revolucia da Chveni Amocanebi" 1928: 1).[1] New modes of dress and consumption became signifiers of the New Soviet Woman. It is notable that in 1928, women in Batumi were forced to remove their chador by decision of Adjara's regional committee (Anaida 1928: 7).

Magazine articles about "backward" people helped shape new self-definitions among readers who presumably wanted to be identified in opposite terms, an ideological maneuver as old as ancient Greece, where "the barbarian is often portrayed as the opposite of the ideal Greek." The idea of who would be "Greek" could be constructed only in relation to the "barbarian," who would be its opposite (Kuper 2005: 20). Similarly, as Chakrabarty (2002) notes, "modernity" must be defined in contrast to those people or practices identified as backward or "non-modern." Following the tenets of the European Enlightenment, Soviet ideologues saw modernity as the rule of institutions that unshackled its citizens from all that was irrational or premodern. Since they saw modernity as coeval with the idea of progress, the backwardness of the old subjects defined the new Soviet subject in terms defined by these very Soviet subjects. Any attempt to subvert this dichotomy implied that the New Soviet Wo/Man was not, after all, so different from the uncivilized backward wo/man. Thus, Soviet ideologues employed the "insistence on difference" — sharp, virtually absolute contrasts between Soviet and pre-Soviet cultures. Similarities between the Soviets and the pre-Soviet independent Republic of Georgia that embraced social democracy and Marxist ideology were systematically ignored in this construction of modern Soviet subjects.

Although the Soviet Union instituted revolutionary changes in nearly all areas of Georgian life, men in general were reluctant to accept women's emancipation. The *Woman Worker* features the case of some Komsomol members who imposed the chador on their wives in Adjara (Ch. 1935: 4).[2] As indicated by the magazine articles, both proletarian and peasant men expressed fears that their wives and daughters would become "degenerates"; they were resistant to change (Bregvadze 1927; Makharadze 1929). Thus, "the woman's question" was a contested issue that many men, unwilling to compromise, dared to resist.

Women's Labor Participation: Emancipation or Encumbrance

The Bolshevik vision of women's emancipation was shaped by the ideas formulated by Marx and Engels in the nineteenth century. For instance, Alexandra Kollontai, following Marx and Engels, argued that the social relations of private property determine family life (Marx and Engels 1965). In distinguishing the bourgeois family (rooted in property relations) from the proletarian family (as held together by affection and "real relations"), Marx and Engels romanticized "propertyless" affection, and overlooked the specific manifestations of women's oppression within the proletarian family (ibid.).

Bolshevik ideologues such as Lenin and Kollontai alluded to Marx and Engels, who argued that women's emancipation was largely contingent upon the abolition of private property and the creation of a communal domestic economy (Goldman 1993: 1–52). The Soviet ideologues viewed the transfer of household labor to the public sphere as crucial to women's emancipation. They believed that communal dining rooms, childcare centers and laundries would free women to enter the public sphere on an equal basis with men, thereby solving the contradiction between productive and reproductive work as it existed in capitalist economies (Lenin 1924: 17). The transfer of household labor to the realm of waged or socialized labor aimed to undermine the family and render it free from its previous social functions. In addition, the Code on Marriage, the Family, and Guardianship, ratified by the Russian Central Committee of the Soviet Union in 1918, made it easy for married couples to separate. Lenin viewed household labor as the most arduous work a woman could do. In Lenin's view, legal equality was a first step, but real emancipation for women required the wholesale transformation of household into socialized labor (Lenin 1924: 17; "Qalta Saertashoriso Dgis 25 Wlistavistvis" 1935). Women's magazines often featured Lenin's views on the need for women's liberation from "the most petty, most menial, most arduous, and most stultifying work of the kitchen" (Lenin 1920: 8; Rva Marti 1933: 3). This theme is captured in this passage from an essay that appears in a 1924 issue of *Chveni Gza*:

> Notwithstanding all the liberating laws that have been passed, women continue to be domestic slaves because petty housework crushes, strangles, stultifies, and degrades her, chains her to the kitchen and to the nursery, and wastes her labor on barbarously unproductive, petty, nerve-racking, stultifying, and crushing drudgery. The real emancipation of women, real communism, will only begin when a mass struggle (led by the proletarian who is in power) begins against this domestic economy—or rather, when it is transformed on a mass scale into a large-scale socialist economy. (Woman Worker Natalia 1924: 20; Marx et al. 1951: 24)

The transfer of household labor to the public sphere in the Soviet Union did not alter in any large way the gendered segregation of labor either in the household or in the public domain. In the household, women retained major responsibility for tasks; and in the public sphere, women tended to perform waged household work. This is not surprising considering Lenin himself insisted that "proletarian women's emancipation is the work of proletarian women themselves." As featured in the magazine, Lenin elaborated further that other proletarian women should perform the services provided to proletarian women to lighten their household load (Lenin 1924: 17; Centraluri Komiteti 1933). Although the household labor was transferred from the private to the public sphere, it remained an exclusively women's domain.

Even as the magazines had an ideological mission, articles in them were ideologically inconsistent and occasionally out of line with the Soviet authorities' purported views on the woman's question. For example, in an issue of the *Woman Worker*, Lenin's words about freeing women from household chores are featured (Lenin 1924: 17). In the same volume, another article endorses the idea that women's domestic labor is important. It describes the role of the peasant woman as the "cornerstone of the family" because of the wide range of tasks in the home that she performs (T-a 1924). The article depicts both tending small livestock and gardening as work belonging to women, since "no one can compete with [them] in performing these tasks." It also naturalizes gendered work in the village household: "Domestic livestock are so much accustomed to women's hands. They love women's tender, kind, and loving treatment so much that it is impossible to look after them without women" (ibid.). Implicit in this and other articles is the idea that women are more "inclined" toward certain kinds of work, whether this be in the private or public sphere. For example, another article reports on an uncommon case of men being compelled to labor on collective tea farms, which was considered women's domain because there were not enough women to put to work (Kalandadze 1935: 7).

During the early 1920s, the magazine *Our Way* identified cultural liberation and economic change as important facets of women's emancipation. Articles featured in the magazine illustrated stories of women's lives that had been transformed by their participation in women-centered, politically inspired social activities developed by Zhenotdel activists. Throughout the 1920s up until 1930 (when the Communist Party deemed the woman's question "solved" and shut down its women's section), Zhenotdel activists used a variety of tactics to engage and attract women at the grassroots level. To galvanize local women from the "backward regions," they developed ways to gain their trust and attention. Providing the women and the community with various forms of social support was a key long-term strategy they used to engage local women, such as establishing an orphanage and accompanying doctors in providing the women and their families with medical services and free medicines. As a result, the local women developed attachments to the Zhenotdel activists, and increasingly reached out to them for help with various issues and concerns ("Saqartvelos Qru Kutxeebshi" 1924: 45).

The opening of women's clubs was among the activities introduced by the Zhenotdels. Initially, the women's clubs were places for local Georgian women to watch performances or to take tea with one another. Later, once women became regular visitors, activists offered academic lectures, political talks, and trainings to raise Georgian women's social and political awareness (Gr. 1924).

The *Woman Worker* featured the stories of women whose lives had changed after going to the women's clubs. For instance, it was at a women's club that Khoreshana, an illiterate Georgian Muslim woman, first learned about the women's equality and freedom and the eradication of illiteracy program, a campaign to eradicate illiteracy in the Soviet Union that offered a range of flexible part-time courses. Subsequently, Khoreshana took the classes and became active in the public sphere (Ivanovi 1927).

One of the main objectives of the Soviet state was to maximize the use of women in the labor force. To ensure this, and to encourage women to accept work as a central life value, the Soviets deployed a variety of activities to encourage women's participation, including holding competitions, providing awards, telling heroic tales about women workers, and offering them special excursions ("Daundoblad Davartqat Qalta Shoris Mushaobis Sheufaseblobas" 1931: 9; Charkviani 1933: 4; Adamia 1936). These efforts escalated in the late 1920s, and the emphasis on "using women's labor" and privileging work over other values intensified (Butkhuzi 1933; Charkviani 1933: 4; Svanidze 1933). In this context, the *Woman Worker* ran life stories illustrating the achievements of the hardest working proletarian women and collective farmers, who were transformed into Soviet media heroines (Adamia 1936). The *Woman Worker* depicted them as icons of Soviet egalitarianism and glorified their tirelessness, despite their overwork and exhaustion (Mgeladze 1934; Sona 1934; Kalandadze 1934).

The women's labor force was needed both on the collective farms and in the industries. In Stalin's words, "the women on the collective farms are a great force. To keep this force down would be criminal. It is our duty to bring the women on the collective farms forward, to make use of this great workforce" (Butkhuzi 1933). Women were also needed as factory workers since the number of factories had drastically increased due to rapid industrialization ("Saqartvelos Mshromel Qalebs" 1929). In fact, women were indispensable for the industrialization project. To be free from the fetters of domestic work was not a trivial matter; the Soviet state was compelled to liberate women from unpaid labor so they could be put to work in building the Socialist state (Nina 1926: 7).

In turn, the women's magazines were put to work in encouraging women to adopt a new worker identity. In their depiction of the New Soviet Woman, the *Woman Worker* showed her as a laborer with no time or interest in beauty treatments or any such indulgences. They held up a portrait of the New Soviet Woman to stand in contrast with the pre-Soviet woman who cared only about her appearance, superficial entertainment and other frivolities (Mgeladze 1934). Those who tried to avoid their duties were depicted in the magazines as a "burden to the society." The magazine also featured articles in which collective farmer women were exhorted to "fight against slacker women" (Surguladze 1933). Letters to the magazine highlighted grievances aired by peasant women complaining about those who avoided work, and calling for ways to address the slackers (Olinka 1927). In these ways, women's participation in waged labor was no longer presented as simply the goal of women's emancipation but constructed as a requirement for the building of the new Socialist state. Encouraging women to mobilize as workers to meet production expectations, the *Woman Worker* also encouraged them to embody "the Bolshevik example," and to even go beyond it (I.A. 1931: 10; "Daundoblad Davartqat Qalta Shoris Mushaobis Sheufaseblobas" 1931: 9; Wilosani 1933a: 18; Wilosani 1933b: 2; M-r 1935: 3–4; Gogoladze-Devadze 1936).

The effort to mobilize women into the labor force was quite successful. Nevertheless, women's participation tended to stagnate at the lowest job levels; women were rarely promoted to managerial positions (Centraluri Komiteti 1933). As women entered the labor force en masse, men found a new basis for masculine identity by acquiring and retaining skilled and supervisory positions in industry, on collective farms and in the Communist Party (Creighton 1996: 323).

These patterns and the factors that explain the dynamics of women's labor force participation were noted in articles published in the *Woman Worker* (I.A. 1931: 10; Butkhuzi 1933; M-r 1935: 3–4). The burden of women's responsibilities in the home and a lack of quality childcare were named as key factors hindering women's advancement in the workplace and in political life. As the decade of the 1920s advanced, the number of childcare centers dropped—they were being forced to close due to a lack of financial support (Jaqeli 1933: 21; Goldman 1993: 74). The paramount solution offered by the *Woman Worker* to address the conflict between work and motherhood was simply to provide more daycare centers (Nina 1926: 7; "Socializmistvis Mebrdzol Saertashoriso Qalta Dzalebis Shemchidroebis Dge" 1931: 4).

Articles in the *Woman Worker* also depicted various forms of discrimination in the workplace, including that women's work was devalued, they were paid lower wages, and there were specific instances where managers cheated women out of their due wages (Butkhuzi 1933). In some articles, workplace discrimination was cited as the reason women were becoming alienated from work (ibid.). Further, the *Woman Worker* cited proletarian and peasant men's sexism as one of the hindrances to Georgian women's waged work and participation in the public sphere (Makharadze 1927b; Ivanovi 1927; M-r 1935: 3–4). They reported on cases where women candidates for political office were silenced, turned down and rejected (Cherqezishvili 1927: 10). They reported on common instances of husbands forbidding their wives and daughters from working on the collective farms (S-dze 1934; M-r 1935: 3–4; Kalandadze 1935: 7). The *Woman Worker* depicted sexist comrades who alienated women by portraying them as "bed equipment," and as carriers of the capitalist agenda (Ts. 1935: 6).

"Proletarian antifeminism" was a widespread phenomenon among European workers that was exacerbated in the nineteenth century when men and women began competing for industrialized jobs, which paid lower wages to women than to men, and when men began to organize against women. Marx and Engels admonished proletarian antifeminism, viewing women's employment as inevitable and irreversible; however, socialist movements across Europe were reluctant to accept their views on women's labor participation, and instead demanded a family wage that would enable women to return to the home (Goldman 1993: 29).

The Soviet state accepted the inevitability of women's labor force participation. At the same time, they did not challenge structural sexism manifest in the practice of segregation of labor by gender and workplace inequity, including the failure to promote women in industry, political organizations, and on the collective farms. Several magazine articles called out this issue as the main failure of the collective farms (Charkviani 1933: 4; M-r 1935: 3–4). Even as women were hailed as labor heroes on the collective farms, they were not promoted to lead these farms in many regions of Georgia (M. 1934: 17; M-r 1935: 3–4). Articles also called out the failure to advance women within the Communist Party itself (Shaverdova 1927; Bakhtadze 1931: 5–6).

On 23 July 1928, the central committee of the Communist Party of the Soviet Union (CPSU) passed a resolution stating it was time to take women's advancement seriously, and outlined special measures to engage women in the "building of the Socialist State" (Nina 1928a). The resolution also called on the women's magazines to highlight the issue by writing on the following topics: those proletarian women who "deserve" promotion; the structural and ideological obstacles to women's promotion; those organizations that did promote women and the means by which they did so; and the work and activities of those women who had been promoted (ibid.). Despite the official declaration in support of women's advancement, to implement it posed an altogether different challenge. For one, delegate women were often ignored by and not accepted into the party (Delegati 1928). There were also practical obstacles that limited women's advancement in public life, including the lack of childcare facilities and the scheduling of late night meetings (Nina 1928b: 6). In short, the numerous resolutions and statements calling for women's advancement remained de jure. Given that those responsible for implementing advancement policies failed to do so, women's de facto advancement was not realized (Shaverdova 1927; Bakhtadze 1931: 5; "Daundoblad Davartqat Qalta Shoris Mushaobis Sheufaseblobas" 1931: 9).

In specific ways, the magazines also failed to meet the promise of the resolutions. Instead of promoting women's advancement in the workplace or politics, they promulgated the idea that women were insufficiently interested in waged work, public life, or self-development and advancement (M-r 1935: 3). Thus, the complex and multifaceted structural and ideological problem was reduced to some kind of lack in women themselves. At times, the blame focused on women's purported lack of interest or aspiration. At other times, women's "ignorance" and "illiteracy" was cited as the reason women failed to advance (Nina 1928a). To illustrate, one article profiled Dariko Berezhiani, the first Georgian woman to become a Doctor of Medicine (Qorqia 1935: 7). Emphasizing her personal traits such as studiousness and aspiration, the article suggests that since structural barriers no longer existed, women who wanted to succeed only needed to adopt attributes like those of Dr. Dariko (ibid.). The message was that the Socialist Revolution had granted women "freedom." After that, it was up to the women to take advantage of those freedoms. The Soviet authorities thus placed the onus on women to "preserve the accomplishments of the revolution" without addressing the way gender structures impeded their ability to accomplish the stated goals (Shaverdova 1927: 12).

If readers today are to believe the Soviet narrative featured in the *Woman Worker*, by the 1930s Soviet Georgian women had become remarkable superwomen who seamlessly managed the multiple roles of waged worker, mother, and wife, which altogether gave women a life fulfilled (Beria 1936: 2; "Udidesi Movaleoba" 1937). It would be as if Soviet Georgia had become, indeed, "the country of the happiest women," a phrase repeated in the magazines. As early as 1924, the women's magazine *Our Way* promulgated the message that women can perfect the balance of housework and waged work: "We do not say that women should fully abandon family duties; on the contrary, we fight to create an opportunity for women to manage both—housework and waged work" (Dolidze 1924).

The discourse of the 1920s did differ from that of the 1930s, reflecting the shift from Leninism to Stalinism and their concomitant ideologies. During the 1920s, magazines such as *Our Way* featured Lenin's critical analysis of women's confinement to home and hearth as an obstacle to her full participation in the public sphere (Woman Worker Natalia 1924: 19–20). During the 1930s, the idea of the New Soviet Woman as "superwoman" fitted with the Stalinist approach. At that point, the key messages conveyed through magazine articles were that women should not resist motherhood, since that was their natural function even as waged labor was also essential. Thus, women who participated only in waged work were reprimanded and those who stayed at home raising children and caring for the household were likewise criticized for living "under their husbands' wings" (Chkhenkeli 1936: 9). Thus, the New Soviet Woman must balance the "two extremes"; anyone unable to manage was simply flawed (ibid.; "Udidesi Movaleoba" 1937).

During the 1930s, the *Woman Worker* also conveyed the message that no woman should expect to advance in the public sphere without first having accomplished the primary, rightful duty of all women—motherhood ("Socialisturi Ojaxi da Dedis Movaleoba" 1938). The burden on women was enormous and at times contradictory. Women were exhorted to be hard-working and emancipated; to play at being men and work like them, and yet never stray too far from them. Women were charged with the responsibility of raising their children and inculcating them with love for the Socialist homeland and hatred of its enemies (ibid.: 1). Georgian women were consistently reminded by the state to remember their place in the world, which included motherhood.

The Soviet Union was the first country in the world to decriminalize abortion, a policy made in 1920. The rationale for the policy had nothing to do with rights. Indeed, the Soviet state did not recognize abortion as a woman's right (Goldman 1993: 256). In fact, abortion was conceived as "evil and unnatural," albeit a necessary evil that resulted from poverty and the lack of social supports for childcare (Tvaradze 1935; Beria 1936). From the start, abortion was conceptualized as a temporary initiative, which would disappear once women's material life circumstances improved (Beria 1936: 1). In 1936, the state recriminalized abortion in order to make "the joy of motherhood available to all [its] citizens," and the magazines framed this as a progressive move by a Socialist state that "takes care of [its] mothers and children" (ibid.: 2).

The Stalinist approach to the woman's question was determined, firstly, by labor force considerations that required women's presence both in the public sphere to fulfill a labor shortage and in the private domain as mothers to ensure the future supply of labor. Secondly, it was largely determined by the bureaucratization of the woman's question without connection to broader revolutionary or emancipatory goals. It is true that the *Woman Worker* made reference to the need to raise Georgian women's political awareness and engage them in politics. However, that "engagement in politics" merely referred to enrolling women in the Communist Party. Thus, to be political and to be a Party member became synonymous (Bakhtadze 1931: 5). Finally, Stalin's approach to the "woman's question" was in part a concession to the "proletarian antifeminism" of the 1920s—a concession to the patriarchal order in Georgia and elsewhere in the Soviet Union. Indeed, women's delegate meetings stopped functioning altogether, existing only on paper (Kidaishi 1933: 9; Akhobadze 1933).

Kollontai's anticipation that women's emancipation would follow from the abolition of private property and the emergence of the communal domestic economy was never realized fully. Stalin put the death knell on that possibility with policies aimed at strengthening and stabilizing the family unit. The Georgian women's magazines of the era affirmed these policies and the idea that the family and the interests of the state were one. As one article put it, "There is none in the world as strong and unfaltering as the Soviet family" (Beria 1936: 2).

Maia Barkaia comes from an interdisciplinary background in Oriental Studies (B.A.), Modern History (M.A.) and Gender Studies (Ph.D.). She studied and worked in Georgia, India, Russia and the United Kingdom. Most recently she has been working on historiography of the Georgian-Abkhazian conflict.

Notes

1. Adjara was an autonomous republic of the Soviet Union within the Georgian Soviet Socialist Republic.
2. Komsomol was the youth wing of the Communist Party of the Soviet Union.

References

Adamia, M. 1936. "Witeli Wigni." *Mshromeli Qali* 3: 24.
Akhobadze, N. 1933. "Qalta Shoris Mushaoba." *Mshromeli Qali* 1: 16.
Anaida. 1928. "Dzveli Zne Chveuleba Khels Ushlis Qalta Gantavisuflebis Saqmes." *Mshromeli Qali* 24: 6–8.
Bakhtadze, V. 1931. "Marxistul-Leninuri Ganatleba Qalta Shoris." *Mshromeli Qali* 9–10: 5–6.
Beria, L. 1936. "Sabchota Ojaxis Ganmtkiceba-Ganvitarebis Stalinuri Kanoni." *Mshromeli Qali* 6–7: 1–2.
Bregvadze, V. 1927. "Meti Kuradgeba Svanetis Qalebs." *Mshromeli Qali* 14: 31.
Butkhuzi, M. 1933. "Rogor Mimdinareobs Qalta Shromis Gamokenebis Saqme." *Mshromeli Qali* 8–9: 15.
Centraluri Komiteti. 1933. "Qalta Saertashoriso Komunisturi Dgis 8 Martis Chatarebis Shesaxeb." *Mshromeli Qali* 2–3: 6.
Ch., M. 1935. "Tavisufali Qveknis Tavisufali Adamianebi." *Mshromeli Qali* 10: 4–5.
Chakrabarty, D. 2002. *Habitations of Modernity: Essays in the Wake of Subaltern Studies*. Chicago: University of Chicago Press.
Charkviani, N. 1933. "Qalta Shromis Gamoqeneba Kolmeurneobashi." *Mshromeli Qali* 10: 4–5.
Cherqezisvhili. 1927. "Mshromel Qalta Monawileoba Sruliad Saqartvelos Sabchota Archevnebshi." *Mshromeli Qali* 9: 9–10.
Chkhenkeli, S. 1936. "Sakutar Tavze." *Mshromeli Qali* 6–7: 9–10.
Ckhakaia, M. 1924. "Oriode Gulrwfeli Sitkva Jurnal Chven Gzas." *Chveni Gza* 3: 2.
Creighton, C. 1996. "The Rise of the Male Breadwinner Family: A Reappraisal." *Comparative Studies in Society and History* 38(2): 310–37.
"Daundoblad Davartqat Qalta Shoris Mushaobis Sheufaseblobas." 1931. *Mshromeli Qali* 7–8: 9–15.

Delegati. 1928. "Aseti Uquradgebobac Xels Ushlis Qalebis Partiashi Shesvlas." *Mshromeli Qali* 25–26: 30.
Dolidze, T. 1924. "Rogor Unda Iqos Qalta Shoris Mushaoba Soflat." *Chveni Gza* 7: 47.
Gaji-Zade. 1935. "Chven Gamogvzarda Sabchota Khelisuflebam." *Mshromeli Qali* 1: 15.
Glekhishvili, V. 1928. "Saidan Warmosdga Saeklesio Dgesaswaulebi." *Mshromeli Qali* 18: 9–11.
Gogoladze-Devadze, E. 1936. "Amxanag Elene Gogoladze-Devadzis Sitqva." *Mshromeli Qali* 4: 7.
Goldman, W. 1993. *Women, the State and Revolution: Soviet Family Policy and Social Life, 1917–1936*. Cambridge: Cambridge University Press.
Gr., L. 1924. "Musulman Qalta Shoris." *Chveni Gza* 5: 44.
I. A. 1931. "Fartod Gamoviqenot Qalta Shroma Kolmeurneobashi." *Mshromeli Qali* 9–10: 10–11.
Ivanovi, K. 1927. "Ra Momca Sadelegato Krebam." *Mshromeli Qali* 13: 27.
Jaqeli, L. 1933. "Qalebis Shesvlas Kolmeurneobashi Win Eghobebian." *Mshromeli Qali* 10: 21–22.
Japaridze, V. 1926. "Editorial." *Mshromeli Qali* 1: 3–4.
Kalandadze, M. 1934. "Ganaxlebuli Soflis Gogona." *Mshromeli Qali* 12: 13.
———. 1935. "Ori Magaliti." *Mshromeli Qali* 7: 7–8.
Kidaishi. 1933. "Delegati Qalis Furtseli." *Mshromeli Qali* 1: 9–10.
Kuper, A. 2005. *The Reinvention of Primitive Society: Transformations of a Myth*. London and New York: Routledge.
Lenin, V. 1920. "On International Women's Day." Retrieved 10 December 2015 from https://www.marxists.org/archive/lenin/works/1920/mar/04.htm.
———. 1924. "Amkhanagi Lenini Musha Qalta Modzraobis Amocanebis Shesaxeb." *Chveni Gza* 4: 16–18.
M. 1934. "Meti Quradgeba Kolmeurne-Qalta Dawinaurebas." *Mshromeli Qali* 4–5: 17.
Makharadze, F. 1924. "Sakartvelos Mshromel Qalebs." *Chveni Gza* 3: 3.
———. 1927a. "Rva Marti anu Mshromel Qalta Saertashoriso Dgesaswauli." *Mshromeli Qali* 8: 1.
———. 1927b. "Oqtombris Revolucia da Mshromeli Qali." *Mshromeli Qali* 15: 2–3.
———. 1929. "Acharel da Turq Qalta Pirveli Qrilobis Shemdeg." *Mshromeli Qali* 2: 5.
Marx, K., and F. Engels. 1965. *A Critique of the German Ideology*. Retrieved 20 December 2015 from https://www.marxists.org/archive/marx/works/download/Marx_The_German_Ideology.pdf.
Marx, K., et al. 1951. *The Woman Question*. New York: International Publishers. Retrieved 10 December 2015 from http://www.revolutionarydemocracy.org/archive/WQ.htm.
Mgeladze, S. 1934. "Mshromel Qalebs." *Mshromeli Qali* 3: 8.
"Mivardnil Kutxeebis Glexis Qalebic Erkvevian." 1926. *Mshromeli Qali* 3: 31.
M-r. 1935. "Qvelaze Gadamwkveti Kapitali." *Mshromeli Qali* 7: 3–5.
N-a. 1928. "Lenini da Kulturuli Revolucia." *Mshromeli Qali* 25–26: 10.
Nina. 1926. "Kooperaciis Mnishvneloba Soplad." *Mshromeli Qali* 1: 6–7.
———. 1928a. "Davawinaurot Qalebi." *Mshromeli Qali* 25–26: 7.
———. 1928b. "Vemzadot Sabchota Archevnebistvis." *Mshromeli Qali* 27: 6–7.
Olinka. 1927. "Glexebs Gazetebs Ukitxavs." *Mshromeli Qali* 9: 24.
"Oqtombris Revolucia da Chveni Amocanebi." 1928. *Mshromeli Qali* 27: 1–2.
"Qalta Saertashoriso dgis 25 Wlistavistvis." 1935. *Mshromeli Qali* 3: 3.
Qorqia, R. 1935. "Pirveli Mercxali." *Mshromeli Qali* 11: 7–8.
"Raze Unda Sweron Qalkorebma." 1927. *Mshromeli Qali* 12: 27.
"Rva Marti." 1933. *Mshromeli Qali* 2–3: 3–5.
"Saqartvelos Mshromel Qalebs." 1929. *Mshromeli Qali* 2: 1.

Saqartvelos Musha da Glex-Qalta Shoris Momushave Ganqofileba. 1927. "Leninis Gzit." *Mshromeli Qali* 15: 4–11.
"Saqartvelos Qru Kutxeebshi." 1924. *Chveni Gza* 4: 44–45.
S-dze. 1934. "Qvarlis Raioni Chamorcha." *Mshromeli Qali* 7: 13.
Shaverdova, S. 1927. "Qalta Shoris MOmushaveta Amierkavkasiis Tatbiris Shedegebi." *Mshromeli Qali* 12: 12–13.
S-i. 1928. "Rusetis Social-Demokratiul Mushata Partiis Meore Qriloba." *Mshromeli Qali* 24: 1–3.
"Socialisturi Ojaxi da Dedis Movaleoba." 1938. *Mshromeli Qali* 11: 1–2.
"Socializmistvis Mebrdzol Saertashoriso Qalta Dzalebis Shemchidroebis Dge." 1931. *Mshromeli Qali* 7–8: 3–5.
Sona. 1934. "Samagalito Kolmeurne Qalebi." *Mshromeli Qali* 11: 14.
Surguladze, T. 1933. "Qalta Dge Samagalitod Chavataret." *Mshromeli Qali* 4: 13.
Svanidze, K. 1933. "Qalta Shromis Gamoqeneba Tandatan Dzlierdeba." *Mshromeli Qali* 8–9: 30.
T-a. 1924. "Qali da Soflis Meorneoba." *Chveni Gza* 4: 30.
Ts., O. 1935. "Sabchota Qali Qvelaze Bednieria Msoflioshi." *Mshromeli Qali* 8: 5–6.
Tvaradze. 1935. "Aborti, Anu Muclis Moshla." *Mshromeli Qali* 6: 14–15.
"Udidesi Movaleoba." 1937. *Mshromeli Qali* 7: 1–2.
"Werili Zemo Rachidan." 1926. *Mshromeli Qali* 2: 31.
Wilosani, A. 1933a. "Qalebi Kolmeurneobashi Didi Dzalaa." *Mshromeli Qali* 2–3: 18–19.
———. 1933b. "Konkursis Pirobebi." *Mshromeli Qali* 4: 2.
Woman Worker Natalia. 1924. "Ras Gvaswavlida Lenini Musha Qalebs." *Chveni Gza* 7: 19–20.
Zorini, L. 1931. "Akhal Cxovrebisaken." *Mshromeli Qali* 7–8: 7–8.

Chapter 3

"The West" and Georgian "Difference"
Discursive Politics of Gender and Sexuality in Georgia

Tamar Tskhadadze

The topic of this chapter first came to mind in the spring of 2003 when I encountered critiques of Western colonialism and imperialism along with feminist theory in a feminist philosophy course at Appalachian State University in North Carolina.[1] The United States was about to launch its invasion of Iraq, which prompted a Georgian colleague to publish a newspaper article titled, "Why I Support the USA War in Iraq" (Tchiaberashvili 2003). Right around that time, our class was set to discuss postcolonial theory. In seminar, I mentioned my colleague's article and its chief argument: the appeal of the "civilizing" mission of the United States and Europe, and their "responsibility" to support the less fortunate peoples in other places around the globe in their fight against local dictatorships and corrupt governments. I will never forget my classmates' reactions—a mix of disbelief and sadness. Neither will I forget my ambivalent feelings in response to their reactions: it was the last year of Eduard Shevardnadze's rule in Georgia, and like all Georgians, I knew in my bones that the only leverage civil society had against the corrupt government would be pressure from the West and international agencies.

Those same feelings surfaced again in 2010. This time I was studying feminist theory at Central European University in Budapest. Some topics and theories were similar to those covered in the feminist philosophy course I had taken seven years earlier. In a discussion on Western hegemony, I raised another uncomfortable point about the important role of NATO and Europe in the immediate aftermath of the August 2008 war,

---

Notes for this chapter begin on page 58.

and how both figured in the Georgian collective imagination as sources of hope as well as disappointment. I am quite certain that if I shared with North American and European university colleagues today the controversies that are ongoing in Georgia around LGBT issues and the poor state of Georgian state labor protections relative to the West, I would likely elicit feelings of unease and perhaps confusion about what I am suggesting about the value of Western intervention in places like Georgia.

Today, no less than ten or twenty years ago, many of us in Georgia know that the only weapon we have to counter oppressive policies and inept government practices is to appeal to international norms, and the only leverage in demanding compliance with them is to invoke pressure from the West.

In Georgia, I sometimes make people uncomfortable by challenging them to think about how colonial thought works, and works on us, and how the normative idea of the West functions in post-Soviet Georgia—which may not necessarily be to our benefit. I am not alone in raising these questions. Political debates in contemporary Georgia include what some might consider an "anti-Western" political stance that some might dismiss as anti-Western propaganda. However one might depict these perspectives, it is clear that Georgians are no longer simply pulling themselves toward the West and no longer see themselves as merely "lacking Westernness." At this juncture, it is no longer possible to take for granted that "the West" is Georgia's destiny or its destination. At the same time—and this is at the center of the discussion I offer here—scholars must face the perhaps long-overdue question of the role of the West as the norm in Georgian discursive politics, and especially in debates related to the emancipation of women and sexual minorities.

Here I will begin by clarifying what I mean by normativity of the idea of "West." It takes no particular acuity to observe that from the start of the transition to democracy in post-Soviet Georgia, the narrative was most intimately related to the idea of the West as the standard—the source of modernization, progress, human rights, and prosperity. Oftentimes, this narrative was framed with tropes of "Georgia's true Europeanness," "Georgia's return to Europe," and "Europe as Georgia's Future."[2]

By the West or Europe, of course, the referent is no actual entity. As Dipesh Chakrabarty has explained, the notion of "the West" (Europe) is a hyperreal idea that refers to "certain figures of imagination whose geographical referents remain somewhat indeterminate" (Chakrabarty 1992: 1). That is, it is not a description of any actual existing social body or geographic space, but it has immensely real power.

The trope of "development" as moving closer to the West has been particularly influential over the past several decades in discourses on gender equality and sexual emancipation in Georgia. It is exactly the dynamics of the problems of gender and sexuality and related politics that raise interesting questions concerning the normative idea of the West: how does the West, as a norm, figure and function in gender politics and related discourses? How, and in the context of which dichotomies, does the idea of the West work; and in what kinds of contexts is it articulated? In which contexts is it opposed to "Georgian," "Eastern," "Soviet," "Russian," or even "anti-Western"? What are the arguments, assumptions, and discursive strategies that create the conceptual space that comes to be known as "the West"? Also, what theoretical models and epistemic structures can we access to think through this aspect of the Georgian context? Without ambition to fully address all of these questions, I will nevertheless attempt to highlight their relevance with Georgian examples and illustrations.

For thinking through these matters, the concepts of the "transition narrative" developed by Dipesh Chakrabarty (1992) and of "the rule of colonial difference" developed by Partha Chatterjee (1993) are particularly useful. Chakrabarty's notion of the transition narrative relates to the idea that the path and destiny of "lesser developed" nations is to move (transition) to more developed, modern forms, models of which are provided by the developed, colonial center. For Chakrabarty, the logic of the transition narrative necessarily implies a kind of moving target—an eternal lagging behind or difference from the model, from the colonial center.

Chatterjee calls "the rule of colonial difference" the cognitive gesture by which the colonial center is imagined as radically different from, and in contrast to, its "other," the particularity of which serves to justify the inevitable ascent of the former. The gesture constructs an essentialized difference between the colony and the center, a difference that implies the backwardness of the former as compared to the latter. At the same time, the history of the modern West is imagined as independent of its participation in colonialism (Chatterjee 1993: 18–22).

Chatterjee developed this concept in the context of an analysis of colonized India and Europe. József Böröcz ingeniously applied it to the relationship between post-Soviet Eastern Europe (namely, Hungary) and Western Europe. Alluding to Chatterjee's idea, Böröcz discusses "the rule of European difference" by which the difference between the West and the East of Europe is constructed. In his article "Goodness is Elsewhere," Böröcz explains that the rule of colonial difference performs two acts of erasure. On the one hand, all evil is erased from the colonial center, while on the other, all historical connections between the colonial center and the periphery are erased—connections that were central to what the center would become in the present (Böröcz 2006: 126). He examines how modernizing Hungarian intellectuals use the idea of the "already developed" or the advanced West as the standard and as a compass for assessing Hungary's status and situation. He shows how these ideas are in turn grounded in the idea of difference between "good" and "bad" Europe. For example, France is "advanced" (the good Europe) whereas Hungary is bad and backward. The dichotomy goes further: the West is full of goodness, but the East is devoid of goodness. Difference also figures within the periphery—a correlate of the construction of West–East difference. In Eastern Europe, for example, intra-Hungarian difference is constructed between the minority of liberal pro-Western Hungarian intellectuals on the one hand, and the rest of the Hungarian population and the government on the other (Böröcz 2006).

Drawing on Chatterjee's notion and Böröcz's adaptation of it, by "Georgian difference" I mean the imagined difference between what is "Georgian" and what is "European." Although not exactly parallel, but by approximate meaning, I believe we can articulate the discursive gesture of "Georgian difference," which performs several operations, as follows. First, there is an insurmountable difference between the West/Europe and Georgia by means of which Georgian backwardness is construed. Second, all evil is erased from the West, which is conceptualized as the central place of goodness. Third, intra-Georgian difference between Western-oriented Georgians and other Georgians (the latter oftentimes referred to alternatively as "*Gruzins*" or "*Savoks*") is similarly constructed.[3] By the logic of the transition narrative, progress is constructed as a consecutive passage following the same steps that the "Western" ("normal") countries have already taken. In what follows, I highlight specific aspects of the Georgian transition narrative, and the workings of "Georgian difference" within it. I also reference the ways in which "Western goodness" and "Georgian difference" are destabilized by anxieties related to gender and sexuality.

Difference or Relatedness?

The Georgian narrative of transition brings together two seemingly contradictory themes: the genuine or ancient Europeanness of Georgia and the difference (relative backwardness) of Georgia as compared to Europe. This contradiction has been resolved by a third narrative theme that is no less essential to the transition narrative; that is, Georgia has digressed from its European destiny and was unable to take the proper sequential steps on the path to European development by means of the anti-Western Soviet Union and Russian Empire. Thus, the competing tropes of Georgian Europeanness and Georgian non-Europeanness coexist comfortably (sometimes within the same text), a contradiction reconciled by the idea that Georgia was derailed in its inevitable move toward progress. For example, in a blog published by Giga Zedania, a prominent Georgian philosopher and public intellectual, he writes, "We ... have missed [the] Enlightenment. Yes, we are a part of European, Western civilization, but we have not passed all of its stages and the main 'missed' stage among these is exactly the Enlightenment" (Zedania 2013), though he does not explain why this is so. On the other hand, the author of a chapter titled "Georgian Enlightenment: In Wake of Europe and in Strictures of the Empire," published in a volume dedicated to unearthing the historical roots of democratic values in Georgian culture, identifies Georgian enlightenment as nourished by European ideas, and identifies the Russian Empire as the main obstacle to its fulfillment (Gaprindashvili 2011). In the same volume, however, another chapter, titled "On the European Orientation of the Georgian Philosophy," identifies the Soviet totalitarian regime as the main obstacle to a European orientation in Georgian philosophy (Mchedlishvili 2011).

This search for European roots and the seesawing between identifying the Russian Empire and Soviet Union as the key obstacle to "progress" is played out in a particularly interesting way in the written histories of Georgian feminism. Scholars of the history of women's rights issues in Georgia highlight the existence of feminist ideas and feminist groups in the second half of the nineteenth and the first decade of the twentieth centuries, which at the same time is a part of a project to legitimize contemporary feminist movements and their European roots (Gaprindashvili 2008). The sovietization of Georgia in 1921 is marked as the moment that brought a tragic end to these developments. There are two assertions underlying this interpretation of the history: (1) that contemporary Georgian feminism has national Georgian roots (an argument put forth against complaints that gender issues are artificially forced from abroad by the West and international donor-driven nongovernmental organizations) at the same time it attaches to its European identity; and (2) that in this context, "Western" is not opposed to Georgian or traditional but to "Soviet."

Lagging Behind and Catching Up

As noted, a central trope in the Georgian transition narrative is "backwardness," or a lagging behind, which requires effort to compensate for and to catch up to (see also Grabowska, this volume). Central to the contemporary discourse on gender equality is an underlying assumption that Georgia must go through a process that Europe has successfully accomplished, a widespread notion in Georgia. We hear this theme expressed by Georgian feminists in various contexts, who make comments such as "we are still in the time of second wave feminism" and "we are behind by half a century." At times they say Georgians are behind by seventy years, which hints that the Soviet regime was the cause of that backwardness. This thinking reflects a blindness to and erasure of the dynamics of gender issues during the Soviet period, and to any causal links between Soviet social history and the present.

The themes of "lagging behind" and "catching up" are illustrated, for example, in the following statement posted by male feminist bloggers on the Heinrich Böll Foundation, South Caucasus blog: "[For women to speak out,] it will take years and cannot be fully solved in the near future (*in this respect, even Western countries have much to do*) [my emphasis; my translation]" (Tskhadaia 2015). Here, the author takes for granted the advanced status of Western countries and their role as the standard bearer for Georgia. This is accomplished in the phrase "even Western countries," suggesting their much greater progress in contrast to Georgia, which is much further behind. It accomplishes Chatterjee's "first act of erasure," and subtly endorses the notion of the normativity of "West." In feminist and other human rights discourse in Georgia, this is the pervasive, underlying assumption.

It is worth noting that there is the rare occasion when pro-Western voices acknowledge that gender equality has not been fully perfected in the West. In fact, gender and economic inequality seem to be the only two issues that surface in discussions that acknowledge a less than perfect "West." In addition, these acknowledgments tend to occur in discussions that still assume the West as the norm.

A Strategic Emphasis on Difference

The idea that Georgia has digressed from the European way and its "true destiny" coexists with a radical stress on Georgian difference. The emphasis on difference idealizes the West against the backdrop of Georgian backwardness, orientalizing that which is Georgian against the "normal" and normative West. This pattern is consistent with Chatterjee's rule of colonial difference (1993: 18).

The popular media serves as an important mouthpiece for producing and reproducing these ideas. For example, in Georgia there is a radio talk show "Why Europe?" (*ratom evropa?*), which is devoted to popularizing Europe and which launched partly in response to the emergence of anti-Western sentiments among some sectors of Georgian society. The radio show constitutes a counter-anti-Western effort and can be seen as a form of "pro-Western" propaganda.

The show features guests who share their wonderful experiences across the continent, which stand in contrast to their experiences at "home." Guests are asked to describe their impressions from their first visits to particular European countries. Most responses are narratives that tend toward positive idealization of those places. In Europe, people observe rules and laws. In Europe, justice and equality reign. In Europe, one can lose a valuable piece of jewelry that gets returned to its rightful owner, a story that suggests no such thing would happen in Georgia. The narratives are gestures that attribute a fundamental morality to Europe, an idea precisely captured by the Böröcz title "Goodness is Elsewhere" (2006). At the same time, it radically empties that which is "Georgian" of morality and goodness.

As this relates to discussions of women's rights and feminism, among some pro-Western Georgian intellectuals there is a tendency to admonish Georgians for engaging in a form of "incorrect feminism," which stands in contrast to the "correct" form found in Western and European feminism. A concrete image of the "Georgian feminist" has emerged, represented as an aggressive, superficial, and uneducated woman who has failed to grasp the "true sense" of feminism. The pronouncements often appear on social media; their authors, some of whom I cite below, position themselves as pro-European intellectuals, and supporters of gender equality. At the same time, they reject and ridicule nearly all moves made by Georgian feminists, dismissing them by invoking the label "Georgian feminism" to signal their inadequacies and ineptitude. Whether the actions of Georgian feminists be to demand gender quotas in parliamentary elections, to identify violence against women as a systemic gender issue, or to critique instances of sexism in language or action, these particular pro-Western Georgian intellectuals summarily disregard Georgian feminists and their demands.

The case of a "progressive" sociology professor offers a case in point. On his Facebook page, Professor Iago Kachkachishvili posted a comment that Georgian feminists are "confused" in their understanding of the meaning of domestic violence, led astray by means of their wrong-headed "iron logic," which he sees as symptomatic of their overall "confusion" (Kachkachishvili 2015). His depiction of how a Georgian feminist frames domestic violence is reduced to caricature, which does not capture the actual perspectives or nuanced discussions of the issues among Georgian and non-Georgian feminists alike.[4]

In a second example, Zaal Andronikashvili, a respected "progressive intellectual," outlines in his blog his version of the state of Georgian feminism in relation to the development of feminism in the West (Andronikashvili 2015). In his view, "Feminism, or, more precisely, the women's movement in Georgia, is in a phase of feminism in which women are competing with men. They want to drive bigger cars, to be better at driving, to spit further, to enter parliament with gender quotas, to have more power, and, in general, to have more balls." Andronikashvili understands "lipstick feminism" to signal the movement's third wave. He concludes that in Georgia, "[w]hat is called red-lipstick feminism is not even feminism because it has no courage to do all that is symbolized by lipstick." In Andronikashvili's words, we see the two abovementioned operations at work: the trope of lagging behind and catching up (feminism in Georgia is currently in a phase that has already been passed through by Western feminism), and of being hopelessly and fundamentally different and inept.

Paata Kurdadze, who is a popular publicist and author, is another blogger who in context of comparing various aspects of social and political life in France and Georgia, remarks on the state of Georgian feminism. He writes:

> Feminism, which totally changed the world in the past century, has virtually substituted the "thief mentality" in Georgia. I am not joking. It has become as dangerous to say "woman" as it is to mention skin color or sexual orientation. ... Asking aloud a question about gender equality is not recommended for one's nervous system. (Kurdadze 2015)

Kurdadze then invokes the way the "French" address gender difference in a description of a television show. The suggestion is clear: the French form of feminism is clearly superior to the form as it appears in Georgia.

Despite their declared allegiance with feminist ideas in general, these male, "public" intellectuals reveal themselves to be in opposition to Georgian feminism. Here, the West functions as a hyperreal idea for which there is no actual, defined prototype, and from which contradiction and history are erased. The repetition is persistent, which serves to reinforce an ideology of difference. Whether or not they are aware of it, they gesture Georgian difference by means of specific discursive devices that orientalize Georgian feminists and delegitimize feminist activities and actions taking place in Georgia.

The Non-Westernness of the Georgian – Russian Empire or the Soviet Past

The "Soviet Union," the "Russian Empire," and the "West" are three iconic concepts constituting the hyperreal against which difference is constructed in Georgia. Within these constructs, it is difficult to tease out what specifically differentiates "Georgian" with the West. In the Georgian context, distinctions between the Soviet Union (with its seventy-year history) and the Russian Empire (with its two-hundred-year history, and which is imagined to include the Soviet period) are often (deliberately) blurred, sometimes to the extent that these signifiers are used interchangeably. This occurs, for example, in discursive linkages between Orthodox Christianity and the Soviets, which at first sight seems strange. The discursive configuration operates as follows: the West stands in opposition to the Russian Empire and to the Soviet Union, as well as to Orthodox Christianity. It is seldom that non-Western roots are sought in Georgian traditions or in some characteristics considered as specifically Georgian, though the effort to articulate Georgian-specific differences did enjoy popularity in the 1990s and early 2000s. At that time, the relationship between Georgia and the West was mainly situated in the context of discussions about Georgia's unique national characteristics, and within an "Asian versus European" dichotomy—highly essentialist discursive frames.

In terms of the "woman's question" and feminism, concerns about gender equality by both its proponents and its opponents are generally understood as a corollary of the European/Western orientation. For advocates, gender equality is an object of aspiration, and for opponents, it is something artificially forced upon Georgia by the West. Projects that link gender equality with a Western orientation tend to be oriented in three key ways. First, efforts to unearth and reclaim origins of Georgian feminism tend to be silent about the Soviet period (see also Gaprindashvili, this volume). These histories tend to begin around the mid nineteenth century and end abruptly in 1921 with the Soviet occupation. Thus, excluded from this history of Georgian feminism are those initiatives and efforts to advance gender equality that took place during the Soviet period, especially during its early years.

Second, most historical analyses of the fight for women's rights in Georgia bypass the Soviet Union's contributions. For example, Natia Gvianishvili, a prominent activist for women and LGBT rights in Georgia, refused to acknowledge Soviet efforts to tackle gender-based violence in an interview on a Georgian talk show (Talk Show *tsiteli zona* 2015; see also Gvianishvili, this volume). At times, analysts follow a paradoxical logic in claiming that feminism is "weak" or "absent" in post-Soviet societies because the Soviets "granted" women equal rights "without the fight" (Sabedashvili 2007). In this version of history, rights were granted from the top–down; thus, Georgian women did not have to "fight" for equal rights—a narrative that erases the historical role of feminist movements in Georgia. There is an opposing view of this history, in which advances in equal rights for women in Georgia is linked to the short-lived independent republic (1918 to 1921). In this narrative, universal suffrage was granted and five women were elected to the Founding Assembly as a result of the previous generations' feminist struggles (i.e., not as a result of charity conferred by benevolent men). Thus, women's rights in Georgia were gained by means of conscious effort and struggle (Gaprindashvili 2008).

Putting aside the question of their political significance and historical accuracy, these analyses exclude Soviet participation in advancing gender equity. They ignore the fact that at some points, the aims of feminists coincided with Soviet gender policies. This occurs even as it is widely known that a significant number of early twentieth century Georgian feminists came from the ranks of Marxists and communists, that women's emancipation was an important concern in the early period of the Soviet Union, and that gender politics and policies in that early period had substantive and positive effects on the lives of worker and peasant women.

Third, the contemporary belief that gender equality is a Western idea ignores the fact that many international agreements that identify gender equity as a value and a goal, such as the 1979 UN Convention on the Elimination of all Forms of Discrimination Against Women (CEDAW) and the 1995 Beijing Platform for Action, were largely initiated and supported by Eastern Bloc countries such as the Soviet Union, as well as China (Fraser 1999: 892, 894, 900). Meanwhile, CEDAW, one of the most important international treaties, has not been ratified by the United States.

Difference in the West

If the assumption about the seamless goodness of the West and Georgian difference dominates modernizing or progressive narratives, one might expect that conservative or reactionary narratives, symmetrically, might be imbued with a negative image of the West and, accordingly, a positive attachment to Georgian difference. In fact, this "progressive versus reactionary" dichotomy has characterized the dominant political discourse in Georgia over the past several decades. Indeed, reactionary discourse in Georgia appeals to the dangers from a threatening Europe (or the West), depicted as a place of perversion and alienation, and as the key enemy of Georgian traditions and Orthodox Christianity.

An interesting turn has been taking place in the past few years. The image of the West as monolithically good, and its mirror image as monolithically evil, is being replaced in some discourses with more diverse and, in a sense, more realistic portraits of the West. In these discourses, Western societies are imagined as places of ongoing contestation and struggle on the very same or similar issues with which Georgia is also struggling. This "more nuanced" picture finds its strategic application primarily in the rhetoric of those groups for which the West had previously served as the chief source of things frightening and threatening.

An early example of this shift is found in controversies related to issues of gender and sexuality. On 17 May 2013, an extraordinary event occurred on the streets of Tbilisi when a small LGBT rights protest resulted in full-scale violence (see Rekhviashvili, this volume). In its immediate aftermath, public discussions and media reports referenced protest marches in France and Italy against the legalization of same-sex marriage—events that drew enormous crowds. In these reports, the West was invoked as a model of and justification for Georgia's own reactionary politics. The suggestion that "even the French are opposed to same-sex marriage" can function as a persuasive argument in a language game predicated on the assumption of the seamless goodness or "rightness" of Europe.

Another example involves the case of a controversial painting with religious references. The painting is the work of a contemporary Georgian feminist artist who depicted a pregnant Virgin Mary pointing a toy gun at her temple. The painting prompted an outcry, as well as a proposal to make it illegal to "insult" religious feelings. A proposed law was drafted by a group of pro-Orthodox Christian Church activists, who then managed to get it presented before the Parliament. In front of a television talk show audience, the author of the proposed law noted that many European countries have similar laws, a point that constituted his main argument ("Politika" 2016). He also noted that in Europe, people are more "conscientious," while those in Georgia have yet to arrive at their level of moral integrity—a truly grotesque invocation of the image of European goodness.

Up to this point, this particular form of appeals to the West has been mobilized predominantly on behalf of reactionary arguments. In this respect, the position of Charles H. Fairbanks, a professor of Soviet and post-Soviet Studies at Ilia State University, is worth noting. Reflecting on the events of May 2013, Fairbanks argues that to retain a Western orientation in Georgia, it is necessary to show to the Georgian public the actual diversity and the real controversies that exist in the West. Otherwise, a false impression will be created that a Western orientation necessarily implies univocal answers to such painful questions as gay and lesbian rights (Fairbanks 2014: 72). Such a position is rare in rejecting a picture of the West as monolithically good, even as it urges a leaning toward the West.

Fairbanks's discussion leads to a central question that has been bypassed throughout the present discussion in terms of narratives that define colonial discourse. Who is responsible for these narratives? Is it the colonial center or the periphery? Fairbanks himself writes on behalf of the West, and can be understood to embody the colonial center. However, should we—can we—apply concepts developed by Chatterjee, Chakrabarty and other postcolonial thinkers for our analysis of the Georgian case, where, unlike in India, a history of Western colonialism is not as evident or uncontroversial? And if we do speak of Western colonialism, which colonial histories do we have in mind? Is this the history of the post-Soviet transition or an older history—history before Sovietization or the Soviet period? How can these concepts, developed for a bipolar model (the Western center and the colony) work in a context where a "third pole" represented by the Russian imperial center also figures? Is not my use of the models of postcolonial thinkers a further instance of colonial thinking? These are the large questions that require deep reflection.

Finally, the assertion that a Western orientation does not by definition translate to overcoming homophobia illustrates Chakrabarty's important observation that the modernization project in India proved to be reconcilable with maintaining the traditional model of the family, the private sphere, and existing gender hierarchies. In other words, the actual process of "transition" is never a process of reaching the hyperreal ideal. It is not required by the logic of the transition narrative, and nor does the logic determine on which aspect of the ideal a compromise can be allowed. As we think about "gender" in Georgia, it is necessary that we remain vigilant, cautious, and questioning in imagining the West as the norm.

Tamar Tskhadadze is associate professor in philosophy at Ilia State University, Tbilisi, Georgia. She served as chair of the Gender Studies Programme at Tbilisi State University (2009–2012), where she continues to teach feminist theory in the graduate program. She has published articles on philosophy of science, philosophy of language, and epistemology. Her edited volumes include *Philosophy of Mind: A Reader* (Ilia State University Press, 2013) and *Knowledge and Morality* (Nekeri, 2012).

Notes

1. I am grateful for the research support provided by the German Academic Exchange Service (DAAD), Ruhr University Bochum, and the Human Rights Education and Monitoring Center (EMC).
2. Adrian Brisku has studied in detail how the idea of Europe figured in the Georgian imaginary from the nineteenth century up to 2008. He isolates three dimensions of the

idea of Europe in Georgian discourse: Europe as a geopolitically important entity; Europe as the source of progress as a politico-economic entity; and Europe as the locus of advanced civilization and culture. He also emphasizes how the sense of "lagging behind" was prevalent in this imaginary. See Brisku 2013: 6, 198.
3. *Gruzin* is the word for Georgian in Russian. *Savok* is a neologism for the Soviet people.
4. Kachkachishvili writes: "[The] 'Iron Logic' of some confused Georgian feminists: a man killing his wife is necessarily consciously perpetrating violence, while a wife killing her husband is necessarily an irrational (temporarily insane) victim defending her rights from the violent husband."

References

Andronikashvili, Z. 2015. "Pomadiani da upomado feminizmi." Zaliko's Blog, 15 April. Retrieved 2 March 2016 from http://andronikashvili.blogspot.com/2015/05/blog-post_15.html.
Böröcz, J. 2006. "Goodness is Elsewhere: The Rule of European Difference." *Comparative Studies in Society and History* 48(1): 110–38.
Brisku, A. 2013. *Bittersweet Europe: Albanian and Georgian Discourses on Europe, 1878–2008*. New York and Oxford: Berghahn Books.
Chakrabarty, D. 1992. "Postcoloniality and the Artifice of History: Who Speaks for 'Indian' Pasts?". *Representations* 37: 1–26.
Chatterjee, P. 1993. *The Nation and Its Fragments: Colonial and Postcolonial Histories*. Princeton, NJ: Princeton University Press.
Fairbanks, C. 2014. "Weighing What We Do for Democracy in the South Caucasus: The Complex Case of Gerogia." In *South Caucasus at the Crossroad: Thorny Realities and Great Expectations*, ed. S. Asatiani and N. Lejava, 69–78. Tbilisi: Heinrich Böll Stiftung, South Caucasus.
Fraser, A.S. 1999. "Becoming Human: The Origins and Development of Women's Human Rights." *Human Rights Quarterly* 21(4): 853–906.
Gaprindashvili, L. (ed.). 2008. "Kartuli feminizmi tu feminizmi sakartveloshi?" In *Evropuli ideebis istoria da kartuli kultura*, ed. P. Papava and Z. Shatirishvili, 193–97. Tbilisi: Universali.
———. 2011. "Kartuli ganmanatlebloba: evropis kvaldakval da imperiis martsukhebshi." In *Demokratiuli ghirebulebebis nakvalevze sakartveloshi*, ed. L. Gaprindashvili, 53–82. Tbilisi: Dobera.
Kachkachishvili, I. 2015. "Verbatim." *Tabula*, 21 December. Retrieved 2 March 2016 from http://www.tabula.ge/ge/verbatim/103052-kachkachishvili-zogi-feminististvis-co lis-mkvleli-modzaladea-qmris-tavs-icavs.
Kurdadze, P. 2015. "Populisturi totalitarizmi." *Liberali*, 29 December. Retrieved 2 March 2016 from http://liberali.ge/articles/view/20148/populisturi-totalitarizmi.
Mchedlishvili, L. 2011. "Kartuli filosofiis evropuli orientaciis shesakheb." In *Demokratiuli ghirebulebebis nakvalevze sakartveloshi*, ed. L. Gaprindashvili, 165–96. Tbilisi: Dobera.
Radio program "Ratom evropa? – evrokavshiris idea," 18 January 2016. Retrieved 29 February 2016 from http://www.radiotavisupleba.ge/content/evrokavshiris-idea/27494657.html.
Sabedashvili, T. 2007. *Gender and Democratization: The Case of Georgia 1991–2006*. Tbilisi: Heinrich Böll Stiftung, South Caucasus.

Talk Show "Politika," 2 February 2016. Retrieved 20 March 2016 from http://imedi.ge/index.php?pg=shs&id_pr=6915&id=59&tp=0.
Talk Show "Tsiteli zona," 11 November 2015. Retrieved 20 March 2016 from http://www.radiotavisupleba.ge/content/red-zone/27395161.html.
Tchiaberashvili, Z. 2003. "Why I Support the USA War in Iraq." *24 Hours*, 5 March.
Tskhadaia, G. 2015. "Obekturad dznelia feministoba, kalistvisac da kacistvisac." Heinrich Böll Stiftung, South Caucasus Blog, 12 August. Retrieved 29 February 2016 from http://www.feminism-boell.org/ka/2015/08/12/obiekturad-znelia-peministoba-kalistvisac-da-kacistvisac.
Zedania, G. 2013. "Antidasavleti." Radiotavisupleba Blog, 9 December. Retrieved 29 February 2016 from http://www.radiotavisupleba.ge/content/blog-giga-zedania-anti-west/25195091.html.

Chapter 4

Overcoming the "Delay" Paradigm
New Approaches to Socialist Women's Activism in Georgia and Poland

Magdalena Grabowska

> Laws alone are not enough ... however, we have done everything required of us to put women in a position of equality, and we have every right to be proud of it. The position of women in Soviet Russia is now ideal as compared with their position in the most advanced states. We tell ourselves, however, that this, of course, is only the beginning.
> —Lenin, "The Tasks of the Working Women's Movement"

I met Tsinovar, an economics professor, at Tbilisi State University during my first visit to Georgia in the winter of 2011 to conduct research on women's activism under socialism. In the course of a two-hour interview, Tsinovar shared that she had enjoyed a good life during the socialist period: "I was very lucky because I had the best things in my life. Intellectually, I had all possibilities ... my generation had all opportunities ... I did not pay anything for my education, the government supported me in my travels abroad. It was a very different life [as compared to today]."[1] Tsinovar described her involvement with the Communist Party as pragmatic, and explained her choices as practical decisions that led to a happy and satisfying life, which laid the ground for her current engagement as a "gender expert" in Georgia. Tsinovar, in her seventies at the time of the interview, noted that:

> My generation was not orthodox communist. Here in Tbilisi, but also in Moscow, we had a very modern imagination. And I never felt uncomfortable with

---

Notes for this chapter begin on page 76.

myself ... I changed my life three times. I studied English philology, and then I entered economics, which was not typical for a woman. I had a very interesting political life. I was a member of a political party. When the Soviet era ended, it was very difficult ... the new economic situation made me think that I had to change something again. In 1996 my colleague told me about an international granting program at the United Nations. And that is how I started to work with "gender." "Gender" appeared in my life as a surprise. And to be honest, I was not very interested at first, but now it is very important to me.

In September 2012, I interviewed Halina, also an economist, who served as the Polish delegate to the 1985 United Nations conference in Nairobi, and was a member of the late socialist government in Poland; she was also former director of the Committee for Household Economics, a nationwide women's organization active in socialist Poland. During the course of a summer afternoon we spent at her apartment in a Warsaw residential district, Halina repeatedly asserted that she had made autonomous choices under state socialism. Even as she noted certain of the system's faults, Halina remarked on the value of her work as a state official and as an activist for women, and argued that the contributions she and her colleagues made to gender equity remains unacknowledged in dominant historical accounts of postwar politics and society. She also talked about contemporary politics in Poland, expressing dismay at how the socialist past is consistently misrepresented, dismissed, and misunderstood. "During the time I was active," Halina said, "all [our actions and activities] were reasonable, though [from the vantage point of the political present] perceptions about our actions have changed." She explained that contemporary revisionist history looks down on women activists of the communist era: "We are all under attack—all the women's movements and other organizations are condemned in this new, harsh, and disparaging historical perspective. That should not be."

This chapter aims to recast "second generation" socialist women's activism as part of the genealogy of women's movements in postsocialism. The findings presented here are part of a larger project based on semi-structured interviews with women who were active in communist parties and women's organizations during the 1970s and 1980s in Poland and Georgia. The project focuses on questions about women's experiences and agency before 1989. In an effort to apply specific grand feminist theory to the context of postsocialism, I critically assess the value of "experience as evidence" as it relates to women's agency in pre-1989 Georgia and Poland. I argue that the women's narratives of the communist past are not to be treated just as accounts of what happened, but more as expressions of lived experiences that can add to our understanding of women's equality issues under state socialism.

To better understand the complexity and diversity of women's equality as a socialist project, I employ aspects of postcolonial theory structured around and in relation to the problematic category of "the West" to challenge existing constructions of postsocialist women's movements as "delayed" as compared to those in the West. I consider ways in which socialist women were positioned within the trajectories of transnational women's movements. By revisiting the problem of the place of pre-1989 women's activism in genealogies of women's movements, I speak partially in an attempt to formulate a response to the dominant approach that represents Western "modernity" and "development" as a paradigm for achieving progress in the area of women's rights, and state socialism as a "lag" in the genealogy of the women's movement—not only in the region, but also transnationally.

Historians of women's movements in postsocialism have only recently started to explore questions about the impact of women's emancipation under socialism on current debates on gender equality. Following critiques about the relevance of existing feminist theoretical frames—developed in Western Europe and the United States—to the postsocialist context, there is now growing scholarly interest in "local" trajectories of women's movements, including those of socialism (Havelkova and Oates-Indruchová 2014).

Works that focus specifically on the period of state socialism challenge the idea that feminism was imported to postsocialist states from the West (Ghodsee 2012), and argue instead that the 1917 Russian Revolution had inspired a wave of revolutionary struggle across Europe and beyond (de Haan 2014a; Fidelis 2010). These studies draw on the previous research by scholars such as Barbara Evans Clements that position Bolshevik women activists such as Alexandra Kollontai and Inessa Armand as original socialist feminists who combined a rejection of Western bourgeois feminism with a struggle on behalf of women workers (Evans Clements 1994; de Haan 2016). These new works by Ghodsee, de Haan, Fidelis, Deskalova and others help inspire contemporary feminist activism in the words of Alexandra Kollontai, who in 1909 argued that "however apparently radical the demands of the feminists, one must not lose sight of the fact that the feminists cannot, on account of their class position, fight for that fundamental transformation of society, without which the liberation of women cannot be complete" (Kollontai 1984).

By means of their archival studies and oral history projects, Evans Clements and Fidelis illuminate how the state socialist project of women's emancipation proposed by Kollontai evolved over time. They document continuities between the state socialist period and postsocialism in terms of the ways "gender equality" strategies have been formulated. Nevertheless, mainstream feminist narratives tend to dismiss or ignore the contributions of feminists such as Kollontai, and of subsequent generations of women who remained loyal to communist ideas as sources of inspiration for struggles for women's equality in both the West and the East. Existing feminist works on "gender" under socialism often operate within what Fidelis calls the "totalitarian paradigm" (de Haan 2014b): where women's rights are concerned, they portray the period of state socialism as a time of stagnation, and rarely consider this period a part of feminist genealogy (Fuszara 2000). Instead, mainstream feminist scholarship tends to stress the ways in which women were victimized by the regime, thereby erasing the positive contributions of the socialist project to the lives of many women, including those who chose to become active participants in the socialist political structure. Such scholarship also fails to make connections between state socialist women's activism and current gender discourse at the local and global level (Funk 2014).

"Women's Experience" under State Socialism: A Critical Approach

The role of critical historians, sociologists, and anthropologists has often been defined in terms of expanding knowledge by embracing the contributions and perspectives of the marginalized individuals and groups—those whose lives were not taken into account in mainstream historical analyses. The notion of "experience" is crucial to knowledge production and to feminist theorizing, which has long been used to bring forward the experiences of women. In feminist studies, "women's experience" emerged in the United States in the 1970s as a tool for incorporating what had previously been unrecognized in studies of history and the social sciences (Harding 1987). Feminist standpoint theory was the epistemological argument for acknowledging distinct "female" or "feminine" knowledge through recourse to the experience of women. Experience became a ground for studies that told "truths" about women's lives, in contrast to the purportedly distorted representations in mainstream, male-dominated social sciences.

Over time, feminist researchers became more attentive to the variety of women's experiences and the multiple positions from which these experiences could be "told." Some, including historian Joan Scott, suggested that "experience" is produced out of different contexts and discourses rather than simply "discovered" during research. She famously argued that experience must be historicized, a product of social structure and ideology (Scott 1991: 26). Knowledge and knowledge production are situated within relationships between existing and available narratives and the collective histories of the various groups to which one belongs. To avoid the trap of the naturalization of difference, studies of marginalized groups of women must account for intersecting identities and the ways contemporaneous narratives of gender, class, and other relevant ideological and material structures shape experience. The concepts of gender, class, and social location must be studied simultaneously as coproducing and reproducing the experience.

A number of feminist scholars, many in postcolonial studies, have argued against abandoning the use of experience as a potential source of critical scrutiny (Narayan 1997; Mohanty 2002). Mohanty, for example, offered a more nuanced approach to "experience" by recognizing various material realities of women's lives around the world. More recently, one goal in studies of postsocialism has been to reconstruct the diversity of women's experiences, as these narratives intersect with official accounts of the socialist past and with culturally accepted ideas about women's roles in political processes (Nowak 2006). Studies of women's activism under state socialism challenge existing representations of womanhood under socialist regimes, while critically approaching the narratives constructed by research participants. In the case of my own research, the narratives I have collected may destabilize dominant visions of women's lives under state socialism by undermining the idea of the homogenous experience of women from the entire Soviet Bloc. My findings challenge the representation of socialist women as passive victims of the regime, and call into question the dominant understanding that contemporary women's activism is separate from their pre-1989 activism. My research suggests that there is continuity between the past and the present.

Destabilizing the homogenous representations of women's experiences and activism during state socialism (both in terms of time and location) is a crucial starting point for the analysis of women's diverse trajectories within state socialism. In the Soviet Union, the socialist concept of equality transformed over time. In 1917, the strike of women textile workers on International Women's Day under the slogan "Opposition to the war, high prices, and the situation of the woman worker," triggered the February Revolution (Evans Clements 1994). Later, Alexandra Kollontai, Inessa Armand, Konkordia Samoliova, and other women played a crucial role in incorporating issues of women's equality into revolutionary goals, arguing that Marxist politics cannot be successful without women's emancipation (ibid.). The Bolsheviks recognized the need for a special body within the party to lead the work on women. They introduced radical provisions after the 1917 revolution, including nominating Alexandra Kollontai as the commissar for social affairs, and established the Zhenotdel (Women's Department of the Russian Communist Party) in 1919. Revolutionaries, both female and male, understood that to free women from full responsibility for the family was a condition for their emancipation. Leo Trotsky argued:

> To institute the political equality of men and women in the Soviet state was one problem and the simplest ... But to achieve the actual equality of man and woman within the family is an infinitely more arduous problem ... All our domestic habits must be revolutionized before that can happen. And yet it is quite obvious that unless there is actual equality of husband and wife in the family, in a normal sense as well as in the conditions of life, we cannot speak seriously of their equality in social work or even in politics. (Trotsky 1923)

During its brief existence, the postrevolutionary government offered a hint of what women's emancipation in socialist society would look like: it introduced laws establishing full social and political equality for women (including the right to vote and to be elected), the right to divorce at the request of either a husband or a wife, the rule of equal pay for equal work, paid maternity leave, and a state-funded childcare system. In 1920 abortion became legal, and women were able to obtain free abortions in state hospitals (Evans Clements 1994). The Stalinist era marked a backlash against women's equality, with oppressive policies including the closure of women's departments in 1929 and delegalizing abortion. The new vision of womanhood promoted during the era of "the thaw" focused on reinventing women's roles primarily as mothers, an idea that was partly supported by *Zhensovety*, state-dependent women's organizations established in 1931. The "stabilization" period of the 1960s and 1970s, the crisis of the 1980s, and perestroika marked further departures from the socialist ideal of women's emancipation (Hrycak 2002).

In Catholic Poland, "radical" socialist solutions were introduced briefly after World War II, and the idea of bringing certain "private" issues into the public domain was rarely discussed. Since certain social policies on women's behalf were required from above, authorities attempted to modify these mandates to fit with the pre-socialist, traditional conceptions of women's social roles that were deeply rooted in Polish society's commitment to Catholicism (Fidelis 2010). Women-centered policies enacted during the postwar period focused on including women in the rebuilding effort (encouraging women to work in "male" professions) and ensuring their high fertility (by building daycare centers, liberalizing divorce and parental leave laws, providing maternity leave and healthcare for pregnant women and infants, offering nursing breaks, and providing breast-milk banks). The major goal of the Women's Department (established in 1946) of the Polish Workers' Party was to encourage women's mass participation in the Communist Party and the League of Women, an autonomous group that was re-established in 1945 as a continuation of the pre-war organization by the same name.

During the "thaw" in Poland that followed Stalin's death, the traditional family structure favored by the Catholic Church was consolidated. The doctrine of "humane socialism" proposed after 1956 aimed at building the new order with old forces: the socialist state was seen as rooted in the traditional family, for which the figure of "Mother Pole" remained crucial. Important legal changes marked this shift. Since 1956, abortion was available only for married women who already had children (Fidelis 2010). New institutions were established to help women manage the "double shift" of work inside and outside the home. For example, in the 1960s and 1970s, the League of Polish Women and the Committee for Home Economic Affairs (established in 1957) promoted "practical activism," designed to help women cope with the challenges of combining full employment with household responsibilities (Nowak 2005).

These national and transnational histories of the transformation of the state socialist women's equality provide context for interpreting the personal narratives of women active as the regime's agents over the decades. Whether actions of the women were instances of feminist consciousness is now vigorously debated by scholars from the region and beyond (de Haan 2016). Some argue that three generations of women politically and socially active under state socialism after the revolution of 1917 were dedicated activists: they fought for social justice and women's equality, and they regarded communism as the best way to achieve these goals. Their role in shaping the socialist state project of equality changed over time, as did their priorities: devoted communists in the Soviet Union of the 1920s were replaced by the "practical activists" of later decades (Nowak 2009). And while the agency of these women often does not meet the standard definition of proactivity based on free will and directed toward radically reshaping social reality, it represents an instance of "reactive" agency, which centered on implementing state design policies and goals (de Haan 2016).

Socialist Women: Stories from Georgia and Poland

Socialist women activists tell stories of the grand historical transformations that intersect with their memories to form personal narratives of a past mediated by contemporaneous constructions of "what happened." Julia, a professor of physics and a native of Tbilisi who had moved to Sukhumi, was a devoted party member. In an interview with me in 2011, Julia's narrative helped tie the experiences of the second and third generation of socialist women's activism to the work of Bolshevik women activists. Her story dismantles a popular belief that women were merely passive witnesses to the workings of the socialist system, manipulated into a "false" ideal of equal participation while they faced the difficult reality of the double burden. Julia describes her experience:

> Originally many things in the Soviet Union were planned according to original East European feminist thought. Some of its elements stayed on formally, but the substance was lost with time ... In my early years I learned about Aleksandra Kollontai—not as a feminist but as an ambassador of the Soviet Union. It was never described by official propaganda as a feminist work, but as the work of an outstanding woman ... I don't know if quotas were officially implemented, but [in the Soviet Union] everybody knew that one vice president of the Communist Party in Abkhazia would have to be Abkhaz, another Georgian and the other Russian. And everybody knew that one should be a woman—at least 30 percent women, altogether.

Julia uses herself as an example of how the formal or informal quota coincided with individual life trajectories, choices, and passions. "When I graduated from university," Julia explains, "I was offered party membership. I was not comfortable with that because the stereotype then was that if you are a bad academic then you join the party to advance your career. So I refused." Yet after a period of consideration, Julia changed her mind about becoming a member of the party. "I was reading a lot then," she explains, "and there were very one-directional studies relating to communism. For me it was important to do something, to be active. And during that time [party membership] was the only option."

Rosa, a gynecologist and endocrinologist—born in Kutaisi, grew up in Moscow, and was retired in Tbilisi at the time I interviewed her—describes her reason for becoming a Communist Party member. "If the person who studied for the doctoral degree wanted to go to international conferences, they had to become a member of the party. So I joined." For Rosa, party membership was a pragmatic move that did not limit her work as an autonomous scientist. "I had knowledge and it was respected. I was never undermined because I was a woman. I was always free to travel. There was no political pressure at work."

Lia, a teacher who lives in Tbilisi, describes herself as "active from a very young age." Born in Abkhazia, Lia became a leader of the Komsomol[2] while in primary school. At later points, she was elected head of the student association, and was the Komsomol leader at her workplace. She was a third and later a first secretary of the City Committee, a unit Lia describes as focused on "working with youth, organizing the free and cultural time of young adults." Lia noted that most of her activities within the party were planned from above. Even so, Lia "felt free."

Nana, a Tbilisi-based historian, described her work in a university Communist Party organization as "The Secretary of Dissidents." Nana, active since 1960, noted that the party unit at her institute helped to publish books, provided assistance to vulnerable members of the community, and facilitated discussions on current events. She pointed out that it was within the party as an organization where important issues, including multiculturalism and ethnic tensions, emerged and were critically debated. Nana recognizes that her position in the party had enabled her to put forward ideas and discuss concepts that she would not have been able to examine otherwise. She argues that the Communist Party provided a space for such examination that did not exist elsewhere outside the system. Nana also noted that her political position had made it possible to defend colleagues who criticized the regime; she had often saved them from going to prison and had helped their families.

Like Nana, Julia describes actions that could be accomplished within the party system. "My party unit in Sukhumi was always very open," Julia explained. "We had people with different opinions. We talked mostly about work because it was a scientific institute. I was lucky not to experience ideological pressure. We were not talking about ideology but about how to improve our scientific work. Of course there was no freedom to do everything. But I think I was quite independent."

Halina, the former director of the Committee for Household Economics, explained that the main purpose of that organization was to implement new government policies. She enjoyed a certain level of autonomy. "Nobody ever imposed what the research program would be," Halina explained. "No one ever told me that I can or cannot work with a factory or a professor. But it is absolutely true that all of these organizations were under the supervision of the party. And all of us had a party 'guardian' who would attend our meetings from time to time. But I never felt forced, or that someone would tell me what I must do."

In terms of the gendered aspects of her social position, Halina commented on the maternity provisions introduced in Poland after World War II that were not as revolutionary as those in the Soviet Union, but nevertheless helped restructure the social gender hierarchy. "I, with three children, had a certainty that no one would fire me; that no one would tell me you can work as long as you don't have children. These problems didn't exist at all. Having children was not an individual choice of women, but the expression of certain attitudes, the recognition of motherhood as a social role, which required support from the society. As a boss I knew exactly how it was when my employees said to me one after another, first child, second child, pregnancy—and maternity leave and parental leave, every time. [Each time] I had to find someone else for their place, but they would say, 'I'm not giving birth for myself. I'm doing it for the society.'"

Eteri, a Tbilisi-born engineer, appreciated the socialist system because it allowed the possibility of having two children while still being a student, and later on it provided her with the opportunity for professional work, despite being a divorcee raising two children alone from the time they were toddlers. In Eteri's words: "The biggest achievement [of the socialist system] was making women and men equal, at the same salary ... The system brought stability that sometimes is more important than autonomy." At the same time, Eteri observed the system's flaws. "There was always discrimination because women used to work in the jobs that were harmful to their health, just to make as much money as men ... You always knew what would happen and that you would have stability ... but we could not organize—we were not in charge of our lives." Likewise, Julia pointed to the double burden that she had experienced as a working mother: "There were obstacles, when you had this additional work at home. My son was very sick at a young age, so I spent a lot of time in hospitals. That influenced my academic career."

Although by and large the women whom I interviewed asserted that the system had provided women not only with legal but also practical equality, they were also aware of its often hidden sexist face. As Lia explained, "[e]quality was often declared, but everybody knew that the men held all the power." Julia also remarked: "I heard comments about me being a woman. I was very surprised by it because equality was something natural to us, so we didn't spend time reflecting on it. We had facilities and formal equality. Ija, an anthropologist and the mother of two children, noted: "The system of state kindergartens freed women and allowed them to work. But in the end, I think I would have achieved more professionally if I hadn't had children."

Lia, Nana, Eteri, Julia and other women have provided narratives that demand recognition of their agency and the multilayered nature of social and professional interaction. Their stories exemplify the complexity of life under state socialism, and challenge the idea of women as passive victims of the system. By providing accounts of experiences of women who lived and worked in the satellite states of the Soviet Union, these narratives provide a new context for discussing the concept of "agency," within the omnipresent influence of culture and socially constructed beliefs. They suggest that the notion of agency as a "socio-culturally mediated capacity to act" is a more suitable interpretative framework for understanding the experiences of women under state socialism than is the romantic idea of free will (Ahrean 2004: 306).

These narratives can also become a starting point for examining the place of state socialist women's activism within the genealogies of feminism, both in the region and transnationally. Many of these women were active during and after the fall of communism as members of organizations acting on behalf of women, refugees, and the poor. Some define their activities under state socialism as feminist; others reject the label. Rosa states, "I am a feminist because my whole life I worked for women." But Eteri argues, "Feminist? I don't know what that means. I am for normal relationships between women and men." As they challenge the applicability of Western-defined notions of "feminism" into postsocialism, these stories reveal the blurred distinction between past and present engagements for women's equality and for "feminist" and "para-feminist" women's agency.

The stories told by my respondents destabilize the existing paradigm that defines the relationship between state socialism and postsocialist gender relationships in terms of disruption and discontinuity. Julia argues that although she had been a member of the Communist Party in the past, she only discovered feminism after the fall of the Iron Curtain. She describes her experience:

> During the Soviet period, feminists such Alexandra Kollontai were represented not as feminists, but as extraordinary women. I started to discover feminism after the [Abkhaz] war [in 1993]. Women took all responsibilities into their hands. They worked professionally and at home. On top of that, they had to take care of the men who felt left out after the war, when many of them started to drink. So for women it was not a double but a triple burden, and they had to find ways to deal with it.

The trajectories from communist activism to feminism that are inscribed in the stories of the women who were then and still are socially and politically active illuminate the neglected connectivities between "then" and "now." As such, these narratives of socialist activists go against existing conceptualizations of the relationship between the post-1945 and post-1989 women's activism as disruption, which renders state socialism as a "gap" period in the history of women's movements. Thus, these narratives provide a basis for understanding the significance of socialist "state feminism" in the genealogy of the European women's movements. It is important to "rediscover" each country's experiences of the past in order to understand current failures and new opportunities in the area of gender equality.

Beyond the "Developmental" Lag: Progress and Regress in "East" and "West"

Contemporary debates in transnational feminist theory remain centered around and in relation to the problematic binary of the "Global North" versus the "Global South." In these debates, the so-called "Second World" remains largely absent. In addition, dominant constructions represent postsocialist states as uniformly on board with processes of Westernization, which tends to exclude Second World critiques of the West and the First World (Regulska and Grabowska 2013). In these constructions, the historical generalizations of the relationship between "transnational," "postcolonial," "postsocialist," "center–periphery," and "Western" and "Eastern" Europe continue to mask particularities in favor of universal categories and binary representations of transnational feminist politics. Stereotypical images of postsocialist societies represent the region as failing to enter the process of modernization, or as delayed in the process of modernization as compared to the "West." Such representations also negate that under state socialism, a mode of modernization alternative to Western capitalism was implemented in the area of gender equality. As we have seen, the state socialist project of "women's equality" that emerged from the work of nineteenth-century Eastern and Western feminists remains unexamined as a source to link resistances that emerged in postcolonial contexts with those developed in Eastern Europe and the former Soviet Union.

Any examination of women's agency under socialism and transnationally must pay attention to the particularities of each social and cultural context while keeping sight of the global processes that emerged from the region and beyond. Postcolonial feminist scholars problematize the category of experience in the context of global feminist theory and practice, and particularly in the context of the production and reproduction of hegemonic representations of non-Western women (Naples and Desai 2002). Pointing to the imperialistic feminist politics that reifies images of Third World women in dominant narratives of the West, these scholars illuminate the crucial role that positionality and location play in feminist knowledge production (Mohanty 2002). Still, these analyses often disregard that similar processes have taken place in the "Second World," a location "invented" by the West European Enlightenment. Larry Wolff (1994) argues that, since the eighteenth century, the countries east of Germany have often played the role of the "little other," a space between the civilized "West" and the barbaric "Orient." This cultural imaginary served the purpose of illuminating the so-called developmental lag that separated the West from all its "others." The division between West and East Europe has persisted with remarkable tenacity for centuries. Its latest embodiment was the "Iron Curtain" that separated the Soviet states from the "civilized" West.

Some of these themes were taken up by the Georgian and Polish women I interviewed. For example, Julia, the professor of physics from Tbilisi, challenges the notion of progress in the area of "women's rights" as attributable solely to the West. Educated in both Soviet history and Western feminist theory, Julia explained that the Soviet Union was in the forefront of providing women's rights and emancipation:

> Under socialism, there was what we call "formal equality." We, as women, also had equal opportunities, at least in the sphere of education. During the Soviet period, certain provisions existed that were supposed to ensure that women who devote a lot of time to their families also have enough time to work. It was good. I'm not sure if women in developed countries have such opportunity even now.

Julia also argued that it was the legacy of Bolshevik women's activism that laid the groundwork for ongoing developments in various areas of women's emancipation, including reproductive rights. In making reference to the "original East European feminist thought," she alludes to the fact that leaders of the 1917 Russian Revolution had from the beginning made combating women's oppression a central aspect of their revolutionary project. Her narrative supports the argument that the early Bolshevik activists can be seen not only as "actors," whose actions were rule-governed, but also as "agents," who exercised power and had the ability to "bring about effects and to (re)constitute the world" (Karp 1986). This changed during the decades of the 1960s and 1970s when sexual politics, as Kollontai understood it, disappeared.

Postsocialist feminisms have yet to reflect critically on the ways in which the images and projections of the West impact the ways in which local feminist pasts and presents are constructed. A tendency among post-1989 women's scholars and activists was to harshly critique the earlier generation for leaving a "gap" in the history of women's movements, both locally and globally. Today, scholars of post-state-socialist feminisms pose different questions, including about how to recognize East European feminisms as an indispensable and original site for the ongoing formulation and reformulation of global gender theory and practice. Recent research such as that produced by Małgorzata Fidelis and Francesca de Haan emerged from the region. Their work represents a departure from the staid conceptualizations of East European women's movements, which represent the state socialist period as a time of "stagnation" as far as women's rights are concerned (de Haan 2014b; Fidelis 2010). They demonstrate that various forms of women's agency were also possible within the socialist state, and suggest that so long as we insist on using "Western" feminist frames to evaluate the existence of feminism under state socialism, various forms of "gender politics" under socialism will remain unrecognized.

The year 2015 marked the twentieth anniversary of the Fourth United Nations Conference of Women in Beijing. On the transnational feminist front, women from the "Global North" and "Global South" are seen as leading mobilizations against discrimination and for greater gender social justice. Scholars are now beginning to recognize the role of state socialist women's emancipation in shaping international women's movements (Popa 2005; de Haan 2014a; Ghodsee 2012), and to understand that the second wave of the feminist movement that emerged in the United States and Western Europe in the 1960s was to some, if not a large, extent shaped by the larger political and cultural frames of the international fight for peace and development. For example, state socialist activism was a leading force behind the foundation of the Women's International Democratic Federation in 1946 (de Haan 2014a), and socialist policies that foregrounded women's equality by implementing constitutional changes and institutionalizing health and social welfare provisions were foundational for future international emancipation discourses, including those of the European Union "gender mainstreaming," which focus on gender economic equality, women in the labor market, and ways to balance work and "life" activities.

Conclusion

In 1990, Teresa de Lauretis argued that a key feature of any feminist critique is that it remains "conscious of itself" — part of our work as feminist scholars is to examine the terms of our own theories and discourses (de Lauretis 1990: 116, 131). In the context of de Lauretis's call for internal feminist critiques, the studies of state socialism that are emerging in the region and beyond have to be examined as twofold projects that: (1) aim at "recovering" forgotten histories while challenging existing conceptual frameworks; and (2) analyze the state socialist experiences of women, including those who argue that, under socialism, agency was only possible outside of the Communist Party power structure.

The ambivalent effects of systemic transformations on women's rights became a critical preoccupation of feminist scholars working in and on Central and Eastern Europe in the 1990s. The question of the impact of the legacies of socialist emancipation projects remains on the margins of postsocialist feminist thought. Previous generations of scholars of gender equality in Central and Eastern Europe stressed the unique political traditions and historical legacies at work during and after state socialism. At the same time, they took for granted that the West was the sole logical point of reference for what were imagined as marginal East European feminisms. In these works, the authors represented women under state socialism as passive witnesses to the workings of the authoritarian system, caught up between the "double burden" of professional work and household responsibilities. They suggest the system did very little to challenge extant gender regimes, and they ignored that under state socialism, women had the right to legal abortion, received maternal provisions and extensive childcare services, and were massively present in the labor market—standard policies in socialist states.

In this chapter I have argued that new conceptualization(s) of women's agency under authoritarian regimes is needed to fully comprehend the complexities of women's lives under socialism in Georgia and in Poland. Emerging scholarship on women's agency under state socialism centers on the female capacity to act within the socialist system, and links state socialist conceptualizations of gender equality with the current struggles for women's rights at regional, national, and supranational levels. By recognizing the state socialist period as one involving a multilayered web of interactions, this new approach contributes to the delineation of the diverse trajectories of women's movements in the region, pointing to its various, often seemingly contradictory, origins.

At the transnational level, acknowledging state socialism as a part of the genealogy of the women's movement after socialism illuminates how local legacies of gender equality intersected with the arrival of global, supranational gender discourses after the fall of state socialism. In consequence, it can also broaden the definition of the transnational women's movement, and expand the dominant understanding of the genealogies of gender equality discourse. Recognizing the role of socialist "state feminism" in the genealogies of the European women's movement, and recognizing state socialism as a part of the genealogy of the women's movement after socialism, can help overcome the enduring tendency to evaluate East European feminisms solely in relationship to the West, and help establish connections with other non-Western locations. The delineation of common effects that genealogies of nationalism and Eastern and Western imperialism had on women—including the complex trajectories of feminisms within anti-imperialist movements, uneasy relations with nationalisms and religious fundamentalisms, the experience of racism, the continuing struggles to negotiate a feminist relationship with local narratives of a motherland, and a transnational positionality vis-à-vis the West—can serve as a stepping stone for establishing transnational solidarities between the feminisms from Eastern Europe and the "Global South" (Jayawardena 1994; Heng 1997; Naples and Desai 2002).

Magdalena Grabowska received her PhD from the Department of Women's and Gender Studies, Rutgers University. She works at the Institute of Philosophy and Sociology, Polish Academy of Sciences, where she is completing a book on women's activism under state socialism in Poland and Georgia. She was European Commission, Marie Curie International Reintegration Fellow at Warsaw University (2010–14), and is the author most recently of "Exploring the Chronology and Intertextuality of Feminist Scholarship on Central and Eastern Europe," in *Signs* (2014). She is cofounder of the Foundation for Equality and Emancipation (STER) where she is conducting research on the prevalence of sexual violence in Poland.

Notes

1. This chapter draws on results of a research project with members of communist parties and women's organizations active before 1989 in Poland and Georgia. The research was conducted between 2010 and 2014, when I was the EC Marie Curie Reintegration Fellow at Warsaw University (grant number 256475). The fieldwork was conducted with the support of the Polish National Science Center for the project "Bits of Freedom: Women's Agency in Socialist Poland and Georgia" (project number N 116673140). The research involved conducting over fifty individual tape-recorded interviews, gathering field notes and conducting archival research. The fieldwork was conducted in several locations, including Tbilisi, Kutiaisi, and Gori in Georgia, and Warsaw, Łódź, Zgierz, and Szczecinek (among other sites) in Poland. The interviews in Georgia were conducted in Russian, and translated into English by the author. The names of all research participants in this chapter are pseudonyms.
2. The Komsomol was a communist youth organization (ages fourteen to twenty-five) founded in 1918. The name of the organization is an acronym of the words Kommunisticheskii soiuz molodezhi / Kommunisticzeskij Sojuz Molodiozy (Communist Youth Association).

References

Ahrean, L.M. 2004. "Literacy, Power, and Agency: Love Letters and Development in Nepal," *Language and Education* 18(4): 305–16.

de Haan, F. 2014a. "Continuing Cold War Paradigms in the Western Historiography of Transnational Women's Organisations: The Case of the Women's International Democratic Federation (WIDF)," *Women's History Review* (September): 547–73.

——— (ed.). 2014b. "Gendering the Cold War in the Region: An Email Conversation between Malgorzata (Gosia) Fidelis, Renata Jambrešić Kirin, Jill Massino, and Libora Oates-Indruchova," *Aspasia* 8: 162–90.

———. 2016. "Ten Years After: Communism and Feminism Revisited," *Aspasia* 10: 102–66.

de Lauretis, T. 1990. "Feminism and Its Differences." *Pacific Coast Philology* 25(1/2): 24–30.

Evans Clements, B. 1994. *Daughters of Revolution: A History of Women in the U.S.S.R.* Wheeling, IL: Harlan Davidson.

Fidelis, M. 2010. *Women, Communism, and Industrialization in Postwar Poland.* New York: Cambridge University Press.
Funk, N. 2014. "A Very Tangled Knot: Official State Socialist Women's Organizations, Women's Agency and Feminism in Eastern European State Socialism," *European Journal of Women's Studies* 21(4): 344–60.
Fuszara, M. 2000. "New Gender Relationships in Poland in 1990s," in *Reproducing Gender: Politics, Publics, and Everyday Life after Socialism,* ed. S. Gal and G. Kligman, 259–85. Princeton, NJ: Princeton University Press.
Ghodsee, K. 2012. "Rethinking State Socialist Mass Women's Organizations: The Committee of the Bulgarian Women's Movement and the United Nations Decade for Women, 1975–1985," *Journal of Women's History* 24(4): 49–73.
Harding, S. 1987. *Science Question in Feminism.* Ithaca, NY: Cornell University Press.
Havelková, H., and L. Oates-Indruchová (eds). 2014. *The Politics of Gender Culture under State Socialism: An Expropriated Voice.* Abingdon and New York: Routledge.
Heng, G. 1997. "'A Great Way to Fly': Nationalism, the State, and the Varieties of Third World Feminism." in *Feminist Genealogies, Colonial Legacies, Democratic Futures,* ed. M.J. Alexander and C.T. Mohanty, 30–45. New York: Routledge.
Hrycak, A. 2002. "From Mothers' Rights to Equal Rights: Post-Soviet Grassroots Women's Associations." In *Women's Activism and Globalization: Linking Local Struggles and Transnational Politics,* ed. N. Naples and M. Desai, 64–82. London: Routledge.
Jayawardena, K. 1994. *Feminism and Nationalism in the Third World.* London: Zed Books.
Karp, I. 1986. "Agency and Social Theory: Review of Anthony Giddens." *American Ethnologist* 13(1): 131–37.
Kollontai, A. 1984. *The Social Basis of the Woman Question. Alexandra Kollontai: Selected Articles and Speeches.* Moscow: Progress Publishers.
Lenin, V.I. 1919. "The Tasks of the Working Women's Movement in the Soviet Republic." Speech delivered at the Fourth Moscow City Conference of Non-Party Working Women, 23 September 1919.
Mohanty, C. 2002. *Learning From Experience: Minority Identities, Multicultural Struggles.* Berkeley: University of California Press.
Naples, N., and M. Desai. 2002. *Women's Activism and Globalization: Linking Local Struggles and Transnational Politics.* New York: Routledge.
Narayan, U. 1997. *Dislocating Cultures: Identities, Traditions and Third World Feminism.* New York and London: Routledge.
Nowak, B. 2005. "'Where Do You Think I Learned How to Style My Own Hair?' Gender and Everyday Lives of Women Activists in Poland's League of Women," in *Gender Politics and Everyday Life in State Socialist Eastern and Central Europe,* ed. S. Penn and J. Massino, 45–58. New York: Palgrave Macmillan.
Popa R.M. 2005. "Translating Equality between Women and Men across Cold War Divides: Women Activists from Hungary and Romania and the Creation of International Women's Year," in *Gender Politics and Everyday Life in State Socialist Eastern and Central Europe,* ed. S. Penn and J. Massino, 59–74. New York: Palgrave Macmillan.
Regulska, J., and M. Grabowska. 2013. "Social Justice, Hegemony, and Women's Mobilizations," in *Postcommunism from Within: Social Justice, Mobilization and Hegemony,* ed. J. Kubik and A. Linch, 139–90. New York: NYU Press.
Scott, J. 1991. "The Evidence of Experience." *Critical Inquiry* 17: 773–97.
Trotsky, L. 1923. "From the Old Family to the New." First Published: *Pravda,* 13 July 1923.
Voronina, O. 1993. "Soviet Patriarchy: Past and Present." *Hypatia* 8(4): 97–99.
Wolff, L. 1994. *Inventing Eastern Europe: The Map of Civilization on the Mind of the Enlightenment.* Stanford, CA: Stanford University Press.

Chapter 5

Women's Political Representation in Post-Soviet Georgia

Ketevan Chkheidze

Introduction

The collapse of the Soviet Union and the subsequent move from "socialism" toward "democracy" brought considerable freedoms and opportunities as well as challenges to women in Georgia. In terms of Georgian women's position, the political arena has been disappointing. Women's hopes for a gender sensitive, multiparty, and inclusive political system has failed to materialize. Considering that women's representation in the Georgian Parliament has not exceeded 12 percent since Georgian independence in the 1990s, it is clear that women have been excluded from party participation and formal decision making, while men hold the key leadership positions in political parties and in the Georgian Parliament. This fact stands out, despite Georgia having declared a strong commitment to so-called European values and democracy.

The processes of democratization and politics more generally are common subjects of Georgian scholarly and public discussion and debate. Even so, the experiences of women in Georgian political life are rarely considered in the scholarly literature. In this chapter, I take up the question of women's political engagement in the Parliament of Georgia in the context of postcommunist Georgia in an effort to identify the key factors that explain their underrepresentation during the democratic transition in Georgia.

Notes for this chapter begin on page 90.

To explore theses issues, I focus on the transition period during the last decade of the twentieth century—an intense time for Georgian society, culture, and politics. During this period, women were active, taking leading roles in various domains in civil society and taking on the family breadwinner role. Even as women found ways to adjust to the new realities by engaging in new and different roles and identities, they continued to be excluded from the formal political sphere. Thus, political processes do not appear to be gender inclusive in the aftermath of the breakup of the Soviet Union and during the democratic transition of Georgia.

The numbers tell the story: in 1995, women represented less than 7 percent of the 250 members of Parliament (only sixteen women); in 1999, it was still approximately 7 percent (seventeen women out of 235 members); in subsequent years, 10 percent of Parliament members were women. After 2008, the number of Parliament seats was reduced to 150. In the four years between 2008 and 2011, women comprised only 6 percent of Parliament members. In 2012, this percentage nearly doubled, as eighteen women appeared in the Parliament of Georgia; but despite the upward trend, the fact remains that men continue to be disproportionately represented in the Parliament, an indicator of a larger gender problem in Georgian politics.

My discussion in this chapter concentrates on exploring low female representation in the Parliament of Georgia during the years 2003–2012, a particularly important period in the democratic development of the country. In 2003, the Rose Revolution brought about a nonviolent regime change as well as Western-driven political power and leadership, and new calls for democracy. I draw on reports from political analysts to examine party-level characteristics and features of the Georgian electoral system that shaped women's low representation in formal politics in the transitional democracy.

The Transition Period: Women in the Political Economy

After the breakup of the Soviet Union, Georgia began the move from communism toward a market economy, and from a subordinated administrative unit of the Soviet Union to representative democracy. The process of political and economic transformation was marked by fervent nationalism and rapid structural change, with implications for the entire population. In this period, Georgians experienced a civil war and two ethnic conflicts resulting in approximately 300,000 internally displaced persons (IDPs), 55 percent of them women (UNHCR 2003: 399). Displaced women suffered physically and economically. They were victims of the wartime crimes of rape and other forms of psychological and physical sexual violence (Sabedashvili 2007). As they sought to rebuild their emotional and material lives in new locations, these women discovered that jobs were scarce, and their identification as IDPs left them marginalized and excluded (Sumbadze and Tarkhan-Mouravi 2003).

In some ways, Georgia's transition has been like that of the other former Soviet countries, all of which have experienced a marked decline in economic production and the availability of jobs, as well as major cultural shifts (Heinen 2006). A majority of Georgians experienced the dramatic downward change in economic conditions. In this context, women across the country—not just those who were IDPs—began to accept low-paying jobs and became increasingly engaged in the informal economy (Sabedashvili 2007). Many became self-employed, running small-scale businesses and selling goods at markets and in the streets, which is a common activity sometimes referred to as "suitcase" merchandizing in certain post-Soviet countries (Ishkanian 2003). Employment in the informal economy provided women with some opportunities to secure a livelihood, though these "opportunities" must be understood as precarious. Even as women appeared to be more independent as solo entrepreneurs, they were in fact becoming increasingly marginalized, both economically and politically.

During the transition period, women did play an active role in the nationalist movements, and they claimed political space through activism as members of civil society and by participating in demonstrations and national movements aimed at the well-being of the entire society during the process of building an independent state. Today, despite their informal political activism, Georgian women's claims on the public sphere and their political power remain weak, as they continue to lack access to formal political power and decision making—in particular, in the national legislative body and local government. Despite a few women occupying positions in the executive government as well as efforts by civil society to increase women's representation in formal politics, the major change that would bring a critical mass of women into politics has not yet taken place.

Women's relative absence from the formal political landscape in the post-Soviet period is a complex issue intertwined with prevailing political, economic, and social factors. Female underrepresentation in formal politics is characteristic of the post-Soviet space more generally. Georgina Waylen notes that the politics of transitional democracy frequently become a male-dominated public sphere where women are seldom present or entirely absent (Waylen 1994).

This pattern is consistent with the situation in Georgia. Research on women's participation in Georgia's emerging political parties conducted in the late 1990s show that in 1997, only 6 percent of political parties were headed by women (ten women out of a total of 158); and in 1999, only 5 percent of the 124 political parties registered were headed by women. During the 1998–2001 period, women's representation in these leadership positions increased slightly, with approximately 10 percent of the parties headed by women (Khomeriki and Chubinidze 1998). It is notable that established political parties did not develop or adopt consistent, clear democratic principles on gender equity.

In the transition period, the Georgian Parliament emerged as a very powerful political institution. Since Georgia gained independence, the Parliament has held utmost legislative power; while the number of MPs had been 235, this figure reduced to 150 in 2008, of which 77 members were elected through proportional lists and 73 through a single-member district plurality system (or single constituencies). In the past decades, women received little support when party lists of candidates were prepared in advance of parliamentary elections. Even when women were included on candidate lists, they seldom appeared among the first ten candidates on the list, and were usually located at the bottom. In the Georgian case, men dominated the legislative institutions while women continued to gain visibility as leaders in civil society organizations.

Taken together, these conditions have hindered the adoption of gender-inclusive political practices in post-Soviet Georgia (Khomeriki 2006). Thus, Georgian women's low representation in formal politics should not be surprising, despite their overall high literacy and educational levels, their high employment rates and contributions to the national economy, and their activism and history of participating in national movements.

There are a number of forces at play that help explain women's underrepresentation in formal politics in most of the Central East European countries, including Georgia. Overall, gender equity did not get adequate attention from the states in transition (Sabedashvili 2007; Regulska and Grabowska 2012). Generally, those who set the political agenda did not deem "women's issues" important (Brunnbauer 2000; Sabedashvili 2007). With men at the helm, women lost ground in terms of the training and preparation in political leadership. At the same time, men were able to expand their political networks and forge informal agreements, helping consolidate male political power. In addition, the dismantling of the social safety net left women with little support for their work in the domestic sphere as mothers and wives, and little time to engage in the wider world of politics (Brunnbauer 2000).

Georgian women held out hope that the transition to "democracy" would ensure women's access to the political sphere. The reality turned out quite differently, as women encountered enormous obstacles in their efforts to exercise their political rights (Walshe 2011). I now turn to the impact of particular attributes of Georgian political parties on women's ability to enter the formal political sphere.

Women's Political Representation and Party Characteristics

It is essential to identify characteristics of the parties that comprise a political system in order to understand the factors that explain the rate of women's participation in formal politics and their representation in a nation's legislative body (Norris and Lovenduski 1995; Chkheidze 2014). Political parties serve as gatekeepers for entering formal politics, determining who is included and who is excluded from their ranks, and at what levels within party hierarchies. A party's organization, its ideology, rules, and degree of centralization are the key characteristics that need to be examined in order to understand the fate of women in parliamentary politics and their representation in the parliaments themselves (Norris and Lovenduski 1995; Caul 2010).

On the heels of the relatively peaceful, nonviolent, and democratic Rose Revolution of 2003, the United National Movement (UNM), Georgia's leading political party at the time, brought much hope for a gender-inclusive political process as the call for high standards of democracy had been declared. Many important reforms aimed at democratic development were implemented, including ending corruption, restructuring the police and introducing new standards for law enforcement, reforming the business sector, and amending and adopting new laws that would bring the country closer to European integration. UNM, which was a leading political party during 2004–2012, declared in early 2005 an active campaign to promote women in political leadership, and several women were appointed in important, high-level positions in the executive government. While women's representation in the Parliament was only around 9 percent, importantly, the speaker of the Parliament, Nino Burjanadze, was a woman. Nevertheless, women political leaders did not recognize gender inequality as an issue, and the ruling party did not have women's inclusion in formal politics on their agenda in subsequent years. A gender quota bill was introduced by civil society in 2008 but it failed to gain the support of the major political forces. No institutionalized practices or policies were introduced to enhance women's real engagement in politics.

By 2012, there were two large political parties—the United National Movement and the Georgian Dream coalition—vying for seats in Parliament. Neither party had addressed the issue of gender representation in Parliament during the election, and neither of the leaders had committed their party to the principle of gender equality. As a result, women remained underrepresented in Parliament. In the 2012 Parliament, seventeen women were elected to 150 seats. Of these, eleven were members of the Georgian Dream coalition and six were members of UNM; ten had been elected through proportional lists and seven had been plurality/majority candidates.

In developing democracies such as Georgia, party leadership tends to be centralized rather than diffuse. This means that power is held in the hands of one person or a very few people. The centralized leadership sets the party agenda and decides whose name appears on candidate lists for municipal and national elections. One may argue that power accumulated in a central authority signals an immature political culture. Regardless of how it is characterized, the leadership in a centralized party structure offers the formal guarantee of women's inclusion or exclusion. Miki Caul (2010) considers centralized leadership and the institutionalization of well-developed and practiced policies, including rules that dictate how party members are recruited, as the determining factors in whether or not women will have representation in party politics.

The absence of explicit gender equality policies and rules, especially within the leading political parties, enhances the likelihood that women will have limited visibility within them. Generally, they lack party support for advancing their political careers, and have weak ties to those individuals and interest groups that are essential to political advancement. Under these conditions, women tend to be alienated from party politics; indeed, they comprise a small proportion of the party membership. It becomes very difficult for women to convince the male leadership to adopt both a platform of gender equity and develop the means to implement it within the political party. Those women who are involved in party politics hold the lowest-level positions and perform the most routine tasks, such as drafting programs, communicating with citizens, and coordinating the work of party activists (Bagratia and Badashvili 2011). They rarely hold executive or important decision-making roles.

This pattern fits with the condition of Georgian political parties in the period between 2004 and 2012. Almost none of the political parties during that period focused on increasing women's leadership positions within their ranks. In general, Georgian political parties address issues around women's advancement and gender parity as social issues rather than as issues to be systematically addressed and institutionalized within the parties themselves. One of the indicators of democracy is the establishment of policies that ensure gender parity, their implementation, and women's political advancement in political parties. Despite some positive steps, this has not yet been accomplished in Georgia. Women's inclusion in politics and political parties has not been based on formal regulations or institutional practices and mechanisms, but is of a more ad hoc character. The system for selecting candidates and how they get on party lists remains grounded in principles that are not favorable to women. While most of the political parties have adopted the principles of democracy in their approaches, strategies, and programs, achieving gender balance remains a serious challenge inside the parties, resulting in low female representation in the national legislative body.

Research conducted by Tamar Bagratia and Medea Badashvili on seven Georgian political parties indicates that all of them made declarative statements supporting gender equality and women's inclusion in party politics, and none provided clear-cut policies or advancement strategies to ensure gender parity. Most of the initiatives were ad hoc and unsystematic. With regard to gender parity policies, the authors identify two types of political parties: those that do and those that do not have mechanisms in place to ensure gender equality. Parties that do have some mechanisms, such as a women's branch, are better able to secure some level of advancement for women in terms of their visibility and levels of responsibility. Even so, no party has institutionalized gender equality by means of its statutes or bylaws (Bagratia and Badashvili 2011). In those parties that have made some effort to be more inclusive by means of special groups or branches, women's standing remains weak.

Furthermore, analysis of political parties from a gender perspective indicates that by 2010 the number of registered political parties had reached two hundred; however, only a few of them were politically active, and general public awareness of their agenda has been rather low (Bagratia and Badashvili 2011). Although parties are fragmented, still the party as an entity remains the main arena and entry point for women's political participation and representation in the Parliament. Therefore, while not all the political parties acknowledge the importance of women's inclusion and have no comprehension of the positive sides of women's engagement in political decision making and party life, establishing gender parity within parties becomes an indicator of a party's level of democracy, and therefore is an important factor for women's political advancement (ibid.; Chkheidze 2014).

It is notable that women comprised 29 percent of the registered candidates for the 2012 parliamentary elections in Georgia. Six of the sixteen registered political parties that participated in these elections responded to the financial incentives incorporated into the Organic Law of Georgia on Political Union of Citizens in 2011 to voluntarily include women in their party lists. The two leading political parties—UNM and the Georgian Dream coalition—put forth the least number of women candidates and did not participate in this voluntary measure (Bagratia 2013). Overall, women won 15 percent of the proportional mandates and 9 percent of the majoritarian mandates in these parliamentary elections. Since women's share of parliamentary seats nearly doubled—from 6 percent to almost 12 percent—the 2012 elections are considered to have been a step forward in women's political representation. Even so, achieving gender balance remains a serious challenge within Georgian political parties, considering the low female representation in the national legislative body.

Gender Equality Policies

Even though the issue of gender equality has failed to gain traction within Georgia's political parties, it did enter into the national discourse in the post-independence transition period. In this regard, the World Conference on Women in 1995 and the adoption of the Beijing Platform for Action have been pivotal to the pursuit and implementation of gender equality policies in Georgia (Chkheidze 2010).

Georgia's commitment to the Beijing Platform for Action is reflected in the establishment of a national commission on women's advancement and the adoption of concrete policies aimed at advancing gender equality. In 1999, the State Commission on Elaboration of State Policy for Women's Advancement was developed by the Security Council of Georgia, and established by the president of Georgia. The commission adopted special decrees and action plans for protecting women's rights in Georgia.[1]

This was indeed a step forward although the promises of these declarations were not fulfilled. The monitoring effort of the National Action Plan for 2001–2004 conducted by a number of NGOs in 2004 found that despite the commitment of the state, goals for women's advancement were not achieved. Only a very few of the activities envisaged by the plan have been implemented (Sabedashvili 2007).

The early efforts to attend to gender equity at the national level have not been sustained. The State Commission on Elaboration of State Policy for Women's Advancement ceased functioning in 2003 after the Rose Revolution. The Gender Advisory Council that was established at the Parliament in 2004, and which comprised parliamentary, government, and NGOs representatives, replaced it. A similar institutional mechanism, the Gender Equality Governmental Commission (GEGC), was created in 2005 with a one-year mandate to ensure coordination among various stakeholders and to develop the State Concept on Gender Equality and the National Action Plan. The concept is based on the Constitution of Georgia and largely reflects the Convention on Elimination of Discrimination against

Women (CEDAW), a major international instrument for combating gender inequality. In this regard, the concept envisages equal rights and opportunities for women and men in all spheres of public and political life (Parliament of Georgia 2006).

The state action to initiate these commissions was a rare demonstration of political will in relation to gender issues. Still, the fact that contributions by international organizations were crucial to the functioning and sustaining of the work of these two entities calls into question the level of state commitment to these issues. In 2006, as a result of a joint working group and the GEGC, a national gender equality strategy was developed that consisted of the State Concept on Gender Equality, the National Action Plan on Gender Equality, and a package of recommendations for gender equality policies to be adopted by the executive and legislative branches of the Parliament (Sabedashvili 2007).

The work of the GEGC ended in 2006, and an Interdisciplinary Commission on Elaboration of State Policy on Gender Equality was established at the Ministry for Reforms Coordination, and was composed of high-level governmental officials (Aladashvili and Chkheidze 2009). The aim of the ministry was to coordinate the work on the implementation of gender equality policies. However, its effectiveness and sustainability were problematic because it was not a permanent institution and lacked state support. These gaps ultimately led to the 2010 Law on Gender Equality, which obliged the creation of a permanent body, the Gender Equality Council, within the Parliament of Georgia, the national legislative body.

In 2006, the Parliament of Georgia adopted two important legislative documents: (1) the Law on Combating Domestic Violence, and the Protection of and Assistance to Domestic Violence Victims; and (2) the Law on Combating Human Trafficking. The period since the establishment of the State Concept of Gender Equality has seen the adoption of relevant national action plans on gender equality. The Gender Equality Council continues to lead the work on the gender equality agenda with an updated National Action Plan on Gender Equality (2007–2009) and by regularly updating action plans for combating domestic violence and protecting and assisting domestic violence victims.

This list of actions and the high level of political representation involved are impressive. Nevertheless, these steps have failed to address a number of burning issues faced by women, have led to few tangible impacts, and have not led to the advancement of women's political position or their socioeconomic status in Georgia (Aladashvili and Chkheidze 2009).

As noted above, the driving forces for gender equity policies have been NGOs and international organizations; the state contributes minimal human and financial resources to the effort, and coordination among responsible government agencies and municipal "focal points" remains weak (Georgia – Beijing +20 2014: 39). UN agencies operating in Georgia have supported the government in monitoring implementation of national action plans since 2006. Results of these assessment reports demonstrate that it is civil society groups and international donor organizations that have been critical to the implementation of the national plans, while the state and its institutions have demonstrated limited commitment to reaching stated objectives (ibid.). Among the key challenges that remain are: the lack of state funding for implementing concrete activities outlined in national action plans (in particular the Gender Equality National Action Plan); that nearly all implementation is driven by donors and international organizations; that there is a lack of clear government monitoring of and reporting on the results of any implementation; and a lack of paid support staff dedicated to ensuring the implementation of the national action plans (ibid.; Chkheidze 2014).

The history of the Gender Equality Council (GEC) offers a case in point. Since 2006, the GEC has played a crucial role in developing and adopting important legislation. Initially a temporary, advisory body, it was charged with coordinating the work of state agencies and NGOs, and introducing legislative amendments. The Advisory Council united seventeen members who brought in representatives of NGOs, including those focused on women's issues, and members of the Parliament (Aladashvili and Chkheidze 2009). When the Advisory Council was transformed into the Gender Equality Council, a permanent institution of the Parliament in 2010, it was composed of members of Parliament, with the vice speaker of Parliament serving as chair. Charged with developing gender equality policy, the GEC developed and adopted the National Action Plan for 2014–2016.

The adoption of the Gender Equality Law of Georgia represents a step forward for gender parity. It defines fundamental guarantees for equal rights, and addresses a range of issues, including maintaining statistics on gender matters, seeking gender equality in labor relations, providing guarantees for gender equality in education and science, as well as equal access to informational resources, ensuring gender equality in healthcare and social security, upholding gender equality in family relations, and guaranteeing equal voting rights (Law of Georgia on Gender Equality 2010).

The Gender Equity Law remains a framing document with general statements of guarantee. Still missing are implementation directives and monitoring mechanisms, which makes it difficult to assess the ways in which the law is being implemented and its efficacy. In terms of women's political participation, the Gender Equity Law includes a general provision guaranteeing equal treatment in the process of assuming public office, but does not specify how that is to be achieved. It does not offer a method by which discrimination in the field of politics can be eliminated, and nor does it suggest that political parties should be regulated.

The 2009 Organic Law on Political Unions of Citizens established the definition, rights, and duties of political parties in Georgia. Two years later, an amendment to the law was introduced, providing financial incentives to implement voluntary measures to increase female participation in political life. Political parties are eligible for a 30 percent increase in funding assuming they include at least the same percentage of women among every ten candidates in proportional lists (Parliament of Georgia 2009). However, the goal of incentivizing political parties to include more women in proportional lists has not been met. In 2012, some political parties did apply this measure and yet did not address low female representation in their parties. Various experts argue that the financial incentive is not an effective measure in solving the issue of low female political representation (Bagratia 2013; Chkheidze 2014; Pataraia 2015).

Although the government of Georgia has adopted a significant gender equality policy, implementation of these policies by the state is lacking. Since independence, women remain underrepresented in political parties because of the deeply gendered election process. Domestic legislation has not been adequately informed by gender analysis nor included specific gender features, which would go a long way in ensuring gender is a basis for and integral to women's participation in every field.

The Election System

The particular characteristics of Georgia's electoral system are another factor in shaping women's political representation. Georgia has a mixed electoral system, allowing candidates to be nominated and elected either through proportional party lists or by means of a plurality system. Generally, the proportional system enables more women to gain seats than they are able to gain in a majoritarian system, a pattern that holds true across nations. Women's political representation in countries with a proportional election system is higher than in countries with any other electoral system (Paxton and Kunovich 2003; Matland and Montgomery 2003).

In Georgia, women's representation through proportional lists has been increasing. For example, in the 2012 election, 14 percent of the seats won by women came through the proportional list, a 4 percent increase since the previous election (Bagratia 2013). Less beneficial to women is the single constituency majoritarian system, in which parties tend to choose as their candidate an authority in the society—someone with a good reputation and access to finances. This leaves less chance for women to be nominated and then elected as majoritarian candidates. As many examples worldwide show, majoritarian/plurality electoral systems offer only modest advantage for women, while proportional representation through party lists results in stronger women's representation (Shedova 2005; Matland 2005). While there are no clear-cut rules in the case of Georgia for recruitment and candidate nomination, in the 2008 election, only one out of the nine women who won a seat in the Parliament got there through the majoritarian system. The fact that after 2012, seven women were elected as majoritarians (a significant increase over 2008) should not lead to the conclusion that the majority system is favorable to women (Bagratia and Badashvili 2011). Other factors account for the increase, including that several advanced on the coattails of the popularity of, and public trust in, the Georgian Dream coalition (Chkheidze 2014). This suggests that if the goal is gender parity in parliamentary political representation, the mixed electoral system does not facilitate reaching the goal.

In context of the state of electoral and party politics in Georgia, significant increases in female political representation in the next elections are not expected. In Georgia, discussions on changing the electoral system abound; gender equality is just one aspect of reforming the system. It will take more than women's advocacy groups to lobby for changes favorable to women in the electoral system (that may include gender quotas), obliging political parties to maintain gender balance in the party lists. Efforts are currently underway, although they are moving at a slow pace.[2] CEDAW's 2014 recommendations that the state undertake special measures to increase women's engagement in political decision making have not been taken up. Still missing is the political will to address the issue in a substantive way.

Conclusion

Women's engagement in formal politics and the extent to which they appear in the national legislative body depends on a complexity of political and legislative factors, as illustrated by the discussion offered in this chapter. As Georgia underwent political, economic, and social change, women made efforts to participate and act as agents of change. However, their opportunities for sharing political power and participating in political decision making have been limited. For the most part, women have been left out of the political sphere, and post-Soviet promises of equality have not been translated into equal rights and opportunities for women.

Women's exclusion from the formal political sphere in Georgia can be attributed in large part to the particular characteristics of Georgian political parties, most of which do not have explicit gender equity principles, mandates, or policies, and there is low-level intraparty democracy. The role of party leaders in deciding who gets recruited to be a party member and who gets to be on the list of candidates for election cannot be underestimated. The lack of institutionalized rules and regulations, the strategy of urging "voluntary" cooperation by the party machine to ensure gender parity, the practice of discretionary decision making in the hands of a centralized leader, and the mixed election system, leave little opportunity for equal justice for women. Under these conditions, the chances are slim that women will reach parity with men in the Georgian Parliament.

There is a clear need for a state-supported national strategy for women's advancement in formal politics. It is also clear that the time has come for Georgian political parties to acknowledge the problem and to muster the political will to initiate positive change for women and society. The question thus remains: what will the Georgian state and the country's established political parties do to ensure that women will be elected to the national legislative body and to local government positions?

Ketevan Chkheidze holds a Master's degree from the Central European University in Budapest, and a PhD in gender studies from Tbilisi State University, where she teaches undergraduate and graduate courses at the Faculty of Social and Political Sciences. Her research interests are women and politics, and gender and development, women and citizenship, and gender and democracy. She also serves as a consultant on gender issues in the Caucasus region for the Asian Development Bank.

Notes

1. The decrees and national action plans that were adopted immediately after the Beijing Platform for Action include Presidential Decree No. 511, On Measures for Strengthening the Protection of Human Rights of Women in Georgia (1999); Presidential Decree No. 308, The National Action Plan on the Measures for Protection of Women's Rights (1998–2000); Three-Year Action Plan to Combat Violence against Women (2000–2002); and The Plan of Action for Improving Women's Conditions (2001–2004).
2. A task force on women's political participation was established in the spring of 2014. The main objectives of the group are to improve coordination among the stakeholders working in the field of women's political empowerment, to assess and analyze the gender situation in terms of women's political participation in Georgia, to establish a platform for joint advocacy, and to strategize for improving women's political participation.

Its members are several international and donor organizations working on women's political participation, such as: the Swedish International Development and Cooperation Agency (SIDA); National Democratic Institute (NDI); Netherlands Institute for Multiparty Democracy (NIMD); International Foundation for Electoral Systems (IFES); International Republican Institute (IRI); Oxfam; United Nations Development Program (UNDP); and UN Women. There are also local organizations, including: Women's Information Centre (WIC); Gender Equality Network; Women's Political Resource Center (WPRC); International Center for Women's Education and Information; and Gender Justice. In addition are experts working on issues of women's political participation. The members of the task force are also representatives from other agencies like the Central Election Commission, Prime Minister's Office, Gender Equality Parliamentary Council and Public Defender's Office. The task force is chaired by NDI. It has developed a strategy, and its first order of business is working on introducing gender quotas for national elections.

References

Aladashvili, I., and K. Chkheidze. 2009. "Review of the Gender Equality Strategy and Monitoring of the 2007–2009 National Action Plan on Gender Equality in Georgia." Tbilisi: UNFPA

Bagratia, T. 2013. "Gender Analysis of 2012 Parliamentary Elections." Tbilisi: NIMD.

Bagratia, T., and M. Badashvili. 2011. "Development of Intraparty Democracy from Gender Perspective." Policy Paper in *Intraparty Democracy and Local Governance,* 7–33. Tbilisi: NIMD.

Brunnbauer, U. 2000. "From Equality Without Democracy to Democracy Without Equality." *South East Europe Review* 3: 151–68.

Caul, M. 2010. "Women's Representation in Parliament: The Role of Political Parties." In *Women, Gender and Politics: A Reader,* ed. M.L. Krook and S. Childs. Oxford: Oxford University Press.

Chkheidze, K. 2010. "Gender Politics in Georgia." *Caucasus Analytical Digest* 21: 2–5.

———. 2014. "Women's Political Participation during Democratic Transformation: The Case of Georgia." PhD dissertation, I. Javakhishvili Tbilisi State University.

Georgia – Beijing +20. 2014. "National Review of Implementation of the Beijing Declaration and Platform for Action." Retrieved 19 December 2015 from http://www2.unwomen .org/~/media/headquarters/attachments/sections/csw/59/national_reviews/georgia_re view_beijing20.ashx?v=1&d=20140917T100730.

Heinen, J. 2006. "Clashes and Ordeals of Women's Citizenship in Central and Eastern Europe." In *Women and Citizenship in Central and Eastern Europe,* ed. J. Lukic, J. Regulska, and D. Zavirsek, 81–100. Aldershot: Ashgate Publishing.

Ishkanian, A. 2003. "Gendered Transitions: The Impact of Post-Soviet Transition on Women in Central Asia and the Caucasus." *Perspectives on Global Development and Technology* 2(3): 465–96.

Khomeriki, L., and N. Chubinidze. 1998. "Women in Political Parties of Georgia." *Directory of Political Parties.* Tbilisi: International Center for Civic Culture.

Khomeriki, L. 2006. "Gender Parameters in Political Parties." In *Gender and Politics Reader,* ed. M. Chitashvili. 10–12. Tbilisi: Center for Social Science.

Law of Georgia on Gender Equality. 2010. Retrieved 28 October 2015 from https://www.ilo .org/dyn/natlex/docs/ELECTRONIC/88314/118643/F601507206/GEO88314%20Eng.pdf.

Matland, R.E. 2005. "Enhancing Women's Political Participation: Legislative Recruitment and Electoral Systems." In *Women in Parliament Beyond Numbers, A Revised Edition*, ed. J. Ballington and A. Kara, 93–106. Stockholm: Trydells Tryckeri AB.

Matland, R.E., and K.A. Montgomery. 2003. *Women's Access to Political Power in Post Communist Europe*. Oxford: Oxford University Press.

Norris, P., and J. Lovenduski. 1995. *Political Recruitment: Gender, Race and Class in the British Parliament*. Cambridge: Cambridge University Press.

Parliament of Georgia. 2006. "The State Concept on Gender Equality." Retrieved 5 September from http://www.parliament.ge/files/gender/Conc.pdf.

———. 2009. "Organic Law on Political Unions of Citizens." Retrieved 21 March 2016 from http://aceproject.org/ero-en/regions/europe/GE/organic-law-of-georgia-on-political-union-of/view.

Pataraia, B. 2015. "Georgian Politics Without Women – Quotas as a Solution to the Problem. Policy Brief." Open Society Georgia Foundation. Retrieved 22 March 2016 from http://www.osgf.ge/files/2015/Publication/EU-Geirgia%20Association%20/Angarishi_A4_3.pdf.

Paxton, P., and S.L. Kunovich. 2003. "Women's Political Representation: The Importance of Ideology." *Social Forces* 82(1): 87–113.

Regulska, J., and M. Grabowska. 2012. "Social Justice, Hegemony and Women's Mobilization." In *Postcommunism from Within: Justice, Hegemony and Mobilization*, ed. J. Kubik and A. Linch, 139–190. New York: New York University Press.

Sabedashvili, T. 2007. *Gender and Democratization: The Case of Georgia 1991–2006*. Tbilisi: Heinrich Boll Foundation.

Shedova, N. 2005. "Obstacles to Women's Participation in Parliament." In *Women in Parliament beyond Numbers. A Revised Edition*, ed. J. Ballington and A. Kara, 34–47. Stockholm: Trydells Tryckeri AB.

Sumbadze, N., and G. Tarkhan-Mouravi. 2003. "Working Paper on IDP Vulnerability and Self-Reliance." Tbilisi: UNDP.

UNHCR. 2003. "Global Report 2002." Retrieved 21 April 2017 from http://www.unhcr.org/en-us/publications/fundraising/4a0c24cf6/global-report-2002.html.

Walshe, D.M. 2011. *Women's Rights in Democratizing States: Just Debate and Gender Justice in the Public Sphere*. Cambridge: Cambridge University Press.

Waylen, G. 1994. "Women and Democratization: Conceptualization Gender Relation in Transition Politics." *World Politics* 46(3): 327–54.

Women's Advice Center Sakhli. 2004. "Monitoring of the Plan of Action for Combating Violence against Women." Tbilisi: Oxfam GB.

Part II
Violence

Chapter 6

The Domestic Violence Challenge to Soviet Women's Empowerment Policies

Tamar Sabedashvili

> Battering [of women] takes place every day. Hang yourself if you like … Factory management ironically smiles … trade unions are touched … The other organizations, as expected, do not even consider helping women out.
> —Varvara Chelnochnitsa, "Vsyem na Pokaz"

"Violence against women" and "domestic violence" were first conceptualized by women's rights activists and feminist scholars as a social issue in the United States and the United Kingdom in the late 1960s (Dobash and Dobash 1992). International recognition of violence against women as a human rights issue began in the late 1980s and became large scale in the early 1990s (Pietilä 2002; Meyersfeld 2010). The focus of this chapter lies in understanding how policy planners in the Soviet Union treated the practice of domestic violence, and how it was perceived and labeled. Thus, I explore Soviet state policies related to gender equality, and consider how these policies may have influenced the recognition (or lack thereof) of domestic violence as a women's rights issue by Soviet policy planners. I also examine the ways in which the rethinking of the concept of family at different points in Soviet history affected whether or not domestic violence was identified and regulated.

Notes for this chapter begin on page 106.

My critical interest lies in uncovering the specific factors that contributed to the identification or the lack of identification of domestic violence, which is important considering that Soviet policies and practices may have preconditioned Georgian society's beliefs and attitudes toward gender equality and women's rights in the period that followed the country's independence from the Soviet Union in 1991. Basing my analysis on a larger study of primary and secondary materials, which include Soviet periodicals published in Russia and in Georgia and stakeholder interviews, I identify key ideological and political factors to account for official recognition or the failure to recognize domestic violence as a social problem in the Soviet Union.[1] I also assess Soviet policymakers' attitudes toward domestic violence and the efficacy of the protection and support mechanisms available to women facing domestic violence in Soviet Georgia. This history is particularly important considering the Soviet Union positioned itself as the world's pioneer state in terms of policies and practices enabling women's liberation (*raskreposhchenie zhenshchin*).

De Facto Domestic Violence versus De Jure Women's Equal Rights in the Soviet Union

Scholars of Soviet state policies—as these relate to women and their rights—divide the history of the Soviet Union into three major periods. The first is the early Bolshevik period, which dates from 1918 to the beginning of the 1930s. The Russian sociologist Igor Kon identifies Bolshevik experimentation in the sphere of sexuality, family, and marital relations as a key characteristic of this period (Kon 1995). During the early Bolshevik period, gender policies aimed at resolving the "Woman Question" were put in place, designed to encourage women to break away from families and become more fully active in the public domain.

The second major period falls between the symbolic years of 1936, the year abortion was outlawed by Stalin's government, and 1955, the year abortion was again legalized. Social scientists Elena Zdravomyslova and Anna Temkina label this second period of Soviet gender policy making "totalitarian androgyny," marked by the economic mobilization of women in both the productive and reproductive spheres (Zdravomyslova and Temkina 2005: 98). The third and final period runs from the Twentieth Congress of the Communist Party in 1956 until the dissolution of the Soviet Union in 1991. This period saw campaigns of mass housing construction and a new, "softer" approach to the "Woman Question." It is marked by state concern about a growing demographic crisis (rising infant mortality and decreasing fertility rates) and persistent pressures on women to produce for the commonwealth and reproduce future generations of Soviet citizens. In the late 1970s research circles in Moscow had come to realize that the "Woman Question," which the founding fathers of the Bolshevik state had claimed had been resolved, demanded further consideration (Buckley 1981: 101). According to Mary Buckley, issues of concern were the famous "double shift": declining fertility rates, and women's underrepresentation among the political elites in decision-making positions (but still with no mention of domestic violence against women).

Soon after the establishment of the Soviet Union, the Soviet government considered the "Woman Question" successfully solved and the equality of the sexes mostly achieved (Lenin [1919] 1969).[2] The Soviet success story in relation to women's liberation was not groundless. The state developed successful literacy campaigns, instituted universal compulsory education for children, and opened up higher education opportunities for women. As a result, the number of women in the higher education system rose steadily (Pickard 1988), and women played important roles in the Bolshevik Revolution and the Russian Civil War, fighting alongside the Red Army soldiers, working as intelligence agents, participating in propaganda activity from rostrums, Agitation trains (*Agitpoezd*) and ships, and serving as Red Guard nurses (Stites 1978: 317–23; Evans Clements 1980). However, as was the case after the French Revolution (Bock 2002), the influence of women in post-revolutionary Soviet politics was extremely weak so that de jure gender equality provisions upheld by Soviet law were not translated into de facto gender equality in all fields of life. According to the historian Richard Stites, from 1917 until 1923 a small group of influential women held decision-making positions in the Bolshevik government; but then between 1923 and 1925 they were removed from the sites of power (Stites 1978: 323). Indeed, until the mid-1950s women were virtually absent from top decision-making positions (Buckley 1981: 103).[3]

The principle of equality of the sexes is found in nearly all Soviet law, including in the Constitution. The political structure of the Union of Soviet Socialist Republics (USSR) required three kinds of constitutions: the Constitution of the Soviet Union, the Constitutions of the Soviet Socialist Republics, and the Constitutions of the Autonomous Republics. The Constitution of the Soviet Union held legal primacy, thus requiring the other constitutions to be in conformity with it. In all three versions of the Constitution of the Soviet Union (1924, 1936, and 1977), women were accorded equal rights with men.[4] The principle of equality of the sexes was upheld also in criminal, administrative, and civil codes of the Soviet republics.

In its *Great Soviet Encyclopedia,* the Soviet state acknowledged that despite constitutional guarantees of women's emancipation in socialist countries, the elimination of inequality in women's actual daily lives would be a lengthy process achievable only by the successful, gradual transformation from socialism to communism (*Bolshaya sovetskaya entsiklopedia* 1972: 172). Against the de jure equality of sexes, women's de facto experiences stand in sharp relief. In what follows, I illustrate these experiences with examples from women's periodicals from the Soviet period. My larger analysis of these periodicals indicates variation in women's experiences across and within the Soviet republics, and suggests that issues they faced, such as domestic violence, were largely ignored by the state (Sabedashvili 2011).

In Georgia, the prevalence of domestic violence is suggested by the kinds of stories published in women's periodicals. For example, stories of domestic violence were common in the monthly women's magazine *Chveni gza*, published in Georgia during the 1920s.[5] The accounts of violence are described by female correspondents (*qalkori*) that *Chveni gza* deployed in different regions of the country. In one story, *Chveni gza* reported on "husbands throwing their wives and children out onto the streets, where hunger and death await them" (Zinaida 1924: 42).[6] Oftentimes, one reads individual or group testimonies of victims of violence. For instance, in one such story, women charge their husbands with "insulting and beating us up; [they] make us work like animals" (Tina 1925: 11). Though not exclusively so, these stories mostly centered on rural women for whom access to the civil registration of marriage, easily obtainable divorce, and generous but highly gendered provisions regarding childbearing and childcare in unregistered relationships was limited, and who were therefore highly dependent on their husbands.

A notable shift in the number of domestic violence stories can be observed in the 1930s. This is true for both Russian-language and Georgian magazines that targeted women readers (Revia 1969: 14; Abashidze 1969: 20; Nakaidze 1991: 1–2). It is hard to believe that domestic violence was simply eradicated. More likely, it was purposefully silenced in an effort to conform with state-sponsored propaganda about the progress made in liberating women. To acknowledge the existence of domestic violence in a society where gender equality had been "achieved" and women's liberation had been "completed" would violate that official narrative.

Family Buried and Resurrected: Political, Economic, and Sociocultural Dimensions

In *The German Ideology* (1845), Karl Marx identified the family as the first form of private property in which the wife and children are slaves of the husband/father (Marx and Engels [1845] 1968: 9). In Marxist terms, the annihilation of private property was the significant precondition for the emergence of communist society; in turn, private property could be abolished through the annihilation of the individual economy. Following this logic, Marx deemed it self-evident that "the abolition of [the] individual economy [was] inseparable from the abolition of the family" (ibid.: 11). Marx understood that the project to eliminate the individual economy could only succeed if a communal domestic economy replaced it. The early Bolshevik government attempted to follow these logical principles by shifting most of the household work from the private realm of the family to the public sphere.

Early Soviet policy planners viewed the family from a political perspective; that is, policies and practices in relation to the family were directly tied to the ultimate goal of obliterating private property by several means: abolishing "the individual economy," liberating women from the drudgery of unpaid domestic labor, and recruiting them into paid labor outside the home. It is notable that the early Bolshevik family abolitionists, who believed the family would "wither away," did not include eliminating marriage. Marriage was viewed as a union of individuals based on mutual love and understanding, free from the kinds of obligations imposed on them via the family in feudal and capitalist settings. The early Bolsheviks institutionalized this new understanding of marriage by replacing religious marriage with civil marriage, and by promoting the idea of a union based on affection and shared ideals rather than on women's subordination and economic dependency (Goldman 1993). Along with routine household work, childrearing was understood as a key social function of the so-called "traditional" family. The Soviet Union enacted its vision to liberate its citizens from parental obligations and household maintenance by establishing public childcare facilities as well as public dining and laundry systems (Kollontai [1920] 1977).

The adoption of a series of decrees in 1917 and of the Code on Marriage, Family, and Guardianship in 1918, soon after the Bolsheviks came to power, established equality of the sexes in marital relations. These legal provisions introduced the civil registration of marriages, granted spouses with equal rights, and made divorce easily obtainable upon initiation of one of the sides. Children born out of wedlock were granted the same rights as children of registered couples. Women were also given the right to name the father of a child and, in certain instances, if she was dating several men and the identity of the father was unclear, she had the right to name a few as potential fathers and assign them with alimony to pay (Goldman 1993: 18). Bolsheviks such as Alexander Goikhbarg, one of the authors of the Code on Marriage, Family, and Guardianship, believed that the code was an essential if temporary measure, because without it "the population would resort to religious ceremonies and the church would flourish" (ibid.: 56). They regarded these legal regulations as temporary until socialism could be fully implanted, eliminating the need for the family—as it was understood in capitalist terms—or for the law to regulate human relations.

The Stalin era was a turning point in Soviet policy making regarding women, and the shift that occurred in family legislation during this period was a shift toward conservative, even authoritarian visions of family and gender roles, representing a major break with the Bolshevik vision of the "withering away" family. The Civil Law of 1936 dramatically altered the radical and subversive regulations of the 1918 and 1926 Civil Codes. Formally maintaining the notion of gender equality, it prohibited abortion, introduced fines on divorce, increased alimony and fined men who failed to pay it, and introduced punitive measures for those who had (illegal) abortions and for those who performed them.

Scholars offer two lines of argument to explain the departure from the Bolshevik blueprint. One argument considers larger political and economic conditions as significantly influencing the shift that started in the mid-1930s (Lapidus 1978: 111). The second locates "the ideological reversal of the 1930s" as largely political, "bearing all the marks of Stalinist policy in other areas" (Goldman 1993: 342). Thus, from the 1930s until the very end of the Soviet Union, the family was considered "the bulwark of the social system, a microcosm of the new socialist society" (Lapidus 1978: 111; see also Stites 1978; Evans Clements 1991; Goldman 1993). According to historian Barbara Evan Clements, policymakers considered the family the "cornerstone of the state, and women were responsible for keeping this cornerstone firmly in place" (Evans Clements 1991: 269). Moreover, as historian Wendy Goldman describes it, "the concepts of socialist family, law and state ... had become the new holy trinity of the Party" (Goldman 1993: 338). Complicated divorce procedures, such that women lacked control over their bodies, and the resurrection of traditional family roles and responsibilities, created an environment in which domestic violence could flourish behind closed doors, without public acknowledgement or social remedies for it.

This political ideology and its practice in relation to marriage and family responsibility remained steady throughout the 1950s and 1960s (Pushkareva 1997: 263). In Georgia, as elsewhere in the Soviet Union, these ideas were reflected in the popular media of the time. This quotation, pulled from an article in *Saqartvelos qali*, the leading Georgian women's periodical during the 1960s, reflects the dominant ideology: "We would like each woman and man to marry only on the basis of love, [but] if love disappears, parents have a responsibility to their children and must ensure the family's stability. One of the most essential functions of the family is the upbringing of children" (Bandzeladze 1964: 18–19).

In Georgia, ideological messages about the family as the key social unit were coupled with the chipping away of public, collective provisions such as childcare. The social infrastructure to free women from household work became substantially insufficient.[7] Soviet sociologists came to label the many hours of housework performed by millions of women the "second shift" (Gordon and Klopov 1972: 98–102). In her 1964 housework survey carried out in the city of Gorky, sociologist Barbara Wolfe Jancar shows that fully employed women who had one or more children spent almost as many hours on housework as they were spending at work (Jancar 1978: 41). As Buckley puts it, women in the Soviet Union had "what amounts to a thirteen to fifteen hour work day" (Buckley 1981: 93). In nearly all the Soviet bloc countries, the gap between the need for housing, daycare, shopping facilities, and labor-saving devices, and their limited supply, resulted in the double burden for women. Several sociological surveys carried out in the Soviet Union during 1960s and 1970s also found that the vast majority of women regarded their husband or another male member of the family as the head of the household (Jancar 1978: 63). These findings suggest that the family as a social unit never fell into oblivion, and that the gender division of work and power dynamics within the family remained unaltered.

In terms of social issues such as domestic violence, the juxtaposition of a lack of opportunities for civil activism free from government control and the home as a site of resistance to the communist state further limited the opportunity to give visibility to such social problems. Gal and Kligman (2000) and Verdery (1996) argue that during the socialist period in Hungary, Czechoslovakia, and Poland, many dissident writers created a space for "public" activity in the "private" space of the family. The household became the only place they could express themselves politically and exercise authority relatively independent of the state's gaze. This development may have deterred some women facing domestic violence from speaking up, because they feared being viewed as a traitor to the family; "people perceived a fundamental distinction between the state, understood as a powerful 'they' who ran the country, and the family, the private 'us' who sacrificed and suffered" (Gal and Kligman 2000: 50). Thus, for many citizens, a strong and united family represented the "'site of resistance' to communism" (ibid.: 69). In such an environment, to come forward with revelations of domestic violence would be devastating on the level of the household, and to identify it as a social problem would be a losing proposition, garnering little or no support from the citizenry.

In addition, women and men in many of the republics of the Soviet Union, including Georgia, resisted the state's invasion into the private sphere by firmly fixing their ethnic identity to the value of the sacredness of family privacy and the primacy of kinship. Already in 1923, the Twelfth Congress of the Russian Communist Party (Bolsheviks) looked to address the "national question"—the large number of nationalities that dwelled on the territory of the Union of Republics and the problem of inequality between the nations through the policy of "indigenization" (*korenizatsya*) that was designed to accommodate national sentiments and aspirations (Martin 2001). In Georgia's case, the "indigenization" policy enabled the course of modern nation building and was itself a process of "Georgianization" that also contributed to affirming the idea of the Georgian family as an important symbol of national pride and honor during the Soviet era as well as in the post-Soviet period (Jones 1988: 616, 627).[8] In this context, to acknowledge the presence of domestic violence and thus bring dishonor to the family constituted a threat to the value orientations of the society and to the foundations of the family.

In the post-Soviet period, this resistance to disclose "private matters" remains. For example, social policy analyst Armine Iskhanian documents that in the decade after the breakup of the Soviet Union, NGOs working on women's issues in Armenia were hesitant to address domestic violence (Iskhanian 2002). She reports that NGO activists emphasized that domestic violence was a "private problem" that needed no interference from the state. "We do not air our dirty laundry in public," and "That is not a problem we wish to discuss in public," is the prevailing perspective (ibid.: 14). The National Research on Domestic Violence in Georgia, carried out in 2009, also found that 78 percent of women considered domestic violence to be a "family issue," and one that should not be brought up in public (Chitashvili et al. 2010: 12, 37).

State-Sponsored Support Mechanisms for Women Facing Domestic Violence in the Soviet Union

Information I pulled from women's periodicals during the Soviet period revealed that cases of domestic violence were reported to the People's Courts, Women's Departments of the Party (*Zhenotdeli*), and local executive committees.[9] Although the Soviet government did not consider domestic violence to be a social or criminal problem requiring state intervention, the Women's Department nevertheless advocated on behalf of women's rights, especially with respect to land ownership, employment rights and opportunities, and rights in marital relations.[10] *Zhenotdel* activists were concerned with the rights of peasant women, women workers, housewives, and unemployed, impoverished women. While the *Zhenotdel* was not independent of Communist Party control, the state did not provide it with the financial or human resources to fulfill its mission. Even so, the Women's Department managed to achieve a great deal, including carrying on the work of women's liberation initiated by prerevolutionary feminist organizations in Russia (Stites 1978).

In terms of the role of the Women's Department in addressing domestic violence, my reading of women's periodicals shows that in Georgia there were a number of situations handled by the *Zhenotdel*. To illustrate this, a brief note appeared in a 1924 edition of *Chveni gza* posted by the Women's Department of the Akhalkalaki Regional Committee in southeast Georgia. The posting indicates the occurrence of domestic violence, while at the same time identifying the important role of the *Zhenotdeli* in protecting women: "[I]n all those villages where there are women delegates, husbands do not dare to beat their wives; they are afraid that women delegates will inform the Women's Departments" (Tekle 1924: 39). This rudimentary reporting mechanism served as a crude warning to husbands, and at the same time it may have provided some benefits to some women. The Women's Department had no clear mandate to address domestic violence issues; ultimately their efforts were limited and insufficient (Zinaida 1924: 42). The *Zhenotdeli* were abolished in 1930, at the very same time that official state policy required women to take on more family responsibilities, even as they labored in the public sphere. It is anyone's guess what might have been in terms of recognizing domestic violence as a systemic violation of women's rights had the proletarian women's movement not ended, and had the *Zhenotdel* not been abolished.

At a later point, some of the functions fulfilled by the *Zhenotdel* were mandated in the Women's Councils (*Zhensoviety*), established during Khrushchev's rule during the late 1950s. The primary mission of the Women's Councils was to help women balance work and home responsibilities (Johnson 2009: 26). More so than had been the case with the Women's Departments, the work priorities of the Women's Councils were determined by the party leadership, which was predominately male. As a result, there remained "almost no non-party, non-state spaces for challenging gender" (ibid.).

At best, the Soviet court system only indirectly provided recourse for women who experienced domestic violence. In its day, the *Zhenotdel* recommended that special courts be established to review divorce cases, which may have elicited attention to domestic violence. Although this recommendation was not accepted, the 1960s saw the establishment of what were called Comrade Courts, which were designed to lighten the heavy workload of the People's Courts.[11] Before the 1960s, Comrade Courts had primarily heard cases that dealt with violations of work discipline in factories or on collective farms, and of the production of defective articles and goods. At the Twenty-Second Session of the Communist Party (17–31 October 1961), the decision was made to broaden the scope of work of the Comrade Courts. In addition to work-related cases, the Comrade Courts were assigned to review private matters brought to it by workers and peasants. As Soviet lawyers S. Afanasiev and M. Panina note, the idea behind addressing private matters was to "help the Soviet people's liberation from the leftovers of previous life, and to nurture among them a Communist consciousness"; the Comrade Courts were not established "to punish but to convince and uplift" (Afanasiev and Panina 1962: 30). In contrast to the People's Courts, the Comrade Courts did not have great enforcement authority. However, those who did not abide by their decisions would find their case transferred to a law enforcement agency (such as the *Militia* [Police] or the Office of the Prosecutor General). The Comrade Courts were very grassroot. Members were elected during large gatherings of workers in factories, peasants on collective farms, residents of apartment buildings, or local villagers. The courts were established literally anywhere people formed a group—working, studying, or living together.

In Georgia, the mandate and procedures of the Comrade Courts were defined by a special Decree of 10 July 1961, according to which members were elected once every two years through an open vote. According to archival documents, the Georgian Comrade Courts were entitled to review issues related to the violation of discipline at the workplace and administrative misbehaviors, cases of the civil law (e.g., damage to buildings, both residential and non-residential), citizens' disputes (e.g., over the utilization of additional storage places), and immoral behavior (e.g., disrespectful attitude toward a woman or a parent) (Academy of Science of Georgia 1975, vol. 1). The wide spectrum of cases reviewed by the Comrade Courts included problems in the family such wife battery, alcoholism, adultery, and failure to pay alimony.

The establishment of the block/district inspector (a police function) provided a means by which to provide some recourse in domestic violence cases that was far more formal than the Comrade Courts. These district inspectors were part of the Soviet Militia, and were appointed by the executive committees of the regional and town councils. Among their other duties and obligations as police, their mandate was to ensure the protection of public order, of socialist property, of the rights and legitimate interests of the citizens, and to prevent crime, especially juvenile crime.[12] The position of district inspector allowed the state to exercise more control over domestic violence cases because such inspectors knew the inhabitants in the district under their jurisdiction personally. They were required to register and respond to each case of family conflict, adolescent crime, and any other activity that was in violation of the law. In an interview I conducted with a former senior officer working for Georgian intelligence during the Soviet period, he described the process as follows:

> District inspectors received no special instruction or training. In cases of domestic violence they were to ensure that the perpetrator signed an official warning issued in his name and in the presence of witnesses, whereby he acknowledged his behavior as wrong. After two warnings, or in the case of extreme brutality, the inspector was to arrest the perpetrator and initiate a criminal case.[13]

Given there was no special domestic violence law, the general provisions of the Criminal Code, which criminalized battering, threatening, physical abuse, murder, blackmail, and hooliganism,[14] were to be applied to crimes committed in the family context. According to Johnson, before 1991 "domestic violence was intermittently regulated under the rubric of 'hooliganism,'" and domestic violence was estimated to constitute up to 40 percent of crimes charged under hooliganism (Johnson 2009: 23). This suggests the state treated domestic violence as a relatively minor crime. The systemic nature of domestic violence and its relation to the broader issue of women's rights and gender equity was not recognized.

There were no procedural measures to apply crimes listed in the Criminal Code to the family context, and nor was there a well-developed infrastructure to help victims of domestic violence. Neither the Comrade Courts nor the district inspector could effectively address the problem. As a result, domestic violence flourished in secrecy, factoring in the reproduction of women's oppression and the maintenance of gender inequality.

Conclusion

The practice of domestic violence was present throughout the Soviet Union, including Soviet Georgia. The complex dynamics surrounding the question of women's liberation, and the redefinition of the concept of family and women's roles in it at different historical points, resulted in a failure of policy to identify domestic violence as a social problem. Consequently there was no centralized or republic-level policy, and no legal response from the government.

This failure was in part a result of a belief in the Soviet grand narrative, in which gender equity had been achieved. Despite initial serious efforts to reconfigure gender roles and the role of the family, in the long run the Soviet policymakers significantly compromised in many areas, including domestic violence. The failure to adequately address domestic violence and to see the important link between domestic violence and gender inequality also signals the decline in Soviet political will to achieve substantive gender equity.

Tamar Sabedashvili holds a PhD in gender studies from Central European University, Budapest. She is chair of the Gender Studies Programme at Tbilisi State University, where she also teaches. She is author of *Gender and Democratization: The Case of Georgia, 1991–2006* (Heinrich Böell Foundation, 2007). Tamar Sabedashvili is programme specialist for the United Nations Entity for Gender Equality and the Empowerment of Women (UN Women) in Georgia.

Notes

1. I have reviewed Soviet-era periodicals targeting women centrally on the Soviet Union-level, as well as periodicals produced for women in the Soviet Socialist Republic of Georgia. I have reviewed the journals *Krestyanka* [Peasant Woman] (all issues of the years 1922, 1934, 1937, 1942, 1956, 1972, 1987) and *Rabotnitsa* [Worker Woman] (all issues of the years 1929, 1944, 1962, 1978) published in Russian, and *chveni gza* [Our Way] (all issues of the years 1924, 1925, 1926), *sabchota qali* [Soviet Woman] (all issues of the year 1958) and *saqartvelos qali* [Woman of Georgia] (all issues of the years 1964, 1969, 1979, 1991) published in Georgian. These mouthpieces of the Communist Party are important data sources as they were designed to shape women's consciousness through the communication of state priorities and policies, and by showing glimpses of the present and the future that the party leadership imagined for women. These journals were widely distributed. The issues were sent to even the most remote rural areas of the Soviet Union.
2. The process of incorporating Georgia into a Soviet Socialist Republic, or what Georgians refer to as Georgia's Sovietization (*gasabchoeba*), began with the country's occupation by the Red Army in 1921. Many important Bolshevik and Communist policymakers were ethnically Georgian. Georgia's route to independence in the late 1980s was among the most painful and bloody of the Soviet Union's former republics.
3. Buckley notes that "before 1956, no woman ever sat on the Politburo or the Presidium, the chief policy body of the Party" (1981: 103). Subsequently, Ekaterina A. Furtseva was the only woman to sit on the Politburo, which was then called the Presidium. She held this post from 1957 to 1960, when she was relieved of it to become minister of culture—a position she held until her death in 1974; see also Stites 1978: 326.
4. Article 122 of the 1936 Constitution states: "Women in the U.S.S.R. are accorded equal rights with men in all spheres of economic, state, cultural, social and political life. The possibility of exercising these rights is ensured to women by granting them an equal right with men to work, payment for work, rest and leisure, social insurance and education, and by state protection of the interests of mother and child, pre-maternity and

maternity leave with full pay, and the provision of a wide network of maternity homes, nurseries and kindergartens" (State Political Publishing House of the USSR 1938). See also *Bolshaya Sovetskaya Entsiklopedia* 1972: 50–51.

5. See, for example, Violeta 1924: 54; Tsintsadze 1924: 35; and Olya 1925: 32.
6. The translations of quotations from all the Georgian and Russian periodicals into English belong to the author.
7. By 1972, throughout the Soviet Union, 50 percent of children under the age of five were attending the pre-school facilities (daycares, nurseries, kindergartens). However, over 78 percent of the enrolled children's families lived in urban areas. This means that the nuclear and/or extended families were primarily responsible for raising children in the rural areas. Research conducted by Soviet sociologists in the 1960s indicates that in the vast majority of families, women were solely responsible for childrearing (Jancar 1978: 46–47).
8. According to Jones, the "indigenization" policies applied to ethnic Georgians and to minorities of other nations residing in Georgia. Policies included the hiring of local people in the administration and government, and the use of native language in schools, newspapers, and books (Jones 1988: 617–18). In 1926, over 96 percent of ethnic Georgians claimed Georgian as their first language (Mars and Altman 1983: 549).
9. The People's Courts were established in November 1917 when the Bolshevik government issued a Decree on Courts. The Constitution of the Soviet Union of 1936 and the laws that were adopted based on this constitution further defined and reaffirmed the mandate of the People's Courts, which were the courts of the first instance and reviewed administrative and civil cases, as well as criminal ones (*Bolshaya Sovetskaya Entsiklopedya* 1973: 284–85). *Zhenotdeli* (Women's Departments) were established in 1919 within local committees of the Communist Party, "to bring up working women in the Communist spirit and to engage them in the building of the socialist society. The Central Committee of the Russian Communist Party eliminated *Zhenotdeli* in 1930; their functions were integrated into the usual work of other party organs" (*Bolshaya sovetskaya entsiklopedia* 1972: 169).
10. For more information on the work of *Zhenotdel* regarding these rights, see Goldman 1993. For further details on the organization and work of *Zhenotdel*, see Stites 1978: 329–45.
11. By October 1963 there were nearly 200,000 Comrade Courts to discipline labor and to defend everyday laws of Soviet life (Jacobson 1963).
12. The Soviet Militia was established in the fall of 1917, and until 1931 was controlled by local councils. From 1931 until 1946 the Militia became part of the People's Commissariat of Internal Affairs. From 1946 until the demise of the Soviet Union, it was an inalienable part of the Ministry of Internal Affairs of the Soviet Union, and of the respective ministries of the union and autonomous republics of the USSR (Eropkin 1974: 258–59).
13. He preferred to remain anonymous. Conducted on 19 July 2006.
14. In the Soviet Union, "hooliganism" was made a criminal offense under the penal codes of the Soviet republics. Article 228 of the Criminal Code of the Soviet Georgia defined hooliganism as "any deliberate behavior that violates public order and expresses explicit disrespect toward the society" (Academy of Science of Georgia 1987, vol. 11: 513).

References

Abashidze, D. 1969. "Tserili rdzals" [Letter to daughter-in-law]. *Saqartvelos qali* 8.
Academy of Science of Georgia. 1975 and 1987. *Qartuli sabtchota entsiklopedia* [Georgian Soviet Encyclopedia]. Tbilisi: Specials Scientific Editorial.

Afanasiev, S. and M. Panina. 1962. "Tovarisheski Sud" [Comrade Courts]. *Rabotnytsa* 3.
Bandzeladze, G. 1964. "Vitskebt saubars sikvarulze, ojakhze, bednierebaze" [We start a conversation about love, family, happiness]. *Saqartvelos qali* 5.
Bock, G. 2002. *Women in European History.* Oxford: Blackwell Publishers.
Bolshaya Sovetskaya Entsiklopedya [The Great Soviet Encyclopedia]. 1972–75. Moscow: Sovetskaya Entsiklopedya, volumes 9, 13, 16, 17.
Buckley, M. 1981. "Women in the Soviet Union." *Feminist Review* 8 (Summer): 79–106.
Chelnochnitsa, V. 1929. "Vsyem na Pokaz" [For Everyone's Gaze]. *Rabotnitsa* 5.
Chitashvili, M., N. Javakhishvili, L. Arutiunov, L. Tsuladze, and S. Chachanidze. 2010. "National Research on Domestic Violence in Georgia." Tbilisi: UNFPA.
Constitution of the Union of Soviet Socialist Republics. 1938. Moscow: State Political Publishing House of the USSR. Retrieved 27 February 2016 from http://www.departments.bucknell.edu/russian/const/1936toc.html.
Dobash, R.E., and R.P. Dobash. 1992. *Women, Violence & Social Change.* London and New York: Routledge.
Eropkin, M.I. 1974. "militsia," *Bolshaya Sovetskaya Entsiklopedya* [The Great Soviet Encyclopedia]. Moscow: Sovetskaya Entsiklopedya, volume 16.
Evans Clements, B. 1980. "Bolshevik Women: The First Generation." In *Women in Eastern Europe and the Soviet Union,* ed. Tova Yedlin, 65–74. New York: Praeger.
———. 1991. "Later Developments: Trends in Soviet Women's History, 1930 to the Present." In *Russia's Women: Accommodation, Resistance, Transformation,* ed. Barbara Evans Clements, Barbara Alpern Engel, and Christine D. Worobec, 267–78. Berkeley: University of California Press.
Gal, S. and G. Kligman. 2000. *The Politics of Gender after Socialism.* Princeton, NJ: Princeton University Press.
Goldman, W. 1993. *Women, the State and Revolution: Soviet Family Policy and Social Life, 1917–1936.* Cambridge: Cambridge University Press.
Gordon, L.A., and E.V. Klopov. 1972. *Chelovek posle raboty* [A Man after his Work]. Moscow: Nauka.
Ishkanian, A. 2002. "Is the Personal Political? The Development of Armenia's NGO Sector during the Post Soviet Period." Working Paper Series. Berkeley: University of California Press.
Jacobson, J. 1963. "Russian Law Enters the 'Final Stages of Communism.'" Retrieved 14 December 2015 from http://www.marxists.org/history/etol/writers/jacobson/1963/xx/russia-law.htm.
Jancar, B. W. 1978. *Women under Communism.* Baltimore, MD and London: The Johns Hopkins University Press.
Johnson, J. E. 2009. *Gender Violence in Russia: The Politics of Feminist Intervention.* Bloomington: Indiana University Press.
Jones, S. 1988. "The Establishment of Soviet Power in Transcaucasia: The Case of Georgia, 1921–1928." *Soviet Studies* 40(4) (October): 616–39.
Kollontai, A. (1920) 1977. "*Selected Writings of Alexandra Kollontai.*" Translated by Alix Holt. Retrieved 16 December 2011 from http://www.marxists.org/archive/kollonta/1920/communism-family.htm.
Kon, I. S. 1995. *The Sexual Revolution in Russia: From the Age of the Czars to Today.* New York: The Free Press.
Lapidus, G. W. 1978. *Women in Soviet Society: Equality, Development, and Social Change.* Berkeley: University of California Press.
Lenin, V.I. (1919) 1969. "Sovetskaya vlast' i polozhenie zhenshchiny" [Soviet rule and the position of woman], *Polnoe Sobranie Sochinenii* [Full collection of essays], vol. 39. Moscow.
Mars, G. and Y. Altman. 1983. "The Cultural Bases of Soviet Georgia's Second Economy." *Soviet Studies* 35(4): 546–60.

Martin, T. 2001. *The Affirmative Action Empire: Nations and Nationalism in the Soviet Union, 1923–1939*. Ithaca, NY and London: Cornell University Press.
Marx, K. and F. Engels. 1845. "The German Ideology." Retrieved 11 December 2015 from http://www.marxists.org/archive/marx/works/1845/german-ideology/ch01a.htm. Source: Progress Publishers, 1968.
Meyersfeld, B. 2010. *Domestic Violence and International Law*. Oxford: Hart Publishing.
Nakaidze, M. 1991. "Gtkhovt momisminot: Tsolis versia" [Please listen to me: Wife's version]. *Saqartvelos qali* 11–12.
Olya. 1925. "Darejan Tandilashvilis dardianoba" [The sorrow of Darejan Tandilashvili]. *Chveni gza* 1(11).
Pickard, J. 1988. "Women in the Soviet Union." Retrieved 10 May 2015 from http://www.marxist.com/oldsite/women/women_in_the_soviet_union.html.
Pietilä, H. 2002. *Engendering the Global Agenda: The Story of Women and the United Nations*. New York: UN Non-Governmental Liaison Service.
Pushkareva, N. 1997. *Women in Russian History: From the Tenth to the Twentieth Century*. Translated and edited by Eve Levin. Armonk, NY: M.E. Sharpe.
Revia, O. 1969. "Mudam skhvebze zrunvashi" [Constantly caring for others]. *Saqartvelos qali* 11.
Sabedashvili, T. 2011. "Identification and Regulation of Domestic Violence in Georgia: 1991–2006." Thesis. Central European University, Budapest.
Stites, R. 1978. *The Women's Liberation Movement in Russia: Feminism, Nihilism and Bolshevism, 1860–1930*. Princeton, NJ: Princeton University Press.
Tekle. 1924. "Akhal qalaqis samazro komitetis qalta gankopileba" [Women's Department of Akhalkalaki Regional Committee]. *Chveni gza* 3.
Tina. 1925. "Rogor miighes glekhis qali Marine rva marts partiashi" [How was peasant woman Marine admitted to the party on 8 March]. *Chveni gza* 12–13.
Tsintsadze, T. 1924. "Qalta shoris mushaoba Telavis mazrashi" [Work among women in Telavi district]. *Chveni gza* 10.
Verdery, K. 1996. *What Was Socialism and What Comes Next*. Princeton, NJ: Princeton University Press.
Violeta. 1924. "Svanetis glekh-qalta tskhovrebidan" (From the lives of Svanetian peasant women]. *Chveni gza* 6.
Zdravomyslova, E. and A.Temkina. 2005. "Gendered Citizenship in Soviet and Post-Soviet Societies." In *Nation and Gender in Contemporary Europe*, ed. Vera Tolz and Stephenie Booth, 96–116. New York: Manchester University Press.
Zinaida, E. 1924. "Tfilisis musliman qalta shoris" [Among the Muslim women of Tbilisi]. *Chveni gza* 4.

Chapter 7

Domestic Violence in Georgia
State and Community Responses, 2006–2015

Nino Javakhishvili and Nino Butsashvili

On 17 October 2014, one news item captured national media attention in Georgia. A man shot his ex-wife and then killed himself on the campus of Ilia State University in Tbilisi, the country's capital city. This stirred the interest of the public. Some people expressed concern about the university security system, while others blasted the media for the sensationalist way it covered the matter. Overall, the main point was that this was a case of domestic violence with a fatal outcome. Moreover, it was not a singular event. In 2014, thirteen Georgian women were killed by their husbands (Public Defender of Georgia 2015: 27).

In all or nearly all parts of the world, women who are subordinated to men are the main victims of domestic violence. The term "gender-based violence" points to existing uneven power relations between men and women, which is a key condition that makes domestic violence possible (UN General Assembly 1993; Council of Europe 2011a).

In Georgia, rates of domestic violence range from 5 percent to 31 percent, depending on the data source (Thomas et al. 2006: 3). National prevalence data on domestic violence for 2010 are as follows: 4 percent of women experienced sexual violence; 6 percent economic violence (women forced to give their husbands part of their earnings); and 14 percent emotional violence. Over a third (36%) said that their husbands or partners controlled their behavior—where to go, what to do; and seven percent said they had been victims of physical violence (Javakhishvili 2010: 34–38). Another study found that over three-quarters (78%) of respondents

---

Notes for this chapter begin on page 121.

declared that domestic violence occurs "often or very often" in Georgia (Sumbadze 2014: 27–28).

As qualitative studies have shown, many women feel shame about declaring they are victims of domestic violence, so it is very difficult to get good data; the abovementioned prevalence figures may therefore understate the true scale of the problem (Thomas et al. 2006: 19; Tsuladze 2010: 74). This is a major reason why there have only been a few prevalence studies in Europe and in the United States (Reingarde et al. 2012: 97–102; Stelmaszek and Fisher 2013: 29).

Nevertheless, available data suggest that domestic violence is a serious problem in Georgia that requires immediate intervention. International best practices for addressing domestic violence highlight the importance of a coordinated response from various agencies (EIGE 2012). The Duluth model is considered a model of best practices in the domestic violence field because it emphasizes the role of the community, governmental and nongovernmental organizations joining forces to address it (Domestic Abuse Intervention Programs 2011).

Indeed, the need for cooperation between governmental and nongovernmental agencies in Georgia is articulated in the 2006 Anti–Domestic Violence Law, which may be considered the start of the country's strategic response to domestic violence. This legislation marks the first time that the Georgian government joined forces with local and international nongovernmental organizations that had been working on the law for several years and had advocated for its adoption (Sabedashvili 2011). One of the authors of this chapter has been following these developments, and highlighting gaps and weaknesses in how domestic violence is addressed in Georgia (Javakhishvili et al. 2011; Javakhishvili and Tsuladze 2011; Javakhishvili and Jibladze 2012; Javakhishvili, Lortkipanidze, and Petriashvili 2012; Javakhishvili 2014).

In what follows, we review the policy and implementation developments over a ten-year period, starting in 2006 when the Anti–Domestic Violence Law was adopted. The social actors charged with implementing the domestic violence response include governmental agencies and nongovernmental organizations, and those whose opinions, attitudes, and actions have weighed in on the issue, such as representatives from local communities, the Orthodox Christian Church, and the mass media. Our analysis shows, however, that these social actors are not adequately equipped to address the problem. We identify the obstacles faced by those who are attempting positive change and action, and we reveal the ways in which specific gaps (e.g., a lack of awareness of gender issues and a failure to acknowledge structural forces) impact the efficacy of existing interventions.

The Status of Government and Community Responses to Domestic Violence

In 2006 the Parliament of Georgia adopted the Law of Georgia on Prevention of Domestic Violence, Protection of and Assistance to Victims of Domestic Violence. The main objectives of the law are to prevent violence and assist victims. The law covers multiple forms of violence: physical, psychological, economic, sexual, and coercion.[1] It also defines legal mechanisms designed to prevent and eliminate it (UNFPA 2010: 13–18).

According to the report of the public defender, the domestic violence law is very broad and needs specification. There are no useful criteria to divide "family conflict" and nonphysical violence. Thus, when policemen arrive at a place in which a dispute is taking place, they need to determine whether violence has or has not taken place. This requires a high degree of training and professionalism (Public Defender of Georgia 2015: 40–41).

Since 2006, more than twenty amendments have been adopted in response to the practical issues that have surfaced, though serious issues still remain. Issues with "legal orders" offer a case in point. The "order" is a key legal mechanism designed to provide victims with protection from abusers. In Georgia, there are two kinds of legal orders—restrictive and protective—the issuance of which is regulated by the Code of Administrative Procedures of Georgia. The "restrictive" order enables an authorized police employee to take immediate action, though it must be submitted to the court for approval within a twenty-four-hour period. The "protective" order is issued by the court of first instance. Those who do not comply with these orders (the abusers) are subject to criminal responsibility (UNFPA 2010: 16–17).

In the first two years (2006–2008), orders were applied very rarely. By 2015, the court ratified 2,598 restrictive orders (Aladashvili, Kiknadze, and Nozadze 2009: 22–23; MOIA 2015). In their application, restrictive orders have not necessarily led to beneficial consequences for the victim. All too often, an order is simply a piece of a paper with no meaningful results. In most cases, the abuser continues to abuse despite the order. In addition, there is no method to monitor what is going on in families for which the order has been issued. If there is monitoring, generally it is conducted by district police officers at their own discretion (Public Defender of Georgia 2015: 43).

At times the fines levied for non-compliance with an order ultimately placed an extra burden on victims. This is illustrated in the case of a woman who called the police for help. The police imposed a fine on the "perpetrator," the woman's husband, who did not have any money. As a result, the woman—the victim—was "required" to pay the fine. As the woman explains: "The 100 GEL was a penalty for my husband, which I had to pay ... and then, my husband came back after two days. So what did I gain? What mechanism is there to protect me?" (Javakhishvili et al. 2011: 32). The woman's words highlight another challenge to addressing domestic violence—the separation of the victim and the perpetrator who are also in a marital and family relationship. If a perpetrator has no place to go, he is left in the street without supervision. In most cases, the woman does not want to leave her husband "out in the cold." In the past, police officers had access to special rooms to accommodate drunken perpetrators; these are no longer available, thus creating difficulties in seeing these orders realized (Public Defender of Georgia 2015: 43).

The National Referral Mechanism (NRM) is another tool developed by the government to address domestic violence. This approach focuses on rehabilitation for both abusers and victims. The main objectives of the NRM are to: prevent domestic violence; facilitate the implementation of the law through efficient and flexible mechanisms to stop the perpetrator; protect victims; provide early intervention; and assist victims in starting a new life and refer them to available services. The NRM names the specific governmental entities responsible for meeting the objectives that are to work in cooperation with each other.[2] Nongovernmental organizations can also become involved in this work if they sign a memorandum of cooperation with governmental institutions (UNFPA 2010: 31–42).

As people working in the nongovernmental organizations report, the requirements of the National Referral Mechanism are not fully implemented. There is little to no cooperation among the responsible government entities and nongovernmental organizations, despite the fact that cooperation has been the main focus of the document since its adoption in 2009 (Javakhishvili 2014).

Since the adoption of the Anti–Domestic Violence Law, the National Action Plans have identified specific goals and activities to be accomplished.[3] However, none contained any information on how these would be financed, which puts into question the feasibility of accomplishing any of the goals outlined in the plans.

The Georgian legislation has been analyzed (Sabedashvili 2011; Ubilava, Tchabukiani and Jibladze 2014: 1–21) from a gender equality perspective to determine whether the following factors underpin the legislation: structural causes of domestic violence; uneven power distribution in gender relations; and gender stereotyping and traditional gender roles as they operate in Georgian society. The analysis was based on an approach developed by a group of European scholars as part of the 2003–2006 Policy Frames and Implementation Problems: The Case of Gender Mainstreaming (MAGEEQ) and the 2007 Quality in Gender+ Equality Policies

(QUING) research projects (Krizsan et al. 2007; Krizsan and Popa 2010; Dombos et al. 2012). Findings indicate that every piece of Georgian legislation falls within a de-gendered frame, which means they all are blind to gender equality. This finding is significant considering that the Council of Europe Convention on preventing and combating violence against women and domestic violence (otherwise known as the Istanbul Convention) and the Declaration on the Elimination of Violence against Women emphasize that domestic violence is gender-based violence (Sabedashvili 2011; Ubilava, Tchabukiani and Jibladze 2014: 13–17; UN General Assembly 1993; Council of Europe 2011a).

These limitations with the law and the National Action Plans are partially caused by a lack of gender awareness among the government representatives who adopted these documents. This point is illustrated by the parliamentary debates on the adoption of the law in 2006. Some Parliament members declared during the debates that they voted for the adoption of the law only because it was required by the European Union, even though they did not see any need for the measure. As one parliamentarian asked, "when a man decides to have sex with his wife, how much time in advance should he inform his wife—should this happen via wire transfer, letter … Governor or who else should be present, I wonder?" (Sabedashvili 2011). To this day, some members of the Georgian Parliament as well as of the Cabinet of Ministers lack gender awareness and, consequently, lack an understanding of the structural causes of domestic violence. The representatives of nongovernmental organizations who do have this understanding lack the power to draw up the strategic policy, both at the national and local levels. Gender inequality as it is played out in Georgian politics is a large problem. Only 12 percent of the Georgian Parliament are women, and a negligible number of women hold positions in the Georgian government, when research in other countries demonstrates that women in power draw attention to women's concerns and are likely to advocate for legislation designed to reduce gender inequality (Kunovich, Paxton, and Hughes 2007: 274–75).

Implementation of Services

The above description of law and legislative process constitute the political context for the implementation of services to domestic violence victims in Georgia. A number of governmental organizations are delegated the task of addressing the domestic violence problem in general, as well as specific cases. The Georgian Ministry of Internal Affairs is charged with combating domestic violence, and victims are instructed to contact the patrol or district police as the first responders in emergency situations when victims need immediate, short-term help. The police are mandated to intervene in order to stop the violence, and if necessary, transfer the victim to a medical center or shelter (UNFPA 2010: 34–37).

There are issues with this criminal justice approach to dealing with domestic violence. For example, the police may not be adequately trained to address sensitive domestic violence issues, and the police themselves may be vested in gender inequality. Moreover, it is often the case that women victims feel shame, which prevents them from reaching out to the police, most of whom are men (Tsuladze 2010: 65; Public Defender of Georgia 2015: 45).

The State Fund for Protection and Assistance of (statutory) Victims of Human Trafficking has been providing services to victims of domestic violence since 2009. The fund receives approximately 6 million GEL annually from the government as well as from donor grants.[4] This state program offers a range of services to domestic violence victims, including shelters located in Tbilisi and in three other regions (Javakhishvili 2014; Atipfund Georgia 2016). The Ministry of Labor, Health and Social Protection of Georgia controls the work of the fund.

One provision of the Anti–Domestic Violence Law was to have a special dedicated group of social workers at the Ministry of Labor, Health and Social Protection, whose mission would be to address domestic violence. Ten years have passed since the law went into effect, but the ministry has yet to produce a plan to recruit social workers who specialize in domestic violence issues. Furthermore, the ministry has no intention of developing the resources needed to support a social work approach to domestic violence (Public Defender of Georgia 2015: 5).

The Ministry of Education and Science of Georgia is responsible for the task of teaching gender sensitivity in schools, an approach that has been identified as crucial for achieving gender equality and, by implication, important for the prevention of domestic violence (Council of Europe 2011a). Georgia has made little, if any, progress in this regard.

In 2008, a Presidential Decree established the State Interagency Council to promote cooperation among different agencies addressing domestic violence. The decree mandated the council to monitor the work of governmental agencies and ensure their compliance with the action plan. The council was also mandated to work closely with nongovernmental organizations, plan future violence prevention interventions, and meet a minimum of twice a year (UNFPA 2010: 52–55). However, after only a few months, the council was deactivated, and with no formal explanation for this step. As one of the representatives of the council said, it had been established only to "attract attention to the problem and to mobilize"—after that, it was only "a formality" (Javakhishvili and Tsuladze 2011). Six years later, the government re-established the Interagency Council, although it does not have a website, it has not issued any public document, and (as of early 2016) its last meeting was held in December 2014 (Newspress 2014).

There are approximately twenty nongovernmental organizations in Georgia that provide assistance to victims of domestic violence. About a half of them began their work prior to the drawing up and enactment of the government's domestic violence policy and legislation. Organizations such as the Sakhli Advice Center for Women, and the Anti-violence Network of Georgia, work directly with victims and also work to raise awareness of domestic violence in the larger society. There are two types of such organizations: the well established and the less developed. The well-established ones have a relatively stable revenue stream, an impressive record of completed or ongoing projects, a range of assistance services (three shelters and three crisis centers out of a total ten are managed by the Anti-violence Network in Georgia, Sakhli and Atinati), well-equipped offices and other facilities, and experienced and well-educated personnel, some of whom specialized in Gender Studies. The less-developed organizations are smaller in size; their personnel often lack qualifications and gender-sensitivity training, they only have capacity for a few projects, and they have limited access to office equipment and financial support (Javakhishvili 2014; Javakhishvili and Jibladze 2012). Approximately ten such organizations folded because they were not able to generate adequate revenue to operate (Javakhishvili 2014; Javakhishvili and Jibladze 2012).

All nongovernmental organizations working on this issue seek funds from international donors. The budget for all the organizations combined in 2014 was approximately 550,000 GEL, which means most services are underfunded.[5] Many rely on volunteers to conduct activities, which is not conducive to stable service provision (Javakhishvili 2014). The reliance on donors makes these organizations subject to the priorities set by the funding agencies. Because resources are scarce, some nongovernmental organizations compete with each other for grants, which results in a lack of cooperation and coordination across organizations (Javakhishvili and Jibladze 2012).

Organizations also differ in terms of their organizing principles and their understanding of the root causes of domestic violence. Some prioritize the role of socioeconomic conditions in triggering the violence, while others consider deep-seated cultural ideology (patriarchal beliefs) as the key factor. Some view domestic violence as a crime; others see it as a symptom of a complex of cultural and economic forces such as a lack of jobs and the poor financial situation in the country overall. Some believe that community attitudes and the environment in which they function influence their decisions, which is reflected in the following quotation: "I might call the police, but it is difficult to say. Despite having worked on these issues since 2000 ... I am a child of this society, you know" (Javakhishvili et al. 2011: 32).

Public Attitudes toward Family, Marriage, Divorce, and Domestic Violence

It is important to understand public attitudes in Georgia about gender, family, and society, since perceptions and beliefs may constitute obstacles in efforts to address domestic violence. In that regard, attitudinal research is helpful, and if tracked over time, can offer insights into changing beliefs. In this section, we offer some findings on attitudes and beliefs as these relate to domestic violence and related issues. What follows is a portrait of findings from qualitative and quantitative research conducted in the post-Soviet period.

Across several studies, there is consensus that Georgian society is "family-oriented," with specific behavioral expectations and identified gender roles that define what constitutes "a good Georgian family" (Tsuladze 2010: 61–76; UNDP 2013: 17). The traditional attitude on gender roles and the gendered division of labor in the family is that husbands have to be breadwinners, and wives housekeepers and caretakers of children. In this gendered system, the husband is designated the main decision maker in the family, and his wishes are to be served by his obedient wife and others in the household (Javakhishvili and Tsuladze 2011; UNDP 2013: 18–19; Sumbadze 2014: 27). In a 2013 UN study, one-third (35%) of women and over half (54%) of men agreed with the statement that "it is important for a man to show his wife/partner who is the head of the family" (UNDP 2013: 20). As in-depth interviews and focus groups in different regions of Georgia have revealed, women tend to believe they must make concessions to their husbands, and that their desires and demands take second place (ibid.: 18–23). Place of residence plays a role in these beliefs. The idea about man's dominant position in a family is more common among women from villages than among those from cities, and is even less common among women from Tbilisi (Javakhishvili 2010: 38).

Attitudes toward divorce offer a glimpse into gender ideologies and potential implications for domestic violence situations. According to one study, three out of five Georgians (58%) believe that "being in a bad marriage is better than being single" (UNDP 2013: 18). The study finds that women tend to believe divorce is "a disaster ... the end of the world"

(Tsuladze 2010: 71). Consequently, society has a negative attitude toward the so-called "returned women," the term often used for divorcees. It is not unusual in Georgia that families will refuse to take in their divorced daughters; in turn, women tend to feel uneasy asking their parents for help (ibid.; Javakhishvili and Tsuladze 2011; UNDP 2013: 18). Another study finds that approximately one-fifth (17%) of Georgians think that women should preserve their marriage, irrespective of any violence (Sumbadze 2014: 7).

A number of studies have been commissioned to examine the social problem of domestic violence in Georgia. Research reported in a study by UNFPA/ACT National Research on Domestic Violence against Women in Georgia in 2010 found that one out of three respondents (34%) believed that "violence in the family is justified"; however, by 2014 that figure had dropped to seventeen percent (17%), indicating that attitudes may be changing (Georgia – Beijing +20 2014: 29). Earlier findings from a 2006 study show that over half (54%) of male respondents believed domestic violence was unjustifiable, which suggests that nearly half may still believe it is justifiable. Indeed, over one-third (38%) of male respondents considered that "a man is justified in using physical force against his wife if she is unfaithful to him" (Thomas et al. 2006: 4). Data also indicate that nine out of ten Georgian men (89%) believed "there is no excuse for a woman to use force against her husband" (ibid.; see also Chitashvili and Javakhishvili 2010: 16), revealing gender asymmetry and a clear double standard.

The research also suggests that verbal abuse is not understood as a form of psychological violence but as normative in marital relations. As one respondent in a qualitative study put it: "When a husband says something, [the wife] should be tolerant ... If my husband curses at me, how can I leave him for this reason? It's not a big deal—it is life" (Tsuladze 2010: 64–65).

One study reports that nearly four-fifths of women (78.3%) believe it is improper to discuss family problems outside one's home (Javakhishvili 2010: 37). That same study reports that half (52%) of respondents believe family members should abstain from meddling in cases where a husband treats his wife "badly"—a vague term that may or may not indicate the presence of violence or other forms of abuse.

Some studies offer insights into the attitudes of victims of domestic violence. Findings from one study indicate that for nearly one-third (31%) of respondents, domestic violence is considered a personal matter that should not be subject to legal intervention (Javakhishvili 2010: 37). Another study reveals that victims hide their situation out of embarrassment, shame, and fear (Chitashvili and Arutinovi 2010: 57). Instead, they "put a mask on, as if nothing has happened" (Sumbadze 2014: 18). These women say they fear for their family's reputation and that they are afraid that speaking out will result in more violence (Chitashvili and Arutinovi 2010: 57).

Nearly three out of five Georgians (57%) consider domestic violence a criminal offense, and nearly seventy percent (69%) believe that wife battery must be punished by the law (Sumbadze 2014: 14, 34–35). It would be very useful to get a deeper understanding of beliefs and understandings of domestic violence and how to address it from those Georgians who do not consider domestic violence a criminal offense (approximately 40% of respondents), or who do not believe that legal punishment is the way to address the problem (30%). The research also suggests that the younger generations are less tolerant of domestic violence than the older generations (Tsuladze 2010: 74–75; UNDP 2013: 4–5; Sumbadze 2014: 7, 42).

In terms of seeking help in situations of domestic violence, one study reports that two-fifths (38%) of women who sought help from members of their social circle never received it. Only a negligible proportion of women from that study reported asking for assistance from: the church (3%); the police (2%); healthcare providers (2%); and women's organizations (1%) (Chitashvili and Arutinovi 2010: 53).

Policymakers and service providers—whether psychologists, social workers, or the police—are not necessarily immune from the prevailing assumptions, attitudes, and beliefs about gender, gender roles, and gender violence. These assumptions may range from a belief that women are "naturally" inferior in terms of intellectual capabilities as compared to men and that gender equality in the family will be detrimental to children (Tsuladze 2010: 63–67; Javakhishvili and Tsuladze, 2011; Javakhishvili, Lortkhipanidze, and Petriashvili 2012; Javakhishvili and Jibladze 2012). Often, such "professionals" may be unaware that they hold contradictory values. For example, they may openly express the need for gender egalitarianism in one moment, and in the next moment reveal assumptions about "who" is the rightful "boss" (the husband) and the rightful "caretaker" (the wife and mother) in the family (Javakhishvili and Tsuladze 2011).

In Georgia, there is insufficient gender sensitivity training, and little specific training in how to handle domestic violence, despite the great need for it. Social workers are in the vanguard in terms of serving domestic violence victims, but they do not receive appropriate and intense training that would enable them to see their own biases and assumptions, and to best address the needs of clients. It is all too common that social workers advise women "to stay home and endure the abuse" (Javakhishvili and Tsuladze 2011). The police do receive some special training although it is not sufficient. While police can "see" instances of overt physical violence, they have trouble discerning more subtle forms of abuse (ibid.). In addition, and on the basis of reports we have received, we believe that judges and prosecutors lack gender sensitivity even more than police officers (Javakhishvili 2014).

At the start of this chapter, we described a case of domestic violence in Georgia that had received attention in the local media. The quality and level of media attention on domestic violence in Georgia is poor on multiple levels. For example, a study designed to assess coverage of domestic violence across all media formats in Georgia over a four-year period (2006–2010) shows that the topic was the subject of only eleven pieces (Javakhishvili, Lortkhipanidze, and Petriashvili 2012). The coverage tends to be sensationalist, exploitive (e.g., victim's identities are not protected), and laden with gender stereotypes (Javakhishvili and Tsuladze 2011; Mskhiladze 2012: 1–10). The media can be used to help advance positive social change with regard to domestic violence, as has occurred in some other parts of the world (Stanko 2001; Berns 2009). Georgia lags in this area.

Some scholars have argued that trusted religious institutions may be a useful community resource in helping shape perceptions about the harms and unacceptability of domestic violence (Franklin and Fong 2011). Most Georgians are followers of the Georgian Orthodox Church, which seems to have no interest in serving in this capacity (Javakhishvili, Lortkhipanidze, and Petriashvili 2012). In fact, church doctrine against divorce and in favor of women's subordination tends to work against efforts to address domestic violence (Sumbadze 2014: 8–9). Priests have called out against domestic violence only in the most severe cases of brutal violence (Javakhishvili and Tsuladze 2011).

Concluding Remarks: The State of Domestic Violence in Georgia up to 2016

In June 2014, Georgia signed the Istanbul Convention, which defines standards for state response to domestic violence, and emphasizes the importance of promoting gender equality (Council of Europe 2011a). The convention calls on governments to provide shelter, easily reachable victim support centers across the country, and a free twenty-four-hour hotline service for domestic violence victims (Council of Europe 2011b). At present, these minimum services are not available for all victims in Georgia (Javakhishvili 2014). The convention also calls for rehabilitation services for men who are abusers (Council of Europe 2011a). In Georgia, there is only one organization that offers such services, which are available on a voluntary, not a mandated basis (Javakhishvili 2014: 23). The Georgian law on domestic violence acknowledges the need for such services, but has not mandated their creation and implementation (UNFPA 2010: 20).

Overall, in Georgia there is a dearth of services available for victims of domestic violence. Moreover, knowledge and awareness of available services are not widespread among the population (Sumbadze 2014: 54–55). The new economy in Georgia has created conditions (high unemployment and reliance on personal income for sustaining the household) that put women at risk of domestic violence. The government provides insufficient services to victims of domestic violence, who ultimately find they have no alternative to living with their abusers (Chitashvili and Arutinovi 2010: 60). At the same time, governmental as well as nongovernmental organizations continue to address the problem by means of various legislative and informational actions, which creates some hope for improved services in future.

Nino Javakhishvili is professor of psychology and director of the Dimitri Uznadze Psychology Institute at Ilia State University. She is widely published in Georgian and international journals, and her research and teaching focus on gender issues, among others.

Nino Butsashvili is an MA student in social psychology at Ilia State University. She is research assistant at the Dimitri Uznadze Psychology Institute, and is involved in several research projects, including studies that focus on domestic violence.

Notes

1. Definition of the five forms of Law of Georgia on the Prevention of Domestic Violence, Protection of and Assistance to Victims of Domestic Violence are as follows: Physical violence (beating, torture, physical injury, illegal restriction of liberty, or any other action that causes physical pain or suffering; failure to meet requirements concerning his/her state of health that may cause harm to the health of the family member, or that may lead to his/her death); Psychological violence (assault, blackmail, degrading treatment, intimidation, or any other act that violates the honor and dignity of a human being); Sexual violence (sexual intercourse through violence, threat of violence, or taking advantage of the vulnerability of a victim, as well as sexual intercourse or other act of a sexual nature or obscene acts to a minor); Economic violence (act of restriction of food,

accommodation, or other conditions for normal subsistence, the right to property, right to engage in labor activities, and the right to enjoy jointly owned possession and to dispose of his/her own share); and Coercion (act of physical or psychological coercion to make a person perform or abstain from performing an act which is their right to perform, or forcing a person to undergo certain influences against his/her will).
2. Entities participating in the process of the elimination and prevention of domestic violence and the protection and rehabilitation of victims of domestic violence are: the Patrol Police Department of the Ministry of Internal Affairs; territorial district units of the Ministry of Internal Affairs; the courts; the State Fund for the Protection and Assistance of Victims of Human Trafficking; state institutions of education, health, and social protection; the Interagency Council for the Prevention of Domestic Violence; and the Prosecutor's Office.
3. The National Action Plans were prepared and adopted for years 2007–2008; 2009–2010; 2011–2012; and 2013–2015.
4. Equals 2.6 million USD at time of writing.
5. Equals 230,000 USD at time of writing.

References

Aladashvili, I., Z. Kiknadze, and N. Nozadze. 2009. "UNPFA Regional Legislative Analysis and Mapping for Regional Partners Country Report – Georgia."

Atipfund Georgia (the State Fund for Protection and Assistance of Victims of Human Trafficking). 2016. "Adjusted and Approved Budget of Administrative Structure." Retrieved 16 December 2015 from http://www.atipfund.gov.ge/index.php/ka/sajaro-info/31 (in Georgian).

Berns, N. 2009. *Framing the Victim: Domestic Violence, Media, and Social Problems.* New Brunswick, NJ: AldineTransaction.

Center for Policy Studies. n.d. "Policy Frames and Implementation Problems: The Case of Gender Mainstreaming (MAGEEQ)." Budapest: Central European University. Retrieved 24 April 2016 from https://cps.ceu.edu/research/mageeq.

Chitashvili, M., and L. Arutiunov. 2010 "Coping with Domestic Violence against Women." In "National Research on Domestic Violence against Women in Georgia. Final Report," 51–58. Tbilisi: Fountain Georgia.

Chitashvili, M., and N. Javakhishvili. 2010. "Introduction." In "National Research on Domestic Violence against Women in Georgia. Final Report," 13–21. Tbilisi: Fountain Georgia.

Council of Europe. 2011a. Istanbul Convention. "Council of Europe Convention on Preventing and Combating Violence against Women and Domestic Violence." Retrieved 6 October 2015 from http://www.coe.int/en/web/conventions/full-list/-/conventions/rms/090000168008482e.

———. 2011b. Istanbul Convention. "Explanatory Report to Council of Europe Convention on Preventing and Combating Violence against Women and Domestic Violence." Retrieved 6 October 2015 from https://rm.coe.int/CoERMPublicCommonSearchServices/DisplayDCTMContent?documentId=09000016800d383a.

Dombos, T., A. Krizsan, M. Verloo, and V. Zentai. 2012. "Critical Frame Analysis: A Comparative Methodology for the 'Quality in Gender+ Equality Policies' (QUING) project." Working Paper. Budapest: Central European University, Center for Policy Studies.

Domestic Abuse Intervention Programs. 2011. "What is the Duluth Model?" Retrieved 20 October 2015 from http://www.theduluthmodel.org/about/index.html.

EIGE (European Institution for Gender Equality). 2012. "Collection of Methods, Tools and Good Practices in the Field of Domestic Violence (as described by area D of Beijing Platform for Action)." Retrieved 5 May 2016 from http://eige.europa.eu/gender-based-vio lence/eiges-studies-gender-based-violence/collection-methods-tools-and-good-practic es-field-domestic-violence-described-area-d-beijing-platform-action.

Franklin, C., and R. Fong. 2011. "Counseling Approaches for Domestic Violence, Child Abuse and Severe Personality Disorders." In *The Church Leader's Counseling Resource Book*, ed. Cynthia Franklin and Rowena Fong, 229–284 . New York: Oxford University Press.

Georgia – Beijing +20. 2014. "National Review of the Implementation of the Beijing Declaration and Platform for Action." 2014. Retrieved 4 April 2016 from http://www.unwomen .org/~/media/headquarters/attachments/sections/csw/59/national_reviews/georgia_re view_beijing20.ashx?v=1&d=20140917T100730.

Javakhishvili, N. 2010. "Prevalence of Violence against Women." In "National Research on Domestic Violence against Women in Georgia. Final Report," 33–41. Tbilisi: Fountain Georgia.

———. 2014. "Georgia – National Report. Georgia Component of a Multi-country Study on Support Services for Women and Girls Subjected to Gender-based Violence." UN Women & Council of Europe. Unpublished report.

Javakhishvili, N., and L. Tsuladze. 2011. "Implementing Domestic Violence Policy in Georgia: Impediments and Their Causes." 6th ECPR General Conference, 25–27 August. University of Iceland.

Javakhishvili, N., et al. 2011. "Interagency United Efforts to Combat Domestic Violence in Georgia: A Local or International Agenda?" Retrieved 16 December 2015 from http:// www.ascn.ch/en/research/Completed-Projects/Completed-Projects-Georgia.html.

Javakhishvili, N., and G. Jibladze. 2012. "Implementation of the Anti-Domestic Violence Law in Georgia: Contextual Interaction Theory Perspective." Fourth Annual Conference on Gender Studies. Center for Social Sciences. Retrieved 4 December 2015 from http://css.ge/files/documents/Papers/Nino_Javakhishvili_Gvantsa_Jibladze_(1).pdf (in Georgian).

Javakhishvili, N., M. Lortkipanidze, and A. Petriashvili. 2012. "Social Capital in Combating Domestic Violence: Church, Mass Media, and Local Community." Fourth Annual Conference in Gender Studies. Center for Social Sciences. Retrieved 6 December 2015 from http://css.ge/index.php?lang_id=ENG&sec_id=52&info_id=718 (in Georgian).

Krizsan, A., et al. 2007. "Domestic Violence: A Public Matter." In *Multiple Meanings of Gender Equality: A Critical Frame Analysis of Gender Policies in Europe*, 141–184. Budapest and New York: Central European University Press.

Krizsan, A., and R.. Popa 2010. "Frames in Contestation: International Human Rights Norms and Domestic Violence Policy Debates in Five Countries of Central and Eastern Europe." Budapest: Central European University, Center for Policy Studies.

Kunovich, S.L., P. Paxton, and M.M. Hughes. 2007. "Gender in Politics." Sociology Research. Retrieved 7 December 2015 from http://digitalrepository.smu.edu/hum_sci_ sociology_research/3.

MOIA (Ministry of Internal Affairs). 2015. "MOIA against Domestic Violence." Retrieved 6 December 2015 from http://police.ge/

Mskhiladze, kh. 2012. "Gender Stereotypes in Georgian Media." The Media Development Foundation. Retrieved 16 December 2015 from http://eurocommunicator.ge/mdf/up loads/Gender_report_II.pdf (in Georgian).

Newspress. 2014. Retrieved 12 December 2015 from http://www.newspress.ge/samar thali/58271-ojakhshi-dzaladobis-aghkvethis-ghonisdziebatha-ganmakhorcielebeli- utsyebathashorisi-sabtcos-skhdoma-gaimartha.html?ar=A (in Georgian).

Public Defender of Georgia. 2015. "Special Report. Violence against Women and Domestic Violence in Georgia." Retrieved 6 October 2015 from http://www.ombudsman.ge/ge/ reports/specialuri-angarishebi/specialuri-angarishi-qalta-mimart-dzaladoba-da-odjax shi-dzaladoba-saqartveloshi.page.

QUING (Quality in Gender+ Equality Policies). "About the Project." Retrieved 24 April 2016 from http://www.quing.eu/content/view/17/34/.

Reingarde, J., et al. 2012. "Review of the Implementation of the Beijing Platform for Action in the EU Member States: Violence against Women – Victim Support." Luxembourg: Publications Office of the European Union.

Sabedashvili, T. 2011. "The Identification and Regulation of Domestic Violence in Georgia (1991–2006)." PhD dissertation. Budapest: Central European University. Retrieved 25 December 2015 from https://www.google.com/url?sa=t&rct=j&q=&esrc=s&source=web&cd=1&ved=0ahUKEwiOwP3UpvfJAhUL2BoKHe90Ai0QFggfMAA&url=http%3A%2F%2Fwww.etd.ceu.hu%2F2012%2Fgphsat01.pdf&usg=AFQjCNFp59p-eq9KpGVFFnl7aH_XgI0D5Q&cad=rja.

Stanko, E.A. 2001. "The Day to Count: Reflections on a Methodology to Raise Awareness about the Impact of Domestic Violence in the UK." Criminology and Criminal Justice 1(2): 215–26.

Stelmaszek, B., and H. Fisher. 2013. "Country Report 2012. Reality Check on Data Collection and European Services for Women and Children Survivors of Violence: A Right for Protection and Support?" Vienna: WAVE (Women Against Violence Europe) / Austrian Women's Shelter Network.

Sumbadze, N. 2014. "Study of the Perception and Attitudes toward Violence against Woman and Domestic Violence in Tbilisi, Kakheti and Samegrelo-ZemoSvanety of Georgia (2013)." Tbilisi: Fountain Georgia.

Thomas, Ch., L. Nelson, M. Ellingen, and N. Sumbadze. 2006. "Domestic Violence and Child Abuse in Georgia: An Assessment of Current Standings of Law and Practice Regarding Domestic Violence and Child Abuse in Georgia, and Recommendations for Future United Nations Country Team Involvement." Tbilisi.

Tsuladze, L. 2010. "Behind the Scenes: Qualitative Research Results." In "National Research on Domestic Violence against Women in Georgia. Final Report," 61–76. Tbilisi: Fountain Georgia.

Ubilava, N., ,N. Tchabukiani and G. Jibladze. 2014. *The Anti-Domestic Violence Policy Analysis in Georgia*. Tbilisi: Women's Fund in Georgia.

UNDP (United Nations Development Programme). 2013. "Research Report. Public Perception on Gender Equality in Politics and Business." Georgia.

UNFPA (United Nations Population Fund). 2010. "The Collection of Normative Acts on Prevention of Domestic Violence, Protection and Assistance of Victims of Domestic Violence in Georgia." Tbilisi.

UN General Assembly. 1993. "Declaration on the Elimination of Violence against Women." Retrieved 6 December 2015 from http://www.un.org/documents/ga/res/48/a48r104.htm.

Chapter 8

Remembering the Past
Narratives of Displaced Women from Abkhazia

Nargiza Arjevanidze

This chapter focuses on life in prewar Abkhazia as experienced, practiced, and remembered by Georgian women displaced as a result of the armed conflict that began in the 1990s. Based on life history interviews with internally displaced persons (IDPs), my goal is to understand how displaced women construct their past prior to the armed conflict, including what they say about it and how they describe it. As an internally displaced person myself, I am an insider who sees the urgency in collecting these narratives before the opportunity is gone.

There were several waves of armed conflict and forced displacement in Georgia, starting from the early 1990s in South Ossetia and then in Abkhazia, both autonomous republics of Georgia. According to some estimates, these conflicts resulted in the forced displacement of more than 370,000 people (IDMC/NRC 2012). A recent estimate indicates there are approximately 232,000 conflict-induced IDPs in Georgia (IDMC 2014), amounting to 6 percent of the country's population (Ferris, Mooney, and Stark 2011). Before the conflict erupted, Abkhazia had the status of Autonomous Soviet Socialist Republic within the Soviet Socialist Republic of Georgia (Cohen 1999). In this chapter, I will use the term "Abkhazia" to refer to the autonomous area of Abkhazia before the conflict began.

My observations suggest that most IDPs—men and women, the young and the old—are struggling to recall and remember the past. This may reflect a process of individual and collective "forgetting" that can be explained in multiple ways. There is the matter of the older generation passing away—the very people with a vivid picture of events before the armed conflict. Those who remain—the relatively younger generation, many in their teens when the war started—tend to place less importance on the past and more on their current everyday lives and problems. Memories fade with time, and people tuck their most painful ones into the deep recesses of their minds and hearts. By means of participating in this life history project, many respondents engaged in a process of remembering. With these concerns in mind, the goal of my ongoing project is to gather rich and diverse portraits of life before and after the conflict.

The scholarly literature on forced displacement and conflict in Georgia has primarily focused on the experiences of the displaced after the armed conflict, which began more than twenty years ago. Much of this literature emphasizes the hardships after displacement: people living in misery and destitution who dream of returning to their former lives without the economic, housing, and other hardships that mark their post-conflict circumstances. By means of sympathetic portraits of Georgia's displaced people, many scholars write compassionately about lives marred, or even devastated, by traumatic experiences. They emphasize women's struggles in assuming ever-greater responsibilities inside and outside the home, while men struggle with alcoholism and unemployment (Buck et al. 2000; Kharashvili 2001; Sabedashvili 2007; Arjevanidze 2009). For example, Kabachnik et al. (2013) document the severe disruption of the status and roles of internally displaced men, resulting in the production of "traumatic masculinities" and the reinforcement of hegemonic masculinities. Other scholars have focused on the relationship IDPs have with their lost homes, their attachment to invisible spaces (Dunn 2014), and the ways they "reproduce the past and future senses of home through various home-making practices that occur within the context of the current places where they reside" (Kabachnik, Regulska, and Mitchneck 2010: 315).

My project adds to this literature by providing a portrait of the past as depicted by this cohort of Georgian women.

Methodological Approach

I began this project inspired by a strong belief "in voice, over silence; *in remembering, over forgetting*" (Waterston 2005: 57, emphasis mine). With this project, I ask Georgian women rarely asked questions to better understand their view of their own lives and past experiences. Rather than focusing on the trauma of the war itself and on their postwar realities and survival strategies, I focus mainly on prewar life prior to their forced displacement, which coincided with the final decades of the Soviet Union. Of course, their memories of the past are filtered by the events that came after, which may influence the stories they tell and the memories they have of that past life (Waterston 2014: 21). My task is to tease out themes that emerge from the narratives, which may provide insight into processes of identity formation and transformation in the context of social and political history.

Feminist scholars and ethnographers have developed innovative approaches to incorporating personal experience in scholarly research. In this project, I draw on intimate ethnography and life story in oral history as approaches to data gathering and interpretation. In terms of theory and method, intimate ethnography is key to my project. Anthropologists Alisse Waterston and Barbara Rylko-Bauer developed intimate ethnography to "enter a deeply private and interior place as ethnographers" (Waterston and Rylko-Bauer 2006: 405). Waterston and Rylko-Bauer had intimate connections with their informants—Waterston's father and Rylko-Bauer's mother. Likewise, my informants are people with whom I have very close relations. In fact, the initial inspiration for this project was my own mother's experience. Like theirs, my life story project involves myself, but it is not autoethnography since my "ultimate goal is to go beyond the reflexive 'I'" (Waterston and Rylko-Bauer 2006: 405).

Feminist scholars have made extensive use of the life story approach as a way to collect women's words. As Marie-Françoise Chanfrault-Duchet notes, life stories help in "reaching a social 'group' that does not often speak on the social stage, or, more precisely, whose discourse has not, until recently, been perceived as legitimate" (Chanfrault-Duchet 1991: 77). She views women's words as embedded in a narrative—a specific scheme that makes sense. Increasingly, these narratives focus on women's everyday lives, and the many tasks they perform on a daily basis, to illustrate their concrete experiences (Brooks 2007). As gender studies scholar Abigail Brooks explains, "[b]y making women's concrete experiences the 'point of entry' for research and scholarship, and exposing the rich array of new knowledge contained within women's experiences, feminist standpoint scholars begin to fill in the gaps on the subject of women in many disciplines" (ibid.: 57). In keeping with themes in historical research and memory studies (Roy 2009), intimate ethnography and the life story approaches I use enable me to learn about respondents' lives from their own perspectives, and help me to gain a deeper understanding of how they make sense of their past and what they deem important. In Chanfrault-Duchet's words, the results reveal "the complexity, the ambiguities, and even the contradictions of relations between the subject and the world" (Chanfrault-Duchet 1991: 89).

My mother is an internally displaced person. She would often talk about her life "back then" and "back there" in prewar Abkhazia when, in her words, "I was young and happy." I would half-listen to her musings, accustomed to hearing what sounded to me like generic, idealized, almost mythological images of her "prosperous life back in Abkhazia." One time, I heard something different in my mother's words. She was telling stories, giving details, and speaking with great emotion. Her tone and the stories she began to tell led me to pay closer attention. Reminiscing about her younger years before she had married, my mother talked about her working-class family and her job as a regular worker in a wine plant. "It felt amazing," she shared; "we didn't have to think about what to have for lunch or breakfast, transportation was free and the state provided us plant workers many other benefits." As she spoke, there was a sparkle in her eyes, and I realized she clung to the memories of this time in her life whenever she felt sad and hopeless. It seemed to be her way to re-experience joy and happiness. There seems to be some deeper truth in her words, even if her happy memories are to some degree a distortion that comes from their contrast to the hardships of her subsequent, post displacement life.

The challenge for me as a daughter and a researcher is the same as that faced by Waterston and Rylko-Bauer: how to chronicle my mother's "rich and complex life while also understanding and accounting for the methodological, emotional, and ethical issues attendant to such intimate life histories, and finding ways of linking the individual stories to larger social processes" (Waterston and Rylko-Bauer 2006: 405). Like Waterston, I wanted to "locate one [wo]man's life in space and time without diminishing [her] own story or denying the uniqueness of the events of her time" (Waterston 2005: 57; see also Waterston 2014).

I began my project by talking to my mother, conducting several lengthy interviews over the first fieldwork phase of my project. This led to interviews with other women—my relatives, family friends, and former neighbors from Abkhazia; only one woman I had not known before. Thus my research evolved into a larger "intimate" project, expanding outward from my mother to others in my circle of intimates. As was true for Waterston and Rylko-Bauer, my relationship with my informants began long ago, and so "the dynamics (of power, duty, and status) in [my] relationship with them were determined long before the projects began" (Waterston and Rylko-Bauer 2006: 405).

Collecting Intimate Life Stories

Waterston and Rylko-Bauer write about the particular challenges of separating out fact from fiction, veracity from idealization, and "truth" from myth in the stories provided to them by their intimate interlocutors (Waterston and Rylko-Bauer 2006: 407), a challenge that resonates with my own as I conducted this research as a native participant observer. In the case of my research, there was the additional concern with what the sociologist Jean Peneff calls "the myth-making process" — especially widespread in societies undergoing rapid development and change. In that context, people tend to frame personal histories as a kind of progress or journey. During the period in question, Georgia has been undergoing rapid social transformation. Thus, it was particularly important that I remained alert "to the existence of this envelope of invention, of approximation or fantasy, which surrounds every life story" (Peneff 1990: 45).

These concerns were offset by the advantages I had in gaining the deep trust and complete access to my research subject because I came from the same group as my informant, and shared the same social status and certain life experiences. As some researchers suggest, "'sameness' is integral to a successful oral history interview ... because different groups within the social order have particular experiences and particular ways of expressing those experiences" (Hesse-Biber 2005: 159). In my project, there were times when the closeness helped the conversation; at other times, the intimacy may have led to avoidance of certain topics, elaborations, or reflections.

The findings presented in this chapter are based on the preliminary results of a larger research project. In 2015, I gathered information from ten women from Abkhazia, all ethnically Georgian and all of them displaced from Abkhazia in 1992–93 as a result of the armed conflict. The women ranged in age from fifty-five to seventy (born between 1946 and 1960). I conducted in-depth interviews and follow-up conversations either in their own apartments, or in former kindergartens and former student dormitories, which had been transformed into living spaces by the state after the war, and are now referred to as collective centers (Buck et al. 2000). In this chapter, all respondents are referred to by pseudonyms, as they requested, and that was part of our confidentiality agreement. All translations from Georgian to English are mine.

All ten respondents were willing participants. Four of the women agreed to participate on the condition that "politics" would not be discussed, though each voluntarily began talking about political issues in the course of the interview. For example, although Liana asserted she did not want to talk about the war or be asked to recall memories of it, she raised the topic herself, describing the time her home city was brutally bombed "from the sea, the land, and the air" while she was trapped at home with her sick father.

Among the participants, five women were widowed, four single, and one married. Two of the widows had lost their husbands to the war in 1992. Both were killed by a bomb explosion—their bodies were never recovered, so there were no bodies to bury. These women belonged to what one might call the lower-middle class (proletariat) or middle class (petty bourgeoisie) social strata, though during their life course those women who married enjoyed a somewhat higher social position and status.

Some of them had moved to Abkhazia as children—two from the mountainous region of Svaneti and one from Samegrelo in the western part of Georgia. The remainder had been born and raised in either the capital city of Abkhazia, Sokhumi, or in the nearby villages of Gagra and Sokhumi, two of Abkhazia's main cities. All had received higher education in institutes or attended professional-technical schools (a type of vocational-technical school that provides training in skilled and semiskilled jobs) from the following institutions: Sokhumi Institute of Subtropical Agriculture, Sokhumi Medical School, Sokhumi Pedagogical Institute (now Sokhumi State University), and Sokhumi People's University of preschool education; only one participant studied in Kutasi, located in the western part of Georgia.

In what follows, I offer a brief sketch of key topics that emerged from the life history narratives offered by Georgian women from Abkhazia—what life was like from childhood to adulthood, with a special emphasis on family, marriage, and work in what was the Abkhaz Autonomous Soviet Socialist Republic.

Childhood and Young Adulthood

Nino and Mari are sisters, whom I interviewed separately. Mari is six years older than her sister, who at the time of the interview was fifty-nine. Mari was a fifteen-year-old teenager when she and her sister Nino moved from the mountains of Svaneti in 1967 to the village in the district of Gagra. The village bordered Russia, and was abundantly multicultural. Armenians, Estonians, and Russians lived alongside Georgians. Both women noted that in those years, people did not pay attention to nationality or national origins. The focus on that came later, after the war began, when tensions between the groups were exacerbated.

"We moved to Salkhino in Abkhazia in search of a better life and better conditions," Mari explains. "In the beginning we were poor, but we loved life in Abkhazia. It was peaceful. We were happy. We were never afraid of war, and we never imagined such a thing could ever happen." Mari's recollections are steeped in nostalgia even as she recalls the hardships. Her father had been taken ill and could not work. The family had supported itself and each other by working in the Kolkhoz, a Soviet form of collective farming.

Mari's narrative reveals the ways in which labor was mobilized for family and community sustenance. "My father had health issues and he could not do hard work," Mari explains. "Instead, my mother replaced him, and she taught us how to work in tobacco. Everyone had to work in the Kolkhoz. It was not voluntary, and we were obliged to." Mari recalls the work in the fondest of terms:

> We performed everything required of us, and it was also fun. We worked together with our neighbors. It's true, we did not have another choice, but no one ever complained about it, because it was the only income we had then. My brothers, me and my sister helped our mother to collect tobacco leaves. Besides the money from the Kolkhoz, we also received a pension after our father passed away. This pension was ninety rubles a month and it was quite enough, because everything was cheap. For instance, you could buy five loaves of bread for one ruble.

Nino, Mari's younger sister, shares her sister's positive recollections even as they both acknowledge the hardships. For the most part, those hardships were shared collectively across the community, which was stratified by wealth differences. Mari explains:

> It was hard, of course. We had to help the family from a very young age. We had to work in the tobacco and breed silkworms. It was not easy. You had to carry heavy baskets, but mother would carry the heaviest baskets. All the families in our village lived under similar conditions and received almost the same pay. The payments also depended on the number of family members working in the Kolkhoz. All families were equal in terms of income. I can only recall one family that was richer than the rest of us—they had a TV-set. I was in the 4th form and had never seen a TV-set before. In Svaneti, we had a radio but not the TV. I remember the times when the whole village gathered in front of the black-and-white television to watch the programs. It was fun. We all lived friendly. It was life in a family-like relationship, in our village, and everyone respected each other. And, despite that the one family was more affluent than us, we never felt this difference. They were always helping others who earned or owned less than they did.

Manana's family moved in 1953 from Samegrelo, located southeast of Abkhazia, to a village near Gagra. Their move was part of a planned migration carried out by a government agency then headed by Lavrentyi Beria, an infamous Soviet official. She also recalls her childhood and school years in relation to physical work. Manana reveals the way in which the work ethic was central to the social prestige pecking order:

> Every able-bodied person without health issues had to work in the Kolkhoz. If he or she was not able to work, if they were sick, they were entitled to the state pension. Our family's main income was the money we received from working in tobacco on the Kolkhoz. People lived on this money. And every man and woman who was not lazy could work physically and earn this living. You could

judge whether a person was lazy or not by their yard and garden, by the way they took care of their home.

In terms of the gendered aspects of their lives, the women made a point of noting that household tasks were not divided by gender. "We never used these words—men's work or women's work. This is not how we approached 'work,'" 65-year-old Mari explained. "Men were called on in those situations where women were not strong enough to carry heavy loads. Otherwise men and women—husbands and wives, and brothers and sisters—all worked, and worked alongside one another."

Nana, fifty-eight at the time of the interview, recalls her childhood as a bright and happy time that offered a strong sense of security, even as people labored intensely:

> Our parents were hard-working people. They didn't have to think about how to provide for their children like I do now. We had a very good life. We worked together. We spent leisure time together. We were happy to help our parents to take care of the cattle, or the yard and garden. I always remember my childhood with positive feelings, and you could work hard and get salary for what you did. Now you work hard but you get *nothing*.

Throughout the interview, Nana's stories of the past were seen through the lens of the present, particularly with reference to her living conditions and economic situation, which no longer felt secure. In this regard, all the women contrasted the past with life in Georgia today. Then, there were no beggars on the streets or in their neighborhoods. None of their acquaintances went around asking for food. "Nobody was hungry then," the women said.

The women I interviewed recalled with great fondness frequent gatherings with neighbors and relatives, living and working in a "family-like environment." They never imagined that war and political instability would affect them. All the women talked about "the land," which once was accessible, but no longer is for these women who live in block apartments. For them, "the land" was something they once could step on and feel securely under their feet.

Studies of Georgian IDPs have noted their tendency to depict the past in positive terms, especially as it contrasts with their present lives and circumstances (Arjevanidze 2009; Dunn 2013). They tend to imagine Abkhazia in three different ways: "as a traumatic, violent place; as a chaotic, flawless realm; and [in its] nostalgic version, as a multicultural and harmonious paradise" (Kabachnik, Regulska, and Mitchneck 2012: 126). The narratives I have collected are to some degree consistent with these findings.

My research also reveals some differences between the working-class women and those who were securely middle class. Five of the middle-class women had been born and raised in the city center. Their families did not migrate from elsewhere in Georgia to Abkhazia in search of a better life. Their lives in Abkhazia were about going out for walks along the seashore with their friends, or out to the movies or theatre—all very positive memories.

These women were class-conscious, aware of inequalities under life in Soviet Georgia. Comparatively well-off urban dwellers, they came from families that could afford to travel (albeit only to Soviet-bloc and Soviet countries) and to pay 60–100 rubles for shoes, even though individual monthly salaries were no more than 120 rubles. They had had the privilege of being financially supported by their families, which meant they had not had the obligation to supplement the income of their parents or contribute financially to the sustenance of their households. This meant they had been free from the burden of paying rent, and could study while living in their parents' homes in the city. They were well educated, and had worked in prestigious occupations and managerial positions. They expressed dissatisfaction with the salaries they had received, which they tended to spend on expensive shoes and foreign brand ("firma") clothes. Their memories stand in contrast to those women who had engaged in physical labor on the farms and manufacturing plants, who had considered it a significant accomplishment when their starting salaries of approximately 35 rubles per month had reached 80–90 rubles.

As compared to their better-off counterparts, in depicting their past the proletariat women expressed more contentment and happiness with life and work centered on family and community cohesiveness, friendly multiculturalism, and commitment to the "collective." Overall, my preliminary findings are consistent with feminist labor scholar Joan Sangster's observations on the significance of the interplay of class and gender in the shaping of experience and in the ordering of memory (Sangster 1994: 7).

In terms of educational experiences, the women pointed to specific class and gender factors that had shaped their educational futures. In higher education, girls had been encouraged to study in the field of philology (Georgian and foreign languages and literature), while boys had been expected to concentrate on history, law, physics, and mathematics as their main fields of study. Mari recalls a strong interest in studying history that was deflected by gender norms. "Only boys studied history," she declared, and besides, "it was really expensive—the bribe—to get into university to study it." Most professional schools—such as for trade, culinary arts, pre-school education, and medicine (with a specialization in obstetrics)—were fields that had been pursued by the women in my study.

The bribe system in Soviet Georgia constituted a form of corruption that dictated who could enter the university and who could not. Officially, higher education was available and free for everyone. The reality stood in stark contrast to this policy, according to the women's reports. Whether the bribe system was real or perceived, it meant the proletarian women in my study had not pursued higher education, even if they had so desired. Mari offers a case in point. Unable to afford to commit to five years of study at the university (institute), she had put aside her scholarly interest in foreign languages for a one-year "professional" school that led to her job as a salesperson and later as a plant worker. The bribe system, which the women claimed was more intense in Georgia than in Russia, was the main obstacle that had prevented Natali from studying at the medical institute, though she said she was qualified to do so. Indeed, parents often strategized, sending their children to study in the Russian schools rather than the Georgian primary schools so that their Russian language proficiency would enable them to enter university in Russia, where parents imagined the corruption was not as concentrated as it was in Georgia.

Marriage and Children

Arranged marriages were prevalent in parts of Georgia at the time when the women I interviewed had come of age. Four of the women said they had not been "in love" with their fiancés; in fact they had met them only three or four times before the marriage was decided upon. They had been introduced to their future husbands by their relatives. Nino explained: "I knew he was a good man. People considered him a respectable and successful man. Besides, I was afraid of my uncle who would get very upset with me if I did not marry him, and I can say for sure that I decided to marry my husband out of respect for my uncle."

For that generation of women, 21–23 years old was considered the ideal age to marry; those not married by age 24 were considered to be "late." They report that the pressure to marry came less from their own parents and more from extended relatives and the wider society. Not everyone succumbed to the pressure. Natali, for example, never married. About marriage, Natali observes: "It was never an obligation for me. Divorce was very rare. If you married, it was expected that you had to spend your whole life with your husband until death, even if there was violence."

Natali's mention of "violence" in the context of marriage is interesting, considering most of the women I spoke with did not raise the issue. It is difficult to know if domestic violence was rare or if it was "there" but unspoken (Sangster 1994). For the women in my study, "domestic violence" seemed to be more of a contemporary phenomenon, something notably absent in prewar Georgia. For example, Nino acknowledged there were occasions when "we could hear shouting, fighting from houses. It meant the husband had gotten drunk and was picking a fight, though not physically attacking his wife. I cannot recall any such case." Divorce was also rare, which contrasts with contemporary norms. The norm then was to preserve the family, and divorce was shameful—a source of stigma for all those involved. Those who married men with an established position in society found themselves with an improved social status.

As was the norm, the women in my study continued to work after marrying and having children. Mari pointed out that she did not return to work out of economic necessity but because working outside the home "meant that I had a status in the society, and people respected me."

To the Present: Dreams of the Past and "Home"

For all the women in my study, there is a stark difference between the time before the war and the time after. Those who managed to escape before witnessing the destruction of their homes and their towns, and who did not lose family members to the war, were much more likely to express a desire to return.

Those who saw the physical destruction of their homes and who lost loved ones to the war were less likely to express interest in returning to the place they once called home. For Natali, the place lost all meaning once it had been destroyed: "I saw my city—the place where I grew up, where I studied, worked, lived, and loved—in ruins. It was no longer my city. I did not recognize it when I walked the ruined streets of Sokhumi." Those who, like Natali, had suffered the greatest losses seemed reluctant to return to the place where only remnants of their old homes remained, and were not eager to confront those they considered the perpetrators of the violence. Nevertheless, if provided the opportunity for "reconciliation and return," all the women said they "would take it."

The women continue to hold dear the people they knew who have survived. "When I see my Abkhaz friends," Liana remarked, "we forget about everything that happened. We hug each other hard and just won't move. We wish to be able to stay there, in that moment, so as not to be separated again."

Each interview closed with the participants talking about how the conversation had made them feel. For some, talking about the past was a stressful process that led to troubled thoughts and sleep disruptions. Most try not to think about the past, but for some the interviews were a pleasant experience that allowed them to return to a time and place they miss greatly.

Concluding Remarks

The stories shared with me by the participants of this study are true for them, even if their narratives cannot be taken as faithful representations of what happened in the past (Roy 2009). At the same time, it is likely their narratives reveal larger truths about the organization of their everyday lives as women situated in a historically constituted social world. The narratives also reveal larger truths about the complexities of their lives before and after the war. The label "internally displaced person" captures only one aspect of the Georgian women in my project. To some degree, the emphasis on their displacement is warranted, as the women themselves understand life "before" and "after" the war and displacement. Yet this emphasis does not capture the full story since, as this chapter reveals, there was life for these women before their displacement. The full complexity of these women's lives must be accounted for. In this chapter, I offer an entry point toward that accounting.

Nargiza Arjevanidze is a doctoral student at the Faculty of Social and Political Sciences, program of sociology, at Tbilisi State University, Georgia who holds a Master's degree in gender studies from Central European University, Budapest. She teaches undergraduate and graduate students in the faculty's Institute for Gender Studies, and was a returning scholar of the Academic Fellowship Program, Open Society Foundations (2010–2015). She is a visiting doctoral student at the Department of Gender Studies at Lund University, Sweden.

References

Arjevanidze, N. 2009. "Changing Gender Relations within the Families of the Internally Displaced Population in Georgia." Master's thesis, Department of Gender Studies, Central European University, Budapest.
Brooks, A. 2007. "Feminist Standpoint Epistemology: Building Knowledge and Empowerment through Women's Lived Experience." In *Feminist Research Practice: A Primer*, ed. S.N. Hesse-Biber and P.L. Leavy, 53–82. SAGE Publications.

Buck, T., A. Morton, S.A. Nan, and F. Zurikaskvili. 2000. "Aftermath: Effects of Conflict on Internally Displaced Women in Georgia." Working Paper 310. Washington, DC: USAID.

Chanfrault-Duchet, M. 1991. "Narrative Structures, Social Models, and Symbolic Representation in the Life Story." In *Women's Words: The Feminist Practice of Oral History*, ed. S. Gluck and D. Patai, 77–92. New York and London: Routledge.

Cohen, J. (ed.). 1999. "A *Question of Sovereignty*: The Georgia–Abkhazia Peace Process." *Accord* 7. London: Conciliation Resources.

Dunn, E.C. 2013. "Invisible Spaces of Lost Homes." American Ethnological Society Conference Paper.

———. 2014. "Humanitarianism, Displacement, and the Politics of Nothing in Postwar Georgia." *Slavic Review* 2: 287–306.

Ferris, E., E. Mooney and C. Stark. 2011. "From Responsibility to Response: Assessing National Approaches to Internal Displacement." The Brookings Institution and London School of Economics.

Hesse-Biber, S.N. 2005. "Oral History: A Collaborative Method of (Auto) Biography Interview." In *The Practice of Qualitative Research*, ed. S.N. Hesse-Biber and P.L. Leavy, 149–94. New York: SAGE Publications.

IDMC/NRC. 2012. "Georgia: Partial Progress towards Durable Solutions for IDPs Internal Displacement Monitoring Centre/Norwegian Refugee Council." Retrieved 10 April 2016 from http://georgia.idp.arizona.edu/docs/idmc_georgia_3_12.pdf.

IDMC. 2014. Georgia IDPs Figure Analysis. Retrieved 8 April 2017 from http://www.internal-displacement.org/europe-the-caucasus-and-central-asia/georgia/figures-analysis.

Kabachnik, P., J. Regulska and B. Mitchneck. 2010. "Where and When is Home? The Double Displacement of Georgian IDPs from Abkhazia." *The Journal of Refugee Studies* 23(3): 315–36.

———. 2012. "Displacing Blame: Georgian Internally Displaced Person Perspectives of the Georgia–Abkhazia Conflict." *Ethnopolitics: Formerly Global Review of Ethnopolitics* 11(2): 123–40.

Kabachnik, P., M. Grabowska, J. Regulska, B. Mitchneck, and O.V. Mayorova. 2013. "Traumatic Masculinities: The Gendered Geographies of Georgian IDPs from Abkhazia." *Gender, Place & Culture: A Journal of Feminist Geography* 20(6): 773–93.

Kharashvili, J. 2001. "Georgia: Coping by Organizing. Displaced Georgians from Abkhazia." *Caught Between Borders: Response Strategies of the Internally Displaced*, ed. M. Vincent and B. Sorensen, 227–249. London: Pluto Press.

Peneff, J. 1990. "Myths in Life Stories." In *The Myths We Live By*, ed. R. Samuel and P.R. Thompson, 36–48. London: Routledge.

Roy, M.S. 2009. "Magic Moments of Struggle: Women's Memory of the Naxalbari Movement in West Bengal, India (1967–1975)." *Indian Journal of Gender Studies* 16(2): 205–232.

Sabedashvili, T. 2007. *Gender and Democratization: The Case of Georgia 1991–1996*. Tbilisi: Heinrich Böll Foundation.

Sangster, J. 1994. "Telling Our Stories: Feminist Debates and the Use of Oral History." *Women's History Review* 3(1): 5–28.

Waterston, A. 2005. "The Story of My Story: An Anthropology of Violence, Dispossession and Diaspora." *Anthropological Quarterly* 78(1): 43–61. Special collection on "Bringing the Past into the Present: Family Narratives of Holocaust, Exile, and Diaspora."

———. 2014. *My Father's Wars*. New York and London: Routledge.

Waterston, A., and B. Rylko-Bauer. 2006. "Out of the Shadows of History and Memory: Personal Family Narratives in Ethnographies of Rediscovery." *American Ethnologist* 330(3): 397–412.

Chapter 9

Displacement, State Violence, and Gender Roles
The Case of Internally Displaced
and Violence-Affected Georgian Women

Joanna Regulska, Beth Mitchneck, and Peter Kabachnik

Introduction

Over the past two decades, Georgia has seen conflict, massive internal displacement, and a major restructuring of its political and economic systems. These processes, we argue, have transformed gender relations and gender roles, and have impacted how Georgian displaced women claim their identities and their agency. Paralleling other post-conflict settings, this new social, cultural, economic, and political context has altered gender dynamics by shifting and expanding women's roles. In many cases, displaced women take on new responsibilities, such as that of the breadwinner and/or engage in numerous other activities as a result of shifts in state support. This increased burden entails new forms of agency and responsibility on the part of displaced women. Yet despite these changes, interviews with displaced women highlight how they continue to understand their agency within the bounds of traditional (and hegemonic) gendered power structures; for example, viewing their new economic roles within the context of their duties as mothers and housewives.

This chapter looks at how conflict, state violence, and displacement can challenge gender norms. Displacement, we claim, unleashed gender role reversals and initiated new conversations at the intersection of identity, values, and responsibilities—but as the evidence gathered has shown,

---

Notes for this chapter begin on page 151.

these shifts are not permanent. In fact, the experiences of conflict and displacement may serve to reinforce patriarchal structures that limit women's influence in the home and beyond.

Our decision to focus on women's agency is prompted in part by our recognition that all too often, displaced women are narrowly represented as passive victims (Khan 2002).[1] The question becomes particularly important in the context of ethnic or identity-based conflicts in which a group is fighting for recognition and women are often understood as caregivers of the family and, by extension, of that group or nation (Krasniqi 2007). The image of women as simply passive victims, highlighted in situations of conflict and displacement, tends to obscure the occasions when women are active agents. Matsuoka and Sorenson (1999) note that the process by which women negotiate new roles and identities is most visible in the context of gendered household practices.

It is in daily practices that women undertake renegotiations of roles, behaviors, and relationships. By examining the narratives of displaced Georgian women, we came to understand the processes through which women claim their agency and, by doing so, embrace their reconfigured but not necessarily fundamentally changed identities.

Defining Agency in Post-Conflict and Displacement Contexts

Scholars have devoted considerable attention to defining and understanding the notion of women's agency. Feminist theorist Lois McNay describes agency as "the capacity of embodied subjects," noteworthy for highlighting the ability of actors to take action rather than emphasizing the action itself (McNay 2010: 513). In this aspect, the definition recalls Hannah Arendt's discussion of power as "potential" and as "energy and competence" (Hartsock 1996: 36). To take action and respond to changing circumstances, subjects need some form of power. A critical analysis of agency requires an understanding that agency is fluid and never static. It is subject to structural constraint, and operates within particular social and cultural contexts; at the same time, it is about individual desire, personal interest, and intentionality (Dissanayake 1996; Mahmood 2005).

In our discussion of agency, we follow the ideas of McNay (2000) to highlight the interplay of internal and external factors. We argue that these multiple, concurrently operating factors shape an individual's actions. McNay elaborates on the internal aspect of agency by emphasizing the important role of identity and identity formation in enabling "the individual's willingness to even consider certain types of action over others, or indeed to prefer inaction to any kind of action" (McNay 2010: 520). She critiques approaches to identity formation that assume individuals are passively reactive rather than proactive and innovative. The active process of identity formation illustrates agency; individuals build on the possibilities, of which gender is one part, to inform decisions about how and in what ways to act. The external factors—institutional structures, such as the state and its political bodies, nongovernmental organizations (NGOs), the church, and international aid organizations—influence one's agency by imposing legal and financial rules, or by fostering certain social norms within the context of hierarchical power relations. Such institutions and regulations create a governance environment that sets rules and standards of behavior, and by doing so, shape individuals' and institutions' practices. Individuals' conscious ability to choose how to internalize, enact, or challenge these rules and norms ultimately constitutes what we call women's agency (Niranjana 2001; Mahmood 2005).

Fundamentally, agency arises out of women's creative ability to negotiate between "freedom and constraint"; the interplay of internal motivations on the one hand, and "cultural sanctions and structural inequalities" or the external context, on the other (McNay 2000). We argue that it is this simultaneity of internal and external factors, rather than privileging one over the other, that shapes how women claim agency in Georgia. Elsewhere, we have examined more thoroughly the external forces that construct the governance environment within which IDPs live and work (Kabachnik, Mitchneck, and Regulska 2015). In this chapter, we will pay more attention to the internal forces that have shaped the conditions that have enabled women to exercise and claim their agency.[2] We are especially interested in understanding how IDP women engage and act within Georgian familial, cultural, and institutional contexts.

The question for us became *how* does conflict and displacement influence IDP women's agency. For IDPs, the experience of violence and trauma, and the resulting loss of one's home or loved ones, of one's economic and social stability, and thus of one's sense of one's place within the larger social and economic context, does cause a significant break with the past. To various degrees, it also alters one's sense of self and relations with others (Riaño-Alcalá 2008; Kabachnik, Regulska, and Mitchneck 2010; Kabachnik et al. 2014). After briefly discussing the context of displacement and conflict in Georgia, and our methods, we demonstrate some ways through which Georgian IDP women enact their agency.

Post-Soviet State Transition, Conflict, and the Broader Context of Displacement in Georgia

The conflict over the separatist regions of Abkhazia and South Ossetia, displacement, and post-Soviet state transition have acted as major forces influencing life in Georgia since independence. In the early 1990s, over 200,000 Georgians were forced to leave their homes in Abkhazia,[3] while the conflict with South Ossetia, in 2008, produced an estimated 60,000 IDPs (Internal Displacement Monitoring Centre 2009). Both territories became de facto separate political entities, and Georgia continues to vie for restoring its territorial integrity and mobility across the borders, as claimed in the state strategy.[4] As a result, the conflict regions remain unstable. IDPs comprise approximately 5 percent of the population in Georgia (Norwegian Refugee Council / Internal Displacement Monitoring Centre 2014), serving as a key symbol of the ongoing challenges the country faces. In addition, the majority of Georgians, not only IDPs, face high poverty and unemployment rates (UNDP 2013; UNHCR 2015). The fall of the Soviet Union brought about major economic shifts, impacting people who had previously enjoyed secure employment and housing (Dudwick 2003).

The post-Soviet context has also seen shifts in gender roles and gendered power dynamics. During the Soviet era, most Georgian women were strongly visible in the public sphere as they took on the double duty of working outside the home and remaining the caregivers for their children (despite the existence of nurseries and state-sponsored childcare facilities) and their families (Chkheidze 2014). At the same time, research suggests that in Soviet East European societies, the dominant view was that a wife's employment was considered secondary to that of her husband, who was the family's main breadwinner (Feischmidt, Magyari-Vincze, and Zentai 1997).

Since Georgia's independence in 1991, the return to traditional attitudes regarding gender roles is quite evident. There is now a strong public perception that women are better suited to taking care of the children and family, that they should not work unless it is financially necessary, that men are the head of the family, and that women should tolerate husband's insults in order to preserve the family unit. These are among the most prevailing attitudes toward women's roles inside and outside the family (Gagoshashvili 2008; de Waal 2011; UNDP 2013: 34).

Methodology

Data collection for this chapter is part of a larger National Science Foundation research project focused on examining the living conditions of Georgian IDPs, their interactions with governmental and nongovernmental organizations, and how these organizations influence IDPs' coping strategies. The research also assesses Georgian IDPs' social networks, livelihoods, and gender roles. Several rounds of interviews were conducted in Tbilisi, Kutaisi, Tskhaltubo, and Zugdidi, with IDPs and non-IDPs, both male and female. For this chapter, we draw on interviews conducted in

2007 with sixty women who had been displaced from Abkhazia. At the time of the interviews, half of these women were living in collective centers,[5] and half in private dwellings.

Agency of Women from Abkhazia Living in Protracted Displacement

Internal Context

How does the internal context of being an IDP shape women's actions? How is this newly acquired involuntary identity performed by IDP women? In what capacity do women exhibit agency? Our narratives collected from displaced women indicated numerous ways through which they claim their mediated agency. Four of these dimensions and practices seem especially prevalent and dominant: (1) taking on a leadership role to protect their families when war broke out and displacement took place; (2) assuming financial responsibilities for their own and their family's well-being; (3) mobilizing networks of support; and (4) showing a greater ability than men to adapt to new life circumstances. We will briefly discuss each in turn.

Taking a Leadership Role to Protect Families

The arrival of war and forced displacement imposed a new gendered division of labor and responsibilities. Women often had to claim sole responsibility for family survival by organizing transportation, protecting their elderly family members and children (including actively confronting military forces) and securing their departure by organizing transportation from the war-affected areas. Men, on the other hand, often stayed behind to actively participate in military activities and to organize the protection of material possessions (land, homes, vehicles, etc.).

Women's stories of flight from the conflict zone reveal the ways they "took charge" of the process to ensure the safety of their families. Nani[6] describes how her mother assured their leaving Abkhazia:

> The city was in panic and it was very difficult to find any means of transport. So we went to the airport, my sister, mother, cousin and I ... My cousin and me were not on this list and my mom was told that they would let her and the youngest child leave, but we (me and my cousin) had to stay, and I remember that very bad moment—we are moving up the airplane steps and Mom is holding the hands of all three of us, and she is being told to take this one and leave the other ones, and this machine gun is pointed at her forehead, saying not to

go and at the same time they announce that this will be the last plane ... and then Mom got very brave and somehow managed to push us into the plane.

And Keta echoed:

> I somehow managed to send the younger one to her place as well, and then I found myself to be shut off from my living place and was forced to leave very quickly. I gave up on everything—on my house and husband. I just thought of saving my children and myself. I left home silently, I actually stole away and all we wanted was just to leave, we didn't care about taking anything.

Both men and women repeatedly described the situation as tense, frightening, violent—not having any knowledge of what would happen next, where they were going or how they would get there. Women left behind everything they had, carrying with them very few belongings, and hoping that their husbands, fathers, and cousins would protect their belongings. These departures ruptured family, friends, and neighbor networks, and made everybody vulnerable and fearful. It was in this period that shifts in gender roles began to take place.

Assuming Financial Responsibility

Securing family well-being, and financial and material stability in the new place, has become a major task for IDP women, and another way for them to exercise their agency. As IDPs' access to jobs, transportation, and social, medical, and educational services and facilities became drastically restricted or even nonexistent (and many of these still remain as such), women's labor had to fill much of this void (UNHCR 2015). Women took upon themselves new and extended responsibilities. They became primary breadwinners and caregivers, and by doing so they were reframing the double burden so well known from the past.

Keta explained: "My load increased, it had increased a lot and that was a big stress for me ... because I have taken upon myself to raise three children and looking after the family." Others added: "Now my husband receives [just a] pension and [so] I am the main breadwinner in the family"; and "My wife works and sustain us." Maia pointed out that not many women had worked outside the home in the past, but now they do: "In early times women did not work and men sustained their families. It is vice versa today. Women work and men are at home, because there is no work for men." Both women and men recognized this shift, as Giorgi acknowledged: "She works more than me ... if anyone does anything in my family, it is the woman. I think [the] woman has more load ... women have a very big responsibility, especially today. A son of Gia observed: "Considering our traditions, men are stronger, more enduring ... though I often see also that, for example, my father does not work now, and my mother is carrying all the burden of a breadwinner ... this has increased much nowadays ... life brings all this."

One could argue that nothing much has changed, as many women in the past did work outside the home and provided caregiving services. Yet, while some tasks may be familiar, new ones have been added; and the conditions under which they were and are delivered have fundamentally changed. The newly acquired involuntary identity of an IDP means sudden and persistent social marginalization, which adds an additional burden to everyday struggles (Human Rights House Network 2012).

Interviewees reported that financial means had become very much limited as well; moreover, that access to services, and to information on service providers, were not only limited, but instructions were unclear or simply did not exist. Overcoming these challenges had resulted in multiple trips to state offices, and hours of waiting in their corridors. The remote location of collective centers and subsequent evictions and relocation to more distant sites had translated into long travels and many hours lost (World Bank 2013). Furthermore, the state withdrawal from providing services and its inability to secure services for IDPs has resulted in the ongoing need for women to negotiate and overcome these obstacles on a daily basis. Women struggle to reintroduce and cultivate normalcy, and by doing so enact their agency.

At the same time, our interviews indicated that women's role as the primary breadwinner has not fundamentally changed the gendered aspects of their identities. The themes of mother and housewife are strongly prevalent in the women's narratives. When asked to describe her role, Marine referred to herself as "a housewife ... I am taking care of my family. This is my number one concern." Others echoed this sentiment by claiming: "I am a Georgian woman who should become a mother"; and "I am an active, good mother of my children, a good housewife." Another revealed: "I am like every housewife ... I do everything at home ... I am kind of [focused on] my family members. I like to work ... I am like many other women of my age." These statements echo the values predominant in contemporary Georgian society, in which being a mother and a housewife is considered by many women as the most important goal in a woman's life (Gagoshashvili 2008; UNDP 2013).

Mobilizing Social Networks

Women's ability to forge and make use of their interpersonal and extended social networks has become not only an asset, but also a way for them to enact their agency, which is a third dominant dimension performed by IDP women. These women are active in creating, maintaining, and mobilizing various networks, comprising relatives, friends, and other members of their communities. These actions have proved essential to their survival and that of their loved ones. Engaging with others has allowed women to shape their agency, both as a response to new external conditions, but also as a capacity to transform these conditions. Women exercise their agency by activating informal support systems; they talk, meet others, exchange ideas, and cultivate an agentic sense of self.

The expressions of women's everyday negotiating capacities were visibly revealed during the dramatic events at the beginning of the war, as described by Nino and Tamuna:

> Some people ... helped our children to escape ... I remained in the city to try to save my husband. I used all the connections through relatives and acquaintances, and after several days, by the end of 1992, my husband was released, and with the help of Abkhazian friends we managed to leave for Tbilisi.
>
> My grandma's friend helped. We didn't know her; she found us on her own, and decided to let us live in her apartment near Delisi until we recover.

Men and women both reconstruct and develop personal networks in displacement; yet, the networks are structured differently and in large part around social support and income generation (Mayorova and Mitchneck 2016). Women, especially those who do not work outside the home, tend to mobilize support networks from close family members with whom they live, while men tend to mobilize their networks for leisure activities with social ties around the city in which they live. Women who work outside the home are likely to use their networks directly to develop income generating opportunities to a much greater degree than men. This suggests that men may see networks as less directly leading to income, but primarily for other activities that may in the end lead to income opportunities. This is not to say that men do not use networks for income, but income opportunities are a derivative of social networks rather than a direct function. We interpret this as suggesting that women are more likely than men to use agency to support their families directly. This is indicated by Anna, who said: "I asked them to help me with finding a job, as I had no other means for living and sustaining my children, while my husband was serving his duty." Likewise, Tamara remarked: "It is thanks to my close friends that I manage to survive. Whatever I am, it is thanks to people from my closest circle." This may come from a sense of urgency women feel because of the new social roles that they play after displacement.

Women do not only interact to gain help or assistance; some do so for pure pleasure, as Eka notes: "[I] very much like to hosts guests ... I really like [it] when guests come to my place." Eka's desire for interaction with others at her home reflects her want to anchor herself in her new place. The relationship between people and place is not simply a question of mobility—even though it is critical when (dis)placement occurs—but it is also a matter of material connections. For the displaced person, their forced migration necessitated them to engage their agency to develop ties with a new place. They did not have much in terms of material resources, but they could preserve and keep up their social ties to (re)establish their individual and collective belonging.

Adaptability to New Circumstances

The final theme in IDP narratives is the clear gendering of adaptability capacities, with women found to be more flexible and adaptable than men (Buck et al. 2000; Sumbadze and Tarkhan-Mouravi 2005: 228). Both men and women indicated that they thought women have adapted better and have had an easier time doing so. They tend to interact more with people (for example, through their children), they have more friends of their own, they take jobs that men would not necessarily take, and they keep busy attempting to fulfill their familial obligations. Diana explained:

> Men felt themselves in a different way, they feel humiliated. Women view it differently, life goes on anyway ... now they also understand that life goes on, but still, for them it was a harder blow (pause) ... defeated, thrown out (laughs) and so on, it is very hard for men.

Irakli echoed these sentiments:

> I think my wife has adapted better, because she has her own friends; also there are parents from the school [that she befriended] ... she has adapted better.

Women's abilities to adapt easily did create some gender identity confusion; should they see themselves as women or men? Yet, at the same time, this gender bending gave them a sense of satisfaction and accomplishment. As Mako explained:

> Sometimes I think ... that I am not sure whether I am a women or a man, because my spouse is in this condition and I have to do whatever is required, I am going to take care of it. And I am happy with the way I am dealing with things. Sometimes I think I can do it, I am strong. If I have a goal I should achieve it, whether this way or another.

IDPs recognize how difficult this transition has been for men, who have experienced great difficulties in accepting women's new economic roles and in recognizing women's abilities to adapt faster and easier (Brun 2000). As Kabachnik et al. argued, "Many Georgian IDP men not only continue to experience trauma, a reverberation from undergoing forced migration, but the trauma becomes embodied as they endure numerous psychological and emotional challenges in the guise of drastically altered gender roles and loss of their privileged patriarchal status" (Kabachnik et al. 2013: 5).

Women's ability to adapt to new circumstances was also reflected in their different understanding of what jobs mean for each gender. Due to displacement and lack of job opportunities, street trade and menial labor are often the only livelihood strategies available to IDPs. Yet, many men have been unwilling to engage in these "lowly" jobs. As a result, they idle away their time, with their lost breadwinner status increasing their passivity and sense of shame that comes with knowing that women have become more economically creative and successful in displacement. Ucha described his predicament as follows:

> These times are a little bit difficult for men, because now women are more active ... it is not something shameful to trade in the market, but this is not in my genes ... I cannot do that ... can't manage ... men cannot cope with it ... IDP women all try to buy and sell something. Women have learned how to deal with this life, [better] than men.

This struggle to renegotiate, adapt, and make sense of gender roles in post-conflict and post-displacement Georgia is captured in Ketevan's story:

> Very often I realize that I am wearing a mask of a strong personality. I am strong ... very strong ... No one can do any harm to me ... as if I were not a woman. As if I am a very strong man and I can attack people and something like that ... I have often asked myself where I have obtained these features from. No one has taught me to be like that. This is a self-defence mechanism worked out by a woman with the help of an instinct. Otherwise I would have been lost. I would not have been able to earn a living and sustain my family. And I am still wearing that mask of a strong woman.

Consequentially this "mask" means that Ketevan's gender identity as a strong woman is not available to her. She uses strength reluctantly as a "self-defence mechanism," and she feels uncomfortable performing this trait typically ascribed to men. Her performance is intimately bound up with questions of economic sustenance and becoming a breadwinner. She provided for her family not because of a desire to take on a new role, but out of the necessity to adapt and take care of her family. While Ketevan is currently not performing the typical or expected gender norms, her implicit idea of what women should be like involves not being the breadwinner and not being strong.

A more complicated and ambiguous discourse emerges when she states that she was able to "sustain" her family through this "mask" of strength because of an instinct. For Ketevan, this instinct is seen to be a natural part of being a woman, and aligns with other accounts of IDPs where the adaptability of women is proclaimed with no corollary attempt to articulate why women are particularly adaptable or why this narrative is so readily relied upon to explain the new role of women.

External Context

From the very beginning of the crisis, the external governance context within which all IDPs functioned was extremely complex. The wide range of institutions involved included Georgian state institutions, Parliament, all key ministries, and local government, as well as non-state actors such as nongovernmental organizations. The international community working in the country comprised donors, humanitarian organizations, private foundations and organizations, and many international organizations (e.g., the European Union and the United Nations). The Orthodox Church gained in visibility, power, and influence. These numerous actors often had contradictory agendas and goals, and they neither communicated well nor coordinated their actions, especially in the early years of the post-conflict period. At the same time, they have exercised tremendous power and control over the everyday lives of IDPs.

From the perspective of the IDPs themselves, Georgian state policies have served to reinforce a sense of displacement (Kabachnik, Mitchneck, and Regulska 2015). IDPs were not allowed to vote in local elections until 2003, and did not have the same access to land or services as the general population. IDPs also continue to have separate schools and health-care sites; this reinforced the double displacement—from their own region and then within Georgia. Since the very first crisis developed in the early 1990s, the state's unclear intentions and its control over the lives of IDPs constitute a form of structural violence, and a violation of their social, economic, and cultural rights. The fact that the conflict in Abkhazia remains unresolved, and that the question of "return" continues to linger, creates a sense of insecurity among IDPs, and this limits their ability to plan for the future and act. The state strategy goals have yet to be met. The Georgian state has rationalized the lack of a consistent, unified, and long-term approach to IDPs by maintaining a discourse that the conflicts will be resolved soon and that the return of IDPs to Abkhazia is the only viable solution to territorial conflict. This stance has perpetuated the crisis, and reinforced the lowly status and poor living conditions of the IDPs.

The women talked about these external conditions, constraints, and uncertainties. Almost all voiced their hope of returning to Abkhazia. One woman stated that among her goals for the future was to return to Abkhazia and reclaim her property and her job. Her words express the tension between her ability to act (her "agency") and the obstacles in her way (the structural forces that impede her ability to reach her goal). Maia claimed, "my goals cannot be implemented by my government"—a statement that suggests that power constraining their implementation lies externally to her motivations. She further declared: "[The implementation of] a goal ... does not depend on me ... I can have a goal, but it may turn out to be unreachable because of circumstances that I cannot control." For these women, the locus of accountability for these circumstances is "the government."[7] Some displaced women see the government as a source of support; as one woman remarked, "I fully trust this government [Noghaideli administration] ... They have done a lot of good." Others have little faith in the government or in particular administrations. Still, they identify "the government" as the locus of structural power that can help or harm them: "The government should stop lying. If it can ensure our return, let them do this or let them tell us directly that we will never return." Indeed, those who know that they will never return, although displaced, will have a more stable and certain future.

Conclusion

The discussion presented here on women's roles and agency in the context of post-conflict displacement and political-economic transformation in Georgia highlights the conditions under which women enact and claim their agency. We might posit that the displacement and political tensions with Russia, which have been pervasive in Georgia since the early 1990s, have created conditions that challenge women's and men's traditional roles and responsibilities, and thus create conditions that favor displaced women's articulation of their agency. Under these circumstances, the new roles can provide displaced women with more decision-making power and freedom to decide how they want to define themselves and their relations with others.

The Georgian case shows that despite their new roles, displaced women continue to define themselves and their actions in relation to their position in the domestic sphere, even as they are also engaged in work activities outside the home. In the context of the family and by means of their extended social networks, Georgian women are creative agents in devising ways to ensure the sustenance and survival of their families under difficult living conditions. After all, the post-conflict period remains unstable. This helps to explain to some degree why Georgian IDP women retain their sense of identity as mothers and housewives, and their desire to maintain a happy family, even as they adopt a new and additional role as the primary family breadwinner.

The disruptions in Georgia as a result of war, displacement, and economic transformation did not result in an entirely new gender order in Georgia, yet these events did rupture gender identities and provided new openings for shifts in gender roles. These openings brought new opportunities for women to claim their agency, but also new calls for a return to so-called "traditional" gender relations. For some Georgian women, the return to "tradition" may be the very enactment of their agency.

Joanna Regulska is a professor in the Gender, Sexuality and Women's Studies Program at University of California Davis, and serves as vice provost and associate chancellor, Global Affairs. She has been working with numerous Georgian institutions since 2002, and conducting research about internally displaced persons (IDPs). In 2011, she received a Doctor Honoris Causa from the Tbilisi State University. She is the author or co-author of seven books (most recently *Women and Gender in Postwar Europe: From Cold War to European Union*, Routledge 2012, co-authored with Bonnie G. Smith) and numerous articles and chapters.

Beth Mitchneck is a professor emerita at the School of Geography and Development at the University of Arizona. She has specialized in migration and economic development in Russia and for over a decade has been working on topics related to displacement and violent conflict in Georgia. Her most recent work focuses on gender, social networks and migration as well as migration policy.

Peter Kabachnik is an associate professor of geography in the Department of Political Science and Global Affairs at the College of Staten Island, The City University of New York (CUNY). He has published on a variety of topics, including Georgian IDPs and discrimination against Roma, Gypsy, and Traveler groups. He is currently working on several research projects examining post-Soviet memory and the memorialized landscape in Georgia, focusing on contemporary understandings of Stalin. He also explores more broadly how personality cults function, how they act as a disciplinary mechanism, and how they engender practices of compliance and resistance.

Notes

The authors would like to acknowledge the assistance of Jeanine White and May Ee Wong in the preparation of this manuscript.
1. For work on Georgian IDPs that illustrates how IDPs are not passive, see Dunn 2012, 2014, and Kabachnik et al. 2013.
2. For more extensive discussion of external context and forces shaping women's agency please see: Dissanayake 1996, Mahmood in Nouraie-Simone, 2005, Niranjana 2001.
3. Figures on the number of IDPs displaced from Abkhazia in the early 1990s vary by source.
4. State strategy outlines two major goals regarding IDPs: (1) to create conditions for the return of IDPs; and (2) to provide decent living conditions for IDPs. http://www.carim-east.eu/media/sociopol_module/Strategy%20on%20IDP-2007-Eng.pdf.
5. Collective centers (CC) are government-allocated accommodations in state or private ownership, usually former hotels or schools.
6. All the names of research participants in this chapter are pseudonyms.
7. Some also blame the Georgian government for the conflict that resulted in their displacement (e.g. Kabachnik, Regulska, and Mitchneck 2012: 132).

References

Brun, C. 2000. "Making Young Displaced Men Visible." *Forced Migration Review* 9 (December): 10–12.
Buck, T., et al. 2000. *Aftermath: Effects of Conflict on Internally Displaced Women in Georgia.* Washington, DC: Center for Development Information and Evaluation, US Agency for International Development.
Chkheidze, K. 2014. "Women's Political Participation during Democratic Transformation: The Case of Georgia." PhD dissertation, Tbilisi State University.
de Waal, T. 2011. *Georgia's Choices: Charting a Future in Uncertain Times.* Washington, DC: Carnegie Endowment for International Peace.
Dissanayake, W. 1996. *Narratives of Agency: Self-making in China, India, and Japan.* Minneapolis: University of Minnesota Press.
Dudwick, N. 2003. "No Guests at Our Table: Social Fragmentation in Georgia." In *When Things Fall Apart: Qualitative Studies of Poverty in the Former Soviet Union,* ed. N. Dudwick et al, 213–57. Washington, DC: The World Bank.
Dunn, E.C. 2012. "The Chaos of Humanitarian Aid: Adhocracy in the Republic of Georgia." *Humanity: An International Journal of Human Rights, Humanitarianism, and Development* 3(1): 1–23.
———. 2014. "Humanitarianism, Displacement, and the Politics of Nothing in Postwar Georgia." *Slavic Review* 73(2): 287–306.
Feischmidt, M., E. Magyari-Vincze and V. Zentai. 1997. *Women and Men in East European Transition: Summer School, Cluj, July 23–28, 1996.* Cluj-Napoca: Editura Fundaţiei pentru Studii Europene.
Gagoshashvili, M. 2008. "Shaping Women's Reproductive Decisions: The Case of Georgia." *Gender and Development* 16(2): 273–85.
Hartsock, N.C.M. 1996. "Community/Sexuality/Gender: Rethinking Power." In *Revisioning the Political: Feminist Reconstructions of Traditional Concepts in Western Political Theory,* ed. N.J. Hirschmann and C. Di Stefano, 27–50. Boulder, CO: Westview Press.
Human Rights House Network. 2012. "Internal Displacement as a Stigma in Georgia." Retrieved 10 May 2016 from http://humanrightshouse.org/Articles/18988.html.

Internal Displacement Monitoring Centre. 2009. "Georgia: IDPs in Georgia Still Need Attention." Retrieved 10 May 2016 from http://www.internal-displacement.org/assets/library/Europe/Georgia/pdf/Georgia-July-2009.pdf.
Kabachnik, P., M. Grabowska, J. Regulska, B. Mitchneck, and O. Mayorova. 2013. "Traumatic Masculinities: The Gendered Geographies of Georgian IDPs from Abkhazia," *Gender, Place, and Culture: A Journal of Feminist Geography* 20(6): 773–93.
Kabachnik, P., B. Mitchneck, O. Mayorova, and J. Regulska. 2014. "The Multiple Geographies of Internal Displacement: The Case of Georgia." *Refugee Survey Quarterly* 33(4): 1–30.
Kabachnik, P., B. Mitchneck, and J. Regulska. 2015. "Return or Integration? Politicizing Displacement in Georgia." In *Security, Democracy and Development in the Southern Caucasus and the Black Sea Region*, ed. G. Nodia and C.H. Stefes, 183–204. Bern: Peter Lang.
Kabachnik, P., J. Regulska, and B. Mitchneck. 2010. "Where and When is Home? The Double Displacement of Georgian IDPs from Abkhazia." *The Journal of Refugee Studies* 23(3): 315–36.
———. 2012. "Displacing Blame: Georgian Internally Displaced Person Perspectives of the Georgia–Abkhazia Conflict," *Ethnopolitics* 11(2): 123–40.
Khan, A. 2002. "Afghan Refugee Women's Experience of Conflict and Disintegration." *Meridians* 3(1): 89–121.
Krasniqi, V. 2007. "Imagery, Gender and Power: The Politics of Representation in Post-War Kosova," *Feminist Review* 86: 1–23.
Mahmood, S. 2005. "Feminist Theory, Agency, and the Liberatory Subject." In *On Shifting Ground: Muslim Women in the Global Era*, ed. F. Nouraie-Simone, 111–52. New York: The Feminist Press at the City University of New York.
Matsuoka, A., and J. Sorenson. 1999. "Eritrean Canadian Refugee Households as Sites of Gender Renegotiation." In *Engendering Forced Migration: Theory and Practice*, ed. D.M. Indra, 218–41. New York and Oxford: Berghahn Books.
Mayorova, O., and B. Mitchneck. 2016. "Geography, Gendered Networks and Well-Being: The Case of Forced Migrant in Georgia." XXXVI Sunbelt Conference of the International Network for Social Network Analysis, 5–10 April, Newport Beach, CA.
McNay, L. 2000. *Gender and Agency: Reconfiguring the Subject in Feminist and Social Theory.* Malden, MA: Blackwell Publishers.
———. 2010. "Feminism and Post-Identity Politics: The Problem of Agency." *Constellations* 17(4): 512–25.
Niranjana, S. 2001. "In the Tracks of Women's Agency." In *Gender and Space: Femininity, Sexualization and the Female Body*, 34–44. London: Sage Publications.
Norwegian Refugee Council / Internal Displacement Monitoring Centre. 2014. "Global Overview 2014: People Internally Displaced by Conflict and Violence – Georgia." Retrieved 10 May 2016 from http://www.refworld.org/docid/5374748414.html.
Riaño-Alcalá, P. 2008. "Journeys and Landscapes of Forced Migration: Memorializing Fear among Refugees and Internally Displaced Colombians." *Social Anthropology* 16(1): 1–18.
Sumbadze, N., and G. Tarkhan-Mouravi. 2005. "Transition to Adulthood in Georgia: Dynamics of Generational and Gender Roles in a Post-totalitarian Society." In *A New Youth? Young People, Generations and Family Life*, ed. C. Leccardi and E. Ruspini, 224–52. Burlington, VT: Ashgate Publishing.
UNDP. 2013. "Public Perceptions on Gender Equality in Politics and Business." Research Report prepared by ACT. Retrieved 10 May 2016 from http://www.ge.undp.org/content/dam/georgia/docs/publications/GE_UNDP_Gender_%20Research_ENG.pdf.
UNHCR. 2015. "2015 UNHCR Subregional Operations Profile – Eastern Europe." Retrieved 10 May 2016 from http://reporting.unhcr.org/node/41?y=2015.
World Bank. 2013. "Supporting the Livelihoods of Internally Displaced Persons in Georgia: A Review of Current Practices and Lessons Learned." Retrieved 10 May 2016 from http://documents.worldbank.org/curated/en/2013/05/17961729/supporting-livelihoods-internally-displaced-persons-georgia-review-current-practices-lessons-learned.

Part III

Identities, Representations, and Resistance

Chapter 10

Images of "The New Woman" in Soviet Georgian Silent Films

Salome Tsopurashvili

In this chapter, I analyze three popular Georgian films from the late 1920s in a discussion of how and in which terms women were represented, and how those representations reflect changes in ideas about femininity in the Soviet context. The Soviet film industry functioned as a significant ideological tool; some argue its most important mission was to "enlighten" what was presumed to be an unenlightened population, and to offer role models for what would become "the New Soviet Man" and "the New Soviet Woman."

The chapter positions the three films in the context of changing norms in Georgian Soviet cinema. In the early to mid-1920s, most cinematic representations of women featured passive heroines situated in melodramatic plots. These films were widely popular among audiences, but were harshly assessed by both Georgian and Russian film critics, many of whom criticized them for being unduly influenced by prerevolutionary Russian and Western films. By the end of the decade, there was a notable shift in the way women were represented in film, as observed in the three films I discuss here, which I argue reflects the Soviet ideological project.

Background

Starting in the early 1920s, cinema was considered a main branch of art, designed to legitimize the revolution, depict the new Soviet system and

---

Notes for this chapter begin on page 170.

way of life, and present models of "the New Soviet Man" and "Woman" respectively (Miller 2010). These desired results and screen representations did not readily appear as intended in Georgian or other Soviet republics' films. A certain Y. Rist, film critic for the publication *Soviet Screen*, remarked in 1925 that the Soviet Union had created a cinema production system such that Moscow produced pictures depicting contemporary life while those in the provinces (Ukraine, Georgia, and Leningrad) were "stewing in the juice of various historical and pseudo-historical productions" (Rist 1925: 2). For the most part, the story lines in these films were taken from classic literary texts that were primarily Russian but occasionally foreign (Western). Featured themes were revolts against the ruling class, and the lives of notorious outlaws depicted as having been forced to lead a brigand life because of the oppressive tsarist and feudal regime, and thereby turned into national social heroes. The crucial task for filmmakers was to provide ideologically "correct" representations.

Across the Soviet Union, film critics focused their attention on how women were represented in these films. For example, Tamara Ignatova, a critic for the publication *Kino Nedelya*, wrote in 1924, in a piece titled "Woman in Soviet Cinematography," that women in Soviet cinema are not portrayed in appropriate roles. Ignatova argued that Russian cinematography does not offer a mirror onto the contemporary Russian woman. Instead of an accurate reflection, it presents a disfigured image of women as either *"batalnaya* heroines" [warrior women featured in civil war films] or innocent peasant girls (Ignatova 1924: 5).

In Georgia, the nature of the criticism and the expressions of dissatisfaction were quite different. Critics complained about the overwhelming exoticization and orientalization of the Eastern republics in film, and they noted the way the historical past was falsified and culture was distorted. One critic for the Georgian journal *The Flag of Art* wrote in 1924 that their "pictures" often did not represent accurately Georgian ways of life, including the way people dressed. The critic attributes this misrepresentation to a form of "cinema production guided by people who are far away from understanding our lives" (Don-Ani 1924: 22). One Russian critic noted about Georgian films: "If we are to believe these films, the peripheral nations of the Soviet Union live like cowboys: they ride horses, and shoot and kidnap women. And women dance in harems and ride horses" (Urazov 1928: 13). The Soviet actress Nato Vachnadze often played female characters in Georgian films, generally depicted as vulnerable, objectified, and passive. In her memoirs, Vachnadze noted her dissatisfaction with the parts she had been given: "I am always playing a passive Georgian woman. It is sad that these roles are so homogenous"

(Tatarashvili 2014). It is notable that Georgia was the third top producer of films in the Soviet Union after Russia and Ukraine, and these films enjoyed huge popularity among audiences in both Georgia and Russia (Youngblood 1992).

The Russian constructivist writer Sergei Tretyiakov (1892–1937) published a letter in the 1928 avant-garde Georgian Futurists journal *Leftism*; it was titled "Let's Not Help our Enemies," and addressed Georgia's State Cinema Industry's kino-workers. The letter encouraged the workers to stop reproducing images of "useless women of the boudoir," and instead suggested giving screen time to the women who are "comrade[s], worker[s] and activist[s]," concluding with the injunction to fight against cinema-eroticism that appeals to the most prurient of interests (Tretyiakov 1928: 56).

At the end of the 1920s, a new phase in Georgian state cinema production began when a new generation of filmmakers and scenarists, many of whom belonged to the Georgian Futurists, brought innovative aesthetics and ideas to cinema production. Some of these films were set during the prerevolutionary period (e.g., *First Cornet Streshnelev*; *Prison Cell 79*) and praised for their innovative directorial approaches. Others dealt with contemporaneous existential issues (e.g., *Saba*; *Youth Wins*), and still others (e.g., *Eliso*) were set in the historical Caucasus; all avoided exoticized representations of the orientalized East. These films were also marked by the appearance of strong, independent women who embodied power and agency in contrast to earlier depictions of women as passive, damsel-in-distress types. Even if not always in contemporaneous settings, the women in these Georgian films fit the image and qualities of the strong "New Soviet Woman" who above all values the public good (revolution, solidarity, society) over the private (maternity, love). Oksana Bulgakowa makes a similar observation regarding Russian film heroines, when discussing Russian films of the 1920s:

> Although many of these films were set in the past, they were still modern; they were concerned with the process of the re-education of the masses, and this did not end when the Bolsheviks came to power, it was only just beginning. That is why the "growth and liberation of consciousness" was so vital, and formed the link between cinema and real life. The purpose of the heroine and that of the plot were identical. (Bulgakowa 1993: 154)

In what follows, I identify "the New Soviet Woman" construct in three aspects: as mother (Zakaria Berishvili's *Prison Cell 79*, 1929), as lover and leader (Nikoloz Shengelaia's *Eliso*, 1928) and as comrade, activist, and citizen (Mikheil Chiaureli's *Saba*, 1929).

The Representation of Woman as Mother in *Prison Cell 79*

On 26 September 1907 almost forty prisoners escaped from the Kutaisi prison through a tunnel dug from a house masked as a shop that stood in front of the prison. The famous female revolutionary Maro Bochoridze, a member of Stalin's "Boevaia Drujina," led the operation (Makharadze 2014). This event is the premise of the revolutionary dramatic film *Prison Cell 79,* directed by Zakaria Berishvili. The film pays tribute to the real event in the name of its heroine: the real person Maro Bochoridze in the film becomes Maro Bochorishvili. Aside from the fact of the prison escape, the rest of the story is imaginary. It describes how Maro Bochorishvili and her group try to save revolutionary prisoners from the trials and tribulations of a hard life, and depicts her confrontation with her son, the prosecutor. Russian critic Lev Shatov offered special praise to the scenarist and the director for successfully combining melodrama with ideological message rooted in the real-life story of the conflict between a revolutionary mother and her tsarist son (Shatov 1930).

The film opens with Maro's husband's death at a factory, caused by management's negligence in not ensuring that safety measures were followed. The story line proceeds with the factory supervisor slapping the shocked Maro who, in a fit of passion, kills him. Consequently, she is arrested and exiled to Siberia. The childless factory owner adopts Maro's now abandoned son, the fact of which the mother is unaware. Years later, upon returning from exile, Maro becomes involved with revolutionary activities; this time the mission is to dig a tunnel to prison cell 79, where the leaders of a workers' strike have been imprisoned and sentenced to death. Maro learns that her son, Akaki, has become a prosecutor, and that his first trial is none other than the workers' strike. She pleads with him to postpone the trial for a day, hoping to enable the revolutionaries enough time to reach cell 79. At first her son agrees, but later changes his mind. During the trial, Maro shoots and kills her son, and is promptly arrested. The next day, the prisoners escape.

This short summary reveals that revolution and family drama are interwoven in the film narrative, and suggests that aspects of the dynamics of revolution may be transpositions of family dynamics. In his psychobiography of the Soviet filmmaker Sergei Eisenstein, the French writer Dominique Fernandez explores the relationship between the filmmaker's Oedipal conflicts and "secret self" and the production of his avant-garde films about revolution (Fernandez 1975). Taking Fernandez's analysis a step further, I suggest that the father conflict as an aspect of the Oedipal conflict and political revolution may be discerned in Berishvili's film. Both revolt against the father in the sense of refusing the "old" social order, traditions, cultural beliefs, and modes of expression, replacing these with something "new." There is a certain correlation between the two, and in the context of the Soviet revolution, the rebellion against the political and artistic symbolic father may not have been coincidental. Vsevolod Pudovkin's classic Soviet avant-garde 1926 film, *Mother,* in which a revolutionary son rebels against both his abusive, patriarchal father and the exploitative, tsarist system (symbolic father), offers such a reading (Mayne 1989). Judith Mayne argues that "some of the dimensions of the Oedipal conflict have been adapted to socialist ends—it is the son who represents a new symbolic order, replacing the corrupt and outmoded order of the father; and the mother–child bond serves the socialist public sphere" (ibid.: 104). During the process, a passive, domesticated mother becomes a politically conscious subject as she sides next to her son and becomes an ally of revolutionaries. The mother is the central figure; her emancipation happens and her revolutionary consciousness grows—not because she is an independent agent but because she is a mother, linked to her son. As Mayne states, "she remains, above and beyond all else, a mother" (ibid.: 105).

I read Berishvili's film in the same psychoanalytical light, which reveals the ways it challenges the "successful resolution" of the Oedipal conflict. In *Prison Cell 79,* the son did not revolt against the father; instead, he perfectly fits in and is an active agent of the system by means of his social position as a prosecutor. The father has become the system and the symbolic order itself, and the son forms a symbiosis with him. This is expressed visually through Akaki's shadow play in the portrait of Nikolas II during the workers' trial (Fig. 10.1). Maro's act of shooting her son can be interpreted as the revenge of the rejected phallic mother who avenges her child who has rejected and betrayed her by means of his forgetting and by breaking his word about postponing the trial. The film also shows a strong, determined woman whose dedication to the revolution enables her to sacrifice her own son, killing him for the sake of the revolution. Even if motherhood had retained a special place in the Soviet order, *Prison Cell 79* challenges its primacy in relation to the revolution and larger social good. This juxtaposition is reminiscent of the story of Pavlik Morozov,[1] in which a rejected, phallic mother, who becomes a symbol of revolution itself, castrates her son as punishment for not rebelling against his father.

Figure 10.1 *Prison Cell 79,* directed by Zakaria Berishvili, 1929 (DVD screen capture)

In *Prison Cell 79*, these tensions are accentuated visually: the rejected mother who embodies social class and the symbolic father who is personified in Nikolas II are juxtaposed in shots of Maro and the tsar's statue, altering their fixed gazes on Akaki, the son, as captured in the screen shots below (Figs. 10.2–10.5).

The court trial scene in the film highlights the tension between the "Law of the Father" and the phallic mother. The symbolic father appears in the courtroom hall in two manifestations: in the form of a statue of Nikolas II and in the immense portrait of the tsar that overhangs the judge's seat. At the moment Akaki fails to keep his promise to his mother, the symbolic father wins. The gendarme announces that "[Justice] is coming," a reference to Maro, who appears in the very next shot dressed in black, walking along a street bathed in whiteness. This shot is followed by a medium shot of the portrait of Nikolas II, which suggests the final struggle between the symbolic father and the forgotten mother is soon to come.

Akaki's shadow falls on the immense portrait of Nikolas II in such a way that Akaki's head replaces that of the tsar (see Fig. 10.1). By means of this visual unification, Akaki is revealed as intertwined with the symbolic father. This shot recurs several times during the prosecutor's speech to the

Figures 10.2–10.5 *Prison Cell 79,* directed by Zakaria Berishvili, 1929 (DVD screen captures)

court, which reinforces the father–son union. Akaki's shadow on the tsar's portrait is held in contrast to Maro's shadow, which is cast first on the white pillars of the court hall and later on the courtroom wall as she enters and moves toward him. The meeting of their eyes appears through shadows: Maro's shadow on the wall stops and the camera moves toward Akaki's, which in turn is cast onto the tsar's portrait. In one dramatic shot, Akaki's gesticulating shadow hand abruptly stops, which suggests the moment he sees his mother. The camera pans to his face, which holds a stupefied expression. He turns around, his back to his mother so as not to see her face. He continues to speak to the court. In the next frame, Akaki's shadow is cast on the portrait, which falls from the wall. People in the courtroom jump up terrified. A gun is shown to fall at Maro's feet. In that moment, the viewer realizes that the mother has shot her son. The prisoners are removed from the court. Maro stands steadily, as a close-up shows the pierced front of the portrait where the bullet that killed Akaki also passed through the head of tsar in the portrait (Fig. 10.6). In this way, Maro has committed a double murder, both real and symbolic. As people are rushing to exit in panic, Maro remains and gazes upon the dead body of her son. Policemen rush in and point their guns at her. She does not move. The frame fades.

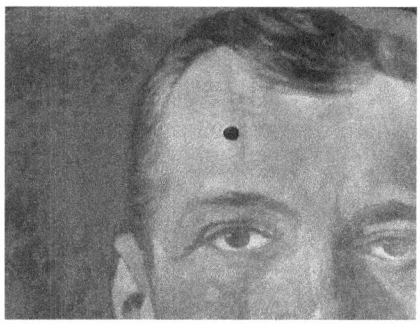

Figure 10.6 *Prison Cell 79*, directed by Zakaria Berishvili, 1929 (DVD screen capture)

Other female characters in the film include the childless factory owner's wife who might represent the sterile condition of the upper classes and the bourgeoisie who, with no heir, have no political future. There is also Akaki's wife as well as Maro's neighbor from whom the heroine learns years later about the fate of her son. As compared to the other female roles in the film, only Maro's character has agency.

Maro is shown to be the active force in the development of the narrative and comes to symbolize the revolution. When she returns from exile, Maro is the one who gathers the revolutionaries at her apartment, having dedicated all her life to revolutionary activities. That she represents the revolution itself is re-emphasized in the closing sequence, which opens with prisoners in the cell who are again in waiting. After speaking with the court representatives, the prison warden announces the emperor's decision to execute the arrested workers by hanging. As the graves are being dug in the prison yard, the gendarmes go to the prison cell. They find it empty. The next scene cuts to the portrait of Nikolas II with the bullet hole in his head, which suggests the graves are being dug to bury the old system. The warden jumps into the hole from which the prisoners have escaped. The camera pans to the irons left behind by the escaped prisoners. A sequence of recurring scenes of hangings and of graves suggest that the gallows are built and the graves are dug for the police and other representatives of the imperial order, and for the whole symbolic order itself.

The Representation of Woman as Lover and Leader in *Eliso*

Eliso, written by Sergei Tretyiakov and Nikoloz Shengelaia, is based on a Georgian classic short story by Alexandre Kazbegi in 1882 under the same title. The original story depicts the fate of lovers in the 1860s, the time of the massive and brutal deportation of the Chechens from North Caucasus. Before releasing *Eliso*, Nikoloz Shengelaia published in *Leftism* an essay titled "Some Preliminary Remarks about the Film *Eliso*" in which he stated that the aim of Tretyiakov and himself was not to produce an adaptation of Kazbegi's "Eliso" (1928). They were interested in the story's main objective to "bring to light the aggressive (colonial) politics of the old regime and its results" (Shengelaia 1928: 57). Shengelaia writes that in preparing for producing the film, the screenwriters studied the locality of Chechnya. They found that Kazbegi had "disfigured the historical truth of the colonial politics for the sake of literary aesthetics ... he did not consider it necessary to include historical truth" (ibid.). Shengelaia claims that the filmmakers studied the historical documents and the secret archive of Tergi's regional governor, accessible only after the revolution. The dramatic conflict in *Eliso* was directly influenced by this research: "We introduced into the script the living conditions and actions of the people ... thus, the film is not a literal translation of "Eliso" ... We took a non-exoticizing approach to depicting the Caucasus" (ibid.).

The plot centers on the love between a Chechen woman (Eliso) and a Mokheve man (Vazhia). In the short story "Eliso," Vazhia's and Eliso's fathers are killed by the Cossacks when they try to escape together. In the film version, Vazhia and Eliso promise each other they will stay together even though Astamir, an elder in the village of Verdi and Eliso's father, forbids Vazhia from marrying Eliso. The key Russian Cossacks want to exile the Chechens in order to appropriate their land. The Russians enlist the help of a Chechen traitor and enemy to Astamir to trick the villagers into signing a document that essentially authorized their own displacement from the land. Vazhia learns about the Cossack's plan, and in an act of solidarity with Eliso's people, confronts the Russian general in charge of the deportation. Vazhia is too late; the Chechens have already been exiled and are on their way to Turkey. Astamir insists the people leave the village untouched. Eliso defies her father when she sneaks out of the traveling group, returns to the village and burns it. The next day, a young mother from the village dies on the journey into exile. When Vazhia reaches the exiled group, he asks Astamir for permission to join them. Astamir refuses and Eliso chooses to stay with her father and her people, but not before she asks her lover to take the child of the dead woman back to the town of Mozdok for safekeeping.

The film *Eliso* transforms an individual tragedy into a tragedy of the masses by focusing not on the misfortune of the lovers, but rather on the brutalized fate of the Chechen minorities at the hand of imperial power. In a rhythmic montage of scenes, the film portrays alliances between two minority groups represented by Eliso and Vazhia, unity among the Chechens who are shown to collectively build a house for a poor widow, and their solidarity in resisting the Cossacks. Their collective tragedy, solidarity, and resistance are dramatically portrayed in the film's climax—a scene in which the exiled villagers mourn the woman's death with the *lezginka*, a traditional Caucasian dance that here represents group catharsis and resurrection.

My focus here is on Eliso's character. Eliso is the film's protagonist even as Shengelaia privileges the tragic story of the collective over individualized drama. Film critic Olgha Tabukashvili argues this point, noting that certain character archetypes are detailed and well developed in this film (Tabukashvili 1974; see also Gray 2014). Eliso is drastically different from all other heroines in Eastern-thematic films. She is depicted as a self-determined woman who is not anybody's victim and makes her own decisions. As Tabukashvili notes, Eliso is the first character in Georgian film to be "strong, and full of dignity and selflessness. She puts public interests above private ones, submitting her individual wants to addressing the needs of the collective" (Tabukashvili 1974: 55). Eliso appears as the master of her body, her affections, and her fate. She chooses Vazhia in defiance of her father's wishes, and commits to her lover that her father's refusal will not influence her own decision. In the act of burning down the village, Eliso articulates her ability to make autonomous decisions. As a woman taking action in a form that is traditionally masculine, Eliso transcends gender expectations. Thus the hero, Eliso, preserves the dignity of her father and her people by means of this act.

Eliso is revealed as a true leader, having power in relation to others as well as within herself. In one scene, the Chechens wrongly blame Vazhia for their exile. Eliso intervenes, placing herself between Vazhia and the growing crowd of people by removing her scarf and throwing it on the ground, a gesture with specific cultural meaning among the various ethnic groups in the region (Figs. 10.7–10.9). No matter the reason, warriors must cease the battle when a woman removes her scarf and throws it between the fighters. Eliso shouts to the hostile group, "It is not his fault! You yourselves signed the document." By means of her powerful and protective body posture, Eliso prevents a fight brought on by the divisive tactics of the imperial forces.

In contrast to other heroines, Eliso is the one who saves a man (Vazhia). In that moment, Vazhia is effectively re-gendered as female, which Slavic scholar Richard Beach Gray also notes occurs later when Eliso gives Vazhia the child to protect and save (Gray 2014). Gray compares Eliso to the biblical figure Moses, referring to her as "a new patriarch of the Chechen community" (ibid.: 8).

In the end, Eliso refuses Vazhia because of her new sense of belonging to the nation. She is reconnected to her roots through the tragedy of the small village Verdi, the exile of its population, and Eliso's own participation in the resistance, including burning down the village. In the original silent film, Eliso's words of refusal appear in the intertitle as "I was living happily with my people. Let me be unhappy with my people as

Figures 10.7–10.9 *Eliso*, directed by Nikoloz Shengelaia, 1928 (DVD screen captures)

well" (Tabukashvili 1974: 54–55). In 1987, Nikoloz Shengelaia's son, Eldar Shengelaia, and Leila Mikeladze restored the film, and changed the intertitle for that sequence. In the new version, Eliso is made to refuse Vazhia with the words, "No, I cannot leave father and my people." In my view, the original is more definitive in capturing the idea that public, social demands supersede individual desires; also, the statement incipiently contains the idea of Georgian nationalism. This resonates with the archetypal image of the Georgian woman who is expected to sacrifice personal happiness (in the form of children and husband) to the nation and nationalist ideals.

The Representation of Woman as Comrade, Activist, and Citizen in *Saba*

Mikheil Chiaureli's *Saba* was a product of the Cultural Revolution that took place during the period of Stalin's five-year-plan between 1928 and 1932. As the Bolshevist version of the Enlightenment, the Cultural Revolution aimed to construct "the New Soviet Man" and "the New Soviet Woman," thereby transforming the people of the Soviet Union. Even though the concept of the "cultural revolution" when first invoked by Lenin referred to competing with the West in terms of technological advancements, by the end of the 1920s it represented utopian notions about culture and politics, including a transformed way of life that was both technological and moral (Kenez 2009). It implied a "complete break with the past," including women's emancipation from patriarchal strictures as well as the eradication of excessive alcohol use, which the Bolsheviks saw "as one of the most troublesome and intractable aspects of … prerevolutionary working-class culture" (Transchel 2006: 74). Slogans like "Alcohol is our Class Enemy" and "Alcohol is the Enemy of the Cultural Revolution" were widely disseminated in the press and on propaganda posters to emphasize the point (Tsopurashvili 2016).

Saba specifically addresses this problem. Shot in Tbilisi in 1929, it was the first film situated in the contemporaneous era, and the only one during the decade that featured an urban woman as comrade. The film depicts the story of an alcoholic Tbilisi tramway driver named Saba, who wastes his salary on buying alcohol to drink with his friends.

At the start of the silent film, Saba is shown trying to resist his friends and coworkers. But they are very persistent, practically dragging him to the tavern by force. When drunk, Saba becomes violent. He beats his wife Veriko and his young son Vakthang, who is portrayed as a pioneer gifted with engineering skills. Personal scandals related to his drinking habits follow Saba, which leads to his being fired from his job. Veriko divorces him, having been encouraged to do so by Olgha, a leader of the Young Pioneers League, the Communist Party's organization for children. At school, Olgha saw that the young Vakthang had been beaten by his father, and is a firsthand witness to Saba's acts of domestic violence. Olgha's intervention signals the entrance of the public realm into the private realm.

Saba is shown becoming increasingly desperate. In one critical scene, Veriko refuses to reconcile with her husband. Saba proceeds to the tavern where he steals the tramway key from a former coworker. Hijacking the tram and driving it recklessly, Saba accidently hits and injures Vakthang, who had been searching tavern by tavern for his father, and who had heroically tried to stop the tram. Saba is arrested. The viewer enters the court for Saba's trial and sees its hallowed halls decorated with anti-drinking posters and placards. Hanging in the center of the hall is the poster that reads, "Alcohol is the Enemy of the Cultural Revolution." As this is a public trial, Saba's case is presented before his coworkers. Details of Saba's domestic life are brought up at the trial, including in Olgha's testimony. The film's narrator speaks for the factory committee representative, who exclaims: "Today we must try not only Saba, but the old world as a whole. Alcohol is our class enemy, which ruins millions of people." In this moment, Saba's case becomes an allegory; alcohol stands as a signifier of the evils of the prerevolutionary order. As his lawyer defends him, the whole community takes Saba's side, realizing that the entire collective must be held responsible for the ways of the past—including Veriko and the injured Vakthang, who appear unexpectedly during the trial. After speaking to the court, Veriko rushes to Saba and holds him along with Vakthang. At that moment, everyone crowds around them; it is not only Vakthang and Veriko who are embracing Saba, but the whole community.

The film ends with the Young Pioneers participating in a demonstration against alcohol. The parade is melodramatic, with the pioneers carrying a coffin in which lies a liquor bottle. The young protesters carry placards damning alcohol. Olgha gives a fiery speech, as do other young pioneers, including Vakthang, who dramatically shakes his bandaged, injured arm. Now transformed, Saba watches the demonstration from the vantage point of the tram and sees Vakthang's message on his placard, "Father, do not drink." In this shot, the viewers glimpse the future represented by Vakthang, and the present represented by Saba, once corrupted by the past but now meeting on common ground. The people, damaged by a corrupt social order that no longer exists, are now rehabilitated, cured, and purified, and able to engage as social beings.

Saba is well known and generally characterized as an anti-alcohol film. It can also be seen as an anti–domestic violence film, although the words "domestic violence" are never invoked and it is never named as a separate problem. The script explicitly connects excessive drinking to what we know as domestic violence, exposing a worker's domestic life and the political effort to address both social problems. Such a coupling suggests that domestic violence would not exist without alcohol—the enemy of socialism as it corrupts the worker. While it is tempting to discuss *Saba* in these terms, given the stated aim of the narrative, my interest here is in examining how "the New Soviet Woman" is represented in and serves the narrative of the film.

The two main female characters are Veriko, Saba's wife, and Olgha, a leader of the Young Pioneers League. Veriko suffers in the domestic realm while Olgha is an agent of the public sphere who appropriately intervenes into that family-domestic space. Olgha personifies the public realm, embodying woman as an active participant in society. Her intervention does not bring immediate results, and requires persistence in order for social transformation to succeed.

When Olgha intervenes, Veriko welcomes her. Social hierarchy does not differentiate the women—both are identified as early twentieth-century working-class women. Their common "modernity" is marked by the same short style of haircut. In all other regards, these two female figures stand at different ends of the spectrum in terms of agency, power, and position. Whereas Veriko is weak, Olgha is strong, a dichotomy that is also expressed in their physical representations. Olgha—more robust and rough—appears stereotypically masculine, while the slim, tender, and vulnerable Veriko appears stereotypically feminine. They also inhabit contrasting locations in terms of their occupations. Olgha, a leader of the Young Pioneers League, is a social activist, whereas Veriko earns a living as a laundress—a traditionally female, domestically centered, laboring-for-others occupation.

These attributes are highlighted in body language, and by camera angles that highlight the gendered contrasts. For example, in a scene that features Olgha and Veriko in conversation, Olgha is shown from a low-angle, medium shot, using what Bulgakowa (*Factory of Gestures* 2008) calls phallic gestures that emphasize her powerfulness and authority (Fig. 10.10). In contrast, Veriko is shown from a high angle, close up, exposing her feminine passivity that indicates her powerlessness and oppression (Fig. 10.11). In a scene composed of multiple shots in which both women are waiting for Saba to appear, they are shown within the same frame, one behind the other. Olgha is in front; Veriko is behind, a smaller presence with her head hanging low (Fig. 10.12). This scene endures for a long fifteen seconds, with no substantive change in the imagery (Figs. 10.13 and 10.14): Olgha remains in front, concentrating, absorbing knowledge by reading, and in this way engaging a larger social sphere. Veriko remains

Figures 10.10–10.14 *Saba,* directed by Mikheil Chiaureli, 1929 (DVD screen captures)

in the same powerless, oppressed position, her head hung low, or eyes staring despairingly into space.

In *Saba*, Veriko is the iconic "damsel in distress." Her vulnerable and powerless position is depicted through cinematic language: when she is alone in the frame, the camera captures her from a high angle or covers her face entirely—such as in the tavern scene after she has been beaten publicly by her husband (Figs. 10.15–10.18). Veriko is not saved by a "knightly" figure but by Olgha, herself the target of Saba's violence. In

Figures 10.15–10.18 *Saba,* directed by Mikheil Chiaureli, 1929 (DVD screen captures)

contrast to Veriko, Olgha is never victimized. By providing Veriko with assistance, encouragement, and support, Olgha stands by Veriko, representing her interest in forging a bond of female solidarity.

With her masculine features and gestures, and her feminine acts of caring and supporting, Olgha is an androgynous agent of the public realm. She captures the image of the modern, "New Soviet Woman" who embodies full agency and independence. Even so, the film never fully escapes from encoding femininity with weakness and passivity, and masculinity with strength and agency.

Conclusion

The three silent films discussed in this chapter, produced in the latter half of the 1920s, reflect an ideological move to the left by the directors and screenwriters of the period. These works stand in contrast to those produced in the early 1920s by a previous generation of filmmakers who the avant-garde considered prerevolutionary and "bourgeois," and against whom the new generation rebelled (Amirejibi 1990: 82). No matter their historical time or geographic setting in Georgia, each of the three films discussed in this chapter present ideas about "the New Soviet Woman" as a strong, self-willed and active agent of social change.

In *Prison Cell 79, Eliso,* and *Saba,* key female protagonists are neither victimized nor objectified in the portrayals or in the camera work. They have agency and possess gaze. As E. Ann Kaplan observes, when a woman becomes a beholder of the gaze—in other words, when she gains power—she loses certain feminine characteristics, a process that corresponds to the above-mentioned films (Kaplan 2000). It is striking that, in general, the characters achieve full agency at the expense of traditional feminine attributes such as maternity, affection, love, sexuality, and beauty. They tend to become active agents denying their femininity. Moreover, this denial tends to be made in the interests of the revolution, the nation, and/or the common good. It is notable that in these films, femininity is not redefined as something positive and powerful; instead women acquire agency by adopting normative masculinity.

Salome Tsopurashvili holds a doctorate in gender studies from Tbilisi State University, Georgia, where she teaches graduate students at the Institute for Gender Studies. She was a returning fellow of the Academic Fellowship Program of the Open Society Foundations (2010–2015). Her thesis, "Women's Representations in 1920s Georgian Soviet Silent Cinema: Modifications, Agency and Social Class," examines themes of orientalization, class, and women's emancipation in 1920s Georgian Soviet silent films.

Note

1. As the story goes, Pavlik Morozov was a 13-year-old dedicated communist and pioneer who supported Stalin's collectivization of farms (the story dates from 1932). He denounced his father to the officials for corruption, and was later killed by his family. Even though the veracity of the story is not certain, Morozov was an actual person who was killed and became a mythic figure in the Soviet Union.

References

Amirejibi, A. 1990. *Screen of Times*. Tbilisi: Khelovneba.
Bulgakowa, O. 1993. "The Hydra of the Soviet Union: The Metamorphosis of the Soviet Film Heroine." In *Red Women on the Silver Screen: Soviet Women and Cinema from the Beginning to the End of the Communist Era*, ed. L. Attwood, 149–174. London: Pandora Press.
Don-Ani. 1924. "Cinema and its Development." *Flag of Art* 1: 20–22.
Factory of Gestures: Body Language in Film, 2008. [DVD]. Stanford: Stanford Humanities Lab. Directed by Oksana Bulgakowa.
Fernandez, D. 1975. *Eisenstein*. Paris: Grasset.
Gray, B. 2014. "Nikoloz Shegngelaia's *Eliso* (1928) and Construction of Soviet Past," Association for Slavic, East European and Eurasian Studies conference, San Antonio, 20–23 November.
Ignatova, T. 1924. "Woman in Soviet Cinematography." *Kino Nedelya* 47: 5.
Kaplan, E.A. 2000. "Is the Gaze Male?" In *Feminism and Film: Oxford Readings in Feminism*, ed. E.A. Kaplan, 119–138. Oxford: Oxford University Press.
Kenez, P. 2009. *Cinema and Soviet Society: From the Revolution to the Death of Stalin*. London: I.B. Tauris.
Makharadze, I. 2014. *History of Georgian Silent Film*. Tbilisi: Bakur Sulakauri Publishing House.
Mayne, J. 1989. *Kino and the Woman Question: Feminism and Soviet Silent Film*. Columbus: Ohio State University Press.
Miller, J. 2010. *Soviet Cinema: Politics and Persuasion under Stalin*. London: I.B. Tauris.
Rist, Y. 1925. "Past and Present." *Soviet Screen* 3: 2.
Shatov, L. 1930. "Prison Cell 79." *Kino* 2 (June): 7.
Shengelaia, N. 1928. "Several Preliminary Notes about Film *Eliso*." *Leftism* 2: 57.
Tabukashvili, O. 1974. *Nikoloz Shegenlaia*. Tbilisi: Khelovneba.
Tatarashvili, T. 2014. "Nato Vachnadze." Retrieved on 4 April 2015 from http://www.feminism-boell.org/ka/2014/06/04/nato-vachnaze.
Transchel, K. 2006. *Under The Influence: Working-Class Drinking, Temperance, and Cultural Revolution in Russia, 1895–1932*. Pittsburgh: University of Pittsburgh Press.
Tretyiakov, S. 1928. "Let's Not Help the Enemies." *Leftism* 2: 55–56.
Tsopurashvili, S. "Modifications of Women's Representations in 1920s Georgian Soviet Silent Films: Orientalisation, Agency, Class." PhD dissertation. Tbilisi State University.
Urazov, I. 1928. "What's on the Screens?" *Soviet Screen* 5: 13.
Youngblood, D.J. 1992. *Movies for the Masses: Popular Cinema and Soviet Society in the 1920s*. Cambridge: Cambridge University Press.

Chapter 11

Gender Equality
Still a Disputed Value in Georgian Society

Nana Sumbadze

Since the dissolution of the Soviet Union in 1991, Georgia has undergone a succession of revolutions, internal wars, and armed conflicts, and a major change in its political and economic system. The twin crises of economic shrinkage and inflation brought on by the dissolution of the Soviet Union resulted in high rates of unemployment across the former Soviet Union, including Georgia (Wyzan 1995: 116). The state and welfare system was incapable of addressing people's basic needs. This led people to search for alternative means of sustaining themselves and their families. Georgian women took the earnings lead in families: they accepted jobs far below their qualification levels or became economic migrants. Women were drawn into relatively unskilled, informal-sector jobs such as street vending (selling goods they had purchased in Turkey), babysitting, and house cleaning; or, as a last resort, leaving the country for similar jobs abroad (CRRC 2014: 7). We might expect that as women engaged in these economic activities, attitudes and beliefs about gender roles may have changed and the power structure of the family reshaped.

Gender equality is one of the most disputed issues in contemporary Georgia. In this chapter I explore attitudes towards gender equality in Georgia, and assert that popular resistance to equality between the sexes in Georgia is rooted in patriarchal ideologies and values.

Equality and inequality can be observed and estimated in both the public and private realms, and reflected in the possibilities for exercising human rights, equal opportunities, and responsibilities. Since gender roles are socially constructed, they may in many respects differ from one society to another as well as from one historical time to another, even as there are universal sex differences and biologically determined functions (Parsons 1965: 36–39).

Gender roles are pervasive in all aspects of life experiences. They are both descriptive, specifying typical gender-related behavior, and prescriptive, defining desirable aspects of women and men (Wood and Eagly 2010: 632). In Georgia, gender divisions conform with a worldwide belief pattern in which the functions of main breadwinner and decision maker are roles allocated to men, and the function of family caretaker is the role allocated to women (Narayan 2000: 181).

Lopez-Claros and Zahidi define gender equality as the "stage of human social development at which rights, responsibilities and opportunities of individuals will not be determined by the fact of being male or female" (Lopez-Claros and Zahidi 2005: 1). Equality implies having equal rights in both public and private spheres. The Constitution of Georgia upholds the principle of equal rights for men and women, and the legislature has passed pro-gender egalitarian laws including "On Gender Equality" (2010) and "On the Elimination of all Forms of Discrimination" (2014). The Gender Inequality Index (GII) measures inequalities in reproductive health, empowerment, and economic status, the three major areas of human development. Georgia's GII ranking for 2014 was 77th out of 188 countries (UNDP 2015: 221). According to the Global Gender Gap Index that measures gender-based gaps across economics, politics, education, and health, Georgia is ranked 82nd out of 145 countries (World Economic Forum 2014). These rankings correspond to the Georgian population's gender perceptions. According to the results of one national survey, less than a quarter of Georgians (25 percent of men, and 21 percent of women) think that there is gender equality in the country (CRRC 2014).

The findings presented in this chapter are based on qualitative research I have conducted ("the Teachers Study") as well as on secondary sources (e.g., from the Georgian Department of Statistics, World Values Surveys, and other surveys carried out by various organizations in the country). The aim of the Teachers Study was to gain insight into the implications of gender equality; I chose teachers as respondents based on my assumption that teachers function as transmitters of culture. The study involved eighteen in-depth interviews with teachers (nine women and nine men) employed in public and private schools in Tbilisi. The questions in the interview guide were phrased in such a way as to evoke widespread practices and attitudes, rather than personal experiences, in an effort to focus on the normative dimension of gender equality.

Results of my research show that seventeen out of the eighteen respondents overtly supported gender equality. They viewed women's labor-force participation, engagement in politics, and the performance of domestic chores as the marks of equality. Five respondents understood gender equality in terms of division of responsibilities and equal decision-making in the home. For five of those interviewed, violence against women, privileging men over women in the church, and barring women from high-level political and occupational positions, were manifestations of gender inequality. Despite their declared belief in equality, respondents tended to endorse attitudes supportive of male supremacy, as indicated by this quote from one respondent: "Equality," the respondent remarked, "is manifested in the fact that a woman works and a man *lets her work*, that a woman's words are respected at home and at work equally" (emphasis mine).

Eight men and five women in the study believed there is gender equality in Georgia. Also, eight of those interviewed (four men and four women) placed importance on traditional gender roles. As one respondent put it: "Men and women should not be equal. Men should have their functions, women theirs. But nowadays women take the men's load on themselves, and the male functions decreased in importance somehow." Two respondents invoked the Holy Scriptures to justify their endorsement of a patriarchal system. They tended to naturalize gender inequality and hierarchy in the family. As one respondent explained, "In the Holy Scriptures, whenever father and mother are mentioned, father is mentioned first. This must be for some reason."

Nearly all (seventeen) respondents in my study believed girls and boys have equal access to education. Findings from a 2014 study reveal that less than half of Georgian men (46 percent) and women (44 percent) believed women and men have equal opportunities to succeed in any field (CRRC 2014). In terms of education, boys (52 percent in 2014 / 54 percent in 2015) slightly outnumber girls (47 percent / 45 percent) in terms of the number of years spent in school and vocational education centers. There are more girls (55 percent) than boys (45 percent) attaining higher levels of education (National Statistical Department of Georgia 2015: 26). Most of the teachers in my study believed girls and boys should be treated equally in the classroom. However, six of the interviewed teachers acknowledged they treat girls and boys differently, which they justified with gender stereotypes. As one teacher noted: "It's an unwritten law that boys have different brains, different attitudes. I forgive laziness in boys, but not in girls. I tell the girls, you need to work harder as you will be mothers and should help your children with homework." Another remarked on differential treatment of students by sex: "We tell girls to be modest and to respect boys." It is notable that these remarks stand against the fact that girls perform better than boys in standardized university entry exams (Sumbadze 2015: 19).

There is a considerable gender gap in average monthly salaries in Georgia, with men earning on average 408 USD, while women earn 257 USD (National Statistical Department of Georgia 2015: 54). This income gap is due to both horizontal and vertical segregation. Women are more concentrated in low-income professions, and are much less likely than men to be found in high-income positions. Women are also more likely than men to be employed in the informal sector. Respondents in my study perceived women as very hard working, and believed there are increasing opportunities for women in employment. As one respondent noted: "In the past, women tried not to be involved fully in work. They were not striving for career advancement, as their prime concern was with family. Nowadays, with the availability of nannies, mothers go to work, even if they pay more to nanny than is their salary."

In terms of women's participation in politics, women comprise only 11 percent of Georgian parliamentarians, and an equally insignificant proportion of women hold positions in local self-governing entities (12 percent). As of December 2014, three out of nineteen cabinet ministers were women (16 percent); and 15 percent of deputy ministers were women. Women comprise over half (51 percent) of all judges in Georgia. Among the country's ambassadors, 10 percent are women (National Statistical Department of Georgia 2015: 67). Respondents in my survey explained the scarcity of women in Georgian politics as reflecting women's inherent "weaknesses" (four respondents), a lack of male support (three respondents), women's lack of desire to become leaders (two respondents), and financial considerations (two respondents).

Power and Resources

Gender equality is most clearly expressed in distribution of power among men and women. In public life, power is mostly reflected in hierarchies. Due to being employed in high positions and being more involved in politics, in the public realm men possess much more power as compared to women. Power in domestic life is less apparent and is not legally determined. It manifests itself in freedom of movement and time use, spending, and decision making.

According to the "Generations and Gender Survey" (Badurashvili, Kapanadze, and Tsiklauri 2010: 23), women and men report having an equal say over decisions concerning shopping for everyday needs, spending, leisure, and children's upbringing, while men's power considerably exceeds women's in decisions about employment arrangements. Women's economic independence increases her power in the family. Findings suggest that the impact of women's employment and hence her share in contributing to family income on her decision power is important. Equality seems to be more widespread in families where women are employed. The results are in line with cross-country comparisons, which demonstrate that women's increased involvement in the labor market is linked with an increase in egalitarian attitudes in the society (Seguino 2007: 1).

A majority of respondents in my study favored normatively equal power in decision making on family matters. At the same time, nine believed that "the final say should be the man's prerogative." As one respondent explained: "When there is a disagreement, it's not good that only the woman's words matter. This diminishes respect to the man. Family is a hierarchical institution, whether we like this or not. And the strength is behind the man, and he has to have a say." Another respondent purported to be in support of gender equality, but when it comes to family decision making she believed that "men should have some kind of supremacy, and should not be ridiculed."

Power rests on resources. These resources can be tangible (e.g., money and possessions) or intangible (e.g., information, contacts, affection). In public life, women hold fewer material resources than men. In 2014, women owned 32 percent of the newly registered businesses in Georgia (National Statistical Department of Georgia 2015: 59). Men hold more tangible resources, and women more intangible ones. Men's command over tangible resources determines their choice of exercising power—in a direct and authoritative manner; in contrast, women try to influence decisions through indirect ways—accommodation and dependence. Affective power rests with women. Their emotional connection with their children is a resource that is often commanded by women (Sumbadze 2006: 324). In Georgian society, mothers and children tend to form a stronger union than do spouses, or fathers and children. According to my respondents, women often exploit their ties with children in bargaining with their husbands, thereby exercising affective power in their marital relations. In contrast, men tend to rely on money and muscle power to exert their will.

Division of Labor in the Home

More than on anything else, family responsibilities rest on gender roles. "Time poverty" is a major issue for women—women worldwide spend more time on household duties and childcare than men (World Bank 2011: 21). According to the CRRC survey, over half of Georgian men (55 percent) and women (59 percent) believe women cannot be as successful in a career as men because of household responsibilities; a large proportion

(79 percent of men, and 76 percent of women) consider that it is difficult for women to combine household duties with work outside the home (CRRC 2014).

Overall, men's involvement in household duties in Georgia is rather low. According to results of one survey, 24 percent of chores are done by men, compared to 46 percent performed by women, 15 percent done by spouses together, and 15 percent by others (Badurashvili, Kapanadze, and Tsiklauri 2010). A majority of respondents in my study supported ideas about the gender division of labor in the family, but their opinions differed on the extent to which household tasks should be shared between husband and wife. Only two of the eighteen respondents believed that both parents should participate in the upbringing of their children. One respondent believed that a sharing of household tasks makes sense: "It should not be like you are a woman and so should stand at the gas cooker or clean the house. Why should men not do these things?" However, twelve respondents approved of the gender division of labor in the household. As one woman said: "A woman should have her role, and a man his. Neither should take the other's role." Another remarked: "Men should do men's work, and women women's work, but they should [also] help each other."

If equality is reflected in the exercise of human rights, power, opportunities, and responsibilities equally enjoyed by both genders, then Georgian society is marked by gender inequality. Women and men have similar access to education, but there is inequality in the types of jobs they are able to get (men tend to get the better jobs), and thus in employment compensation. Few women can be found among Georgia's political leadership, or in high-level positions. In the private realm, preference is expressed to have men as decision makers. The traditional division of responsibilities is still preferred. Notwithstanding the fact that many women do now take on traditionally male responsibilities, men do not respond by fulfilling obligations ascribed to women.

Changes in Attitudes toward Gender Equality

Slowly but steadily, Georgian society is moving toward gender equality as indicated by the results of the World Values Survey (WVS) carried out in Georgia in 1996, 2009, and 2014. The 2014 WVS study revealed that 65 percent of the population subscribed to the idea that having a job is the best way for women to be independent. Results by age and gender suggest that women and the younger generation are spearheading changes in attitudes toward gender equality in Georgia. In most cases, more women and younger respondents subscribe to egalitarian attitudes.

All respondents in the WVS study agreed that important changes have occurred since Georgia became an independent nation. They pointed out that women have become more active both in private and public domains. Changes are visible in the streets, with a considerable increase in the number of women at the wheel, as well as in the media, the labor market, and politics. Respondents perceived that more women are employed in high positions, that they have gained more independence, that they have become stronger, and that their influence in society has increased. They perceive the greatest change in the family power structure in households, where women have become the main breadwinners. However, they have gained their power at the expense of having to take on the extra load of providing for their families, often having to go abroad in search of work and leave their families behind. While women have taken traditionally male responsibilities, men have not responded in the same manner, leaving women to fulfill both the traditionally ascribed roles of caring and homemaking as well as providing for their families.

Among respondents in my study, most believed that household work has become more evenly distributed by gender. Only one believed that nothing has changed, while most talked about women's growing power and autonomy in the home, which they believed is a positive change even though it has some negative consequences. Notable among the difficulties for women who gain more independence in the home are their heavier workloads—and for those who work abroad, estrangement from their families. Women gaining power is often twinned with men losing power. Unemployed men who cannot provide for their families can lose their social purpose, power, self-respect, and the respect of others. As one respondent in my study observed: "In many families, men have lost their role. Women have taken the load of providing for the families. Many men do not have money and ask their wives to give it to them every day. Children see that their mother has money and their father does not. As a consequence, the father loses his authority in the children's eyes." Another respondent, who disapproved of the changes over the last two decades, remarked: "Values changed. If before you could not separate child from mother, nowadays mothers who are in high positions leave children in the hands of nannies or send them abroad, and children are not brought up under parent's supervision anymore." In terms of "gender equality," one respondent sees progress, but "we are not there yet, and won't be able to get there easily." Even as some note positive changes that can result from gender equality, both men and women fear this change might go too far and may result in the replacement of "male supremacy" with "female supremacy."

Conclusion

This review of existing data on gender equality and the results of my qualitative study of teachers' attitudes suggest a shift in attitudes toward gender equality in Georgia. Even as respondents in my study openly declared belief in egalitarian ideals, their attitudes and behaviors often revealed traditional gender beliefs and discriminative behavior. These findings suggest that the country still has a long way to go before it attains gender parity.

Survey data suggest that women and younger people are steering the change process. There seems to be more acceptance of the notion of gender equality in employment and politics than within the domestic realm. This is in part due to current economic realities, which drive more women into the workforce even as there is high unemployment among men. The greatest resistance to the idea of gender equality seems to be rooted in a fear that male supremacy will lose out to female supremacy. Even as gender equality remains a disputed value, it is certain that attitudes, ideas, and ideologies, brought to Georgians by means of the media, global networking, emerging economic realities, international organizations operating in the country, and requirements of international treaties signed by Georgia, will continue to see change.

Nana Sumbadze is a professor of psychology at Tbilisi State University, and co-director of the Institute for Policy Studies. She holds a PhD in social sciences from Leiden University, and is author of approximately eighty publications on gender, public policy, social and human capital, interpersonal relationships, forced migration, education, and disability.

References

Badurashvili, I., E. Kapanadze, and Sh. Tsiklauri. 2010. "Generations and Gender Survey in Georgia." II wave Report. Tbilisi: Georgian Centre of Population Research / UNFPA.

CRRC (Caucasus Research Resource Center). 2014. NDI: Women's Political Participation in Georgia, 2014. Retrieved on 15 October 2015 from www.caucasusbarometer.org./en/no2014ge.

———. 2013. Caucasus Barometer 2013. Retrieved on 12 August 2015 from www.caucasusbarometer.org./cb2015.

———. 2008. "Migration and Return in Georgia 2007." Retrieved on 25 September 2015 from crrccenters.org/2054..

Freedom House. 2015. "Freedom in the World, 2015." Retrieved on 4 January 2016 from https://freedomhouse.org/report/freedom-world/freedom-world-2015#.WPE0747_qYU.
Lopez-Claros, A., and S. Zahidi. 2005. "Women's Empowerment: Measuring the Global Gender Gap." Geneva: World Economic Forum.
Narayan, D. 2000. *Voices of the Poor: Can Anyone Hear Us?* New York: Oxford University Press.
National Statistical Department of Georgia. 2015. "Woman and Man in Georgia: Statistical Publication" (in Georgian), Retrieved on 10 September 2015 from http://www.geostat.ge/?action-page&p_id=1171&lang=geo.
Parsons, T. 1965. "The Normal American Family." In *Men and Civilization: The Families Search for Survival*, ed. M. Farber, 34–36. New York: McGraw-Hill.
Seguino, S. 2007. "Plus Ca Change?: Evidence on Global Trends in Gender Norms and Stereotypes." *Feminist Economist* 13(2): 1–28.
Sumbadze, N. 2006. "Georgia." In *Families Across Cultures: A 30-Nation Psychological Study*, ed. J. Georgas, J.W. Berry, F. van de Vijver, C.Kagitcibasi, and Y.H. Poortinga, 319–26. Cambridge: Cambridge University Press.
———. 2015. *Access to University Education: Barriers and Ways of Overcoming Them.* Tbilisi: IPS.
UNDP. 2015. "Human Development Report 2015." Retrieved on 6 January 2016 from http://hdr.undp.org/en/rethinking-work-for-human-development.
Wood, W., and A. Eagly. 2010. "Gender." In *Handbook of Social Psychology*, Vol. 1, 5th edn, ed. S.T. Fiske, D.T. Gilbert, and G. Lindzey, 629–67. New York: McGraw-Hill.
World Bank. 2011. "World Development Report 2012. Gender, Equality and Development." Washington, DC.
World Economic Forum. 2014. "The Global Gender Gap Report 2014." Retrieved on 7 January 2015 from http://www3.weforum.org/docs/GGGR14/GGGR_CompleteReport_2014.pdf.
World Values Survey. 2014. Wave 6 2010-2014 Official Aggregate v.20150418. World Values Survey Association. Aggregate File Producer: Asep/JDS, Madrid SPAIN. Retrieved on 10 September 2015 from http://www.worldvaluessurvey.org/WVSDocumentationWV6.jsp.
Wyzan, M.L. 1995. *First Steps Towards Economic Independence: New States of the Postcommunist World.* Westport, CT: Praeger Publishers.

Chapter 12

Georgian Women Migrants
Experiences Abroad and at Home

Tamar Zurabishvili, Maia Mestvirishvili, and Tinatin Zurabishvili

Introduction

After the dissolution of the Soviet Union, international labor migration became a major survival strategy for many Georgian households. Since that time, the composition and direction of migratory flows have changed drastically. In the first years of independence, migratory flows were mostly composed of men migrating, primarily to Russia, finding employment in construction and petty trade. Factors that facilitated migration to Russia included the existence of already established networks, ease of travel (visa-free regime), language proficiency, and certain cultural similarities that had emerged over the course of seventy years of the Soviet experience.

In the early 2000s, the composition of migratory flows from Georgia began to change; this was in part due to increased tension between Russia and Georgia, and in part due to the opening up of new destinations for Georgian migrants. More Georgians began migrating to geographically and/or culturally distant locations. Gradually, the predominant pattern of male migration shifted as more women began migrating to the European Union, Turkey, Israel and North America, mainly taking jobs as domestics in the receiving countries. These women migrated not as dependent migrants accompanying their male family members (fathers, brothers, husbands), but as primary migrants, who went abroad independently and alone. Over time, some have returned, looking to re-establish themselves in their home country.

The feminization of emigration from Georgia resulted in a new body of scholarship that focuses on the interplay of gender and migration in the

Georgian case (see, for example, Zurabishvili and Zurabishvili 2010; Hoffman and Buckley 2013). Less attention has been paid to the experiences of Georgian women migrants abroad and upon their return. This chapter contributes to the scholarship in this area. We offer qualitative data on the migration experiences of return Georgian female migrants, and how those experiences shaped their sense of self in relation to dominant gender ideologies. In order to better understand how migratory experiences inform identity and the personal values of women returnees, we provide findings from a study that explores why women migrate and the impacts of their migration experiences.

The chapter is based on qualitative data gathered in Georgia over a three-month period in 2015. Seventeen in-depth interviews were conducted with return female migrants, whose ages ranged from eighteen to forty-seven at the time of emigration, and from twenty-six to fifty-nine at the time of return. Overall in this sample, the women migrants were highly educated. Over half (eleven of the seventeen) had had some post-secondary education, three had had vocational education, and three had completed secondary education.

Slightly less than half of all respondents (eight of the seventeen) migrated to Greece; of the others, three went to Germany, two to Russia, one to Turkey, one to Cyprus, one to Kazakhstan, and one to Italy. Before migrating, eight respondents had been employed. Among these, three had been working in services and sales, and one as an operator in a call center. Others had been employed as skilled professionals: there was a journalist, librarian, interpreter, and an engineer. During the period of their emigration, most respondents had worked as domestics (house cleaning and childcare/nannies). At the time they migrated, six were married, eight were not, two were divorced, and one was widowed. Eight women had children. During the emigration period two migrant women got divorced, and two got married.

Respondents were selected using a combination of snowball and purposive sampling techniques in Tbilisi, the capital of Georgia. Data analysis was conducted using NVivo 9 software that enabled us to undertake thematic analysis and identify patterns.

Why Georgian Women Migrate

For this cohort of women, the main reason they emigrated was to address financial problems for themselves or their families, which is not a surprising find. A closer look at their responses suggests there was a range of ways in which they articulated those economic-related reasons for migrating. Nearly all of them spoke bluntly about the ways economic hardships had triggered their decision to emigrate. For example, a 44-year-old émigré noted that she had left for Russia "to find a job. We did not have an apartment, and [I needed money] to buy an apartment." Another was prompted by the need to finance her child's education. In the words of a 52-year-old woman who had migrated to Greece, the key consideration was that her child "was graduating from high school and [I migrated] only for this, so my child could continue with studies." She added: "My apartment was also in a dire state. Everything needed to be upgraded—the windows, and bathroom." Another woman who migrated to Greece framed her explanation as a search for a better life: "It was better [in Greece] to improve my situation because there are more possibilities ... [and] your work is valued."

In addition to citing financial factors, a handful of women were also motivated by an interest in having new experiences, exploring a new place, or looking for a "self-realization" experience (four out of seventeen). One 28-year-old woman noted: "Maybe everybody at some stage needs a change, and this is not only financial. Simply put, I did not feel well [in Georgia] during that period. Because I had problems with my job, I could not achieve self-realization the way I wanted." She migrated to Greece. Another woman who migrated to Greece said she "did not have a difficult material situation. I really did not. Maybe it was a need to discover something new." Three other women left Georgia to reunify with family members who had already migrated (a spouse, a mother, and sisters).

In nearly all cases, the respondents said their decision to migrate had been made autonomously; it was not a decision influenced by others, and family members had not tried to stop them from leaving. As one 39-year-old woman explained: "It was my decision—I just told them [family members]. I did ask my brother and sister for advice, and in that way I informed them of my plan." Likewise, a 28-year-old who migrated to Germany said: "It was all my decision. But we still sat down and discussed it. My family members did not want me to go. Nobody wanted me to leave. But I wanted it very much—I was already an adult, and I could take my own decisions. And so I left quite easily."

For most among this cohort of relatively highly educated women, difficult economic conditions were a key factor in prompting them to emigrate, but it was not the only factor. Those who were married and who had children were more likely to cite financial considerations in prompting their decision to migrate, while those who were single were more likely to cite learning about new cultures and a desire for new experiences as being important to their decision. For a very few, economic reasons hardly played into their decision. This finding stands in contrast to most of the literature on Georgian migrants, which focuses solely on social, political and economic factors in driving migration (see, for example, Hofmann and Buckley 2013).

Return to Georgia

For all but two among this cohort of return migrants, family reunification and the pull of emotional ties served as two key factors that played into their decision to move back to Georgia. This is illustrated in the words of a married Georgian woman who had migrated to Russia with her husband. They had no plans to return until "my father-in-law passed away and my mother-in-law became really persistent, insisting we have to come back. She did not let us stay there and we came back." Others returned to pursue educational or career goals in their home country. One émigré to Greece returned to Georgia "to finish my tertiary education ... I was on an academic leave for almost two years, and did not want to abandon [my studies] really. I returned to finish my studies, and I did."

For all the respondents, the whole of their migration experience—leaving and returning—constituted a new way of being in the world; but it was not without its worries, confusions, and ambivalences. Nearly all the returnees reported concerns that the return might result in setting back their hopes and dreams. As one 50-year-old émigré to Cyprus reported, her career had blossomed abroad. Upon returning to Georgia, she worried about being able to continue to work in the profession in which she had found success outside her home country. For another, the migration experience had made her realize the fragility of her sense of "home" as a comfortable dwelling place. This 32-year-old, who had migrated to Greece, explains her ambivalence: "I did not feel at home there. I felt as a stranger. But [now] I feel as a stranger here as well, despite the fact that this is my country."

Not surprisingly, the immigrant experience was life changing for this cohort of women. For many, it was the first time they had encountered a different culture, different ways of doing things, and the need to adapt to a new place and to create a new identity, which also required them to reassess their own attitudes and values. For nearly all, the experience contributed positively to their sense of self, and raised their self-esteem. For many, returning to Georgia also provoked a new set of challenges, which will be discussed in the following sections. The findings presented here are consistent with other studies that have looked at the complex relationship between migration and the stories migrants tell about their personal changes and transitions (see, for example, Van Tonder 2013).

Becoming Independent

The stories told by the women in this study reveal the role of becoming financially independent in prompting a change in the women's sense of self, their confidence, and their new-found autonomy. In this regard, being employed is itself an important factor. "I started to value work—that's huge. When you have your own money, your salary, I realized how independence feels," remarked a 34-year-old who had migrated to Greece. On this same theme, another who had emigrated from Georgia to Greece noted: "You have your own salary. Nobody is cheating you on your money. You will get your money and you will distribute it yourself." Several women stressed the importance of being able to independently structure their lives abroad—finding employment, establishing effective working relationships, and managing their financial resources. As one woman put it: "I managed to do everything independently. I can go to any country again. Frankly I am not afraid." For the nine women who prior to emigration had either had no labor market participation experience or had been low-wage employees (thus, they were not primary family income providers), their migration employment experiences played an especially important role in building confidence and bringing to the women a sense of fulfillment and satisfaction. The fact that almost all the women in this study were able to receive what they considered to be "decent" remuneration, that allowed them to support themselves and their families, constituted a major source of emotional satisfaction and pride.

Even as the women gained more independence, they retained strong family ties. To a large degree, the lives of women migrants abroad were structured around their families back in Georgia. Many of the women sent remittances home. Those whose remittances were used to improve housing conditions for their families or to finance family members' education or medical needs, or were put into savings, reported more satisfaction and pride than those who had not had much say in how family members spent those remittances. We heard expressions of satisfaction from those women who were providing for their families, such as this 39-year-old Georgian woman who had migrated to Russia: "When somebody leaves Georgia, you have a drive to achieve something. When you call via Skype or phone and you know that your family does not need anything—they have everything, like food, for example—that's what makes you happy [knowing] that they sleep peacefully and have no need for anything and are not hungry." This reveals the ways in which their independence in decision making and increased self-realization is articulated in their ability to satisfy family needs. As one woman described it:

> I could solve all [financial] problems from there. There was no problem I could not solve from there. [In Georgia], I should have worked at least five to six months to accumulate the amount I was getting [in Greece] as a one-month salary. I sent so much stuff to my family, you know, [ensured] all the comfort, [vacations] sea, mountains, and birthdays. I took care of everybody and cheered them on from abroad. That brought me satisfaction somehow. For instance, when I knew that my grandchild was going on a tour, I was somehow glad as if I was going myself.

For many of the women in this study, their newfound financial independence and the pride and joy that came along with it was challenged upon their return to Georgia, where employment was hard to come by, especially employment with good compensation. They experienced this as more than just a financial loss; it was also a blow to their sense of purpose. Fourteen of the seventeen women reported that they had not been able to find the kind of job with the kind of compensation they had wanted to secure upon their return to Georgia. Only three reported finding a "good" job with adequate compensation: one runs a house cleaning company, another works as a cleaning lady for foreigners, and the third is a student who also works for an NGO.

For those who did find employment or were able to establish their own business, the emigration experience was instrumental in providing them with the knowledge and experience they needed to land a position in their homeland, and to effectively manage their entrepreneurial efforts. Some were able to avail themselves of resources, including programs of the International Organization for Migration (IOM) in Georgia, as in the case of the returnee who applied for and received a grant to start her own home cleaning business.

Changes in Identity

If prior to emigrating the majority of the women in our study had self-identified primarily in terms of their roles as mothers, wives, and daughters, the migration experience produced at least two new identities that represents a change in their self concept: as friend and as businesswoman. Comparing herself before and after migrating, a 32-year-old returnee described herself as follows:

> I have changed one hundred times. I became active. If before I did not have time for certain things, now I do my best to find time for everything. Before I was mainly staying at home, [and] did not socialize much, even with my friends. I would only attend birthdays. Since I am back, I am more active. I come and go. I do not miss anything.

Others attributed the migration experience to their ability to seek and achieve success, as captured in this quote by a 44-year-old returnee:

> I became more independent, and more adult. I learned how to stand on my own feet, to cope with loneliness, and to value work. I worked and it brought results. I knew that if I did something today then the day was not wasted. I did not know if [upon my return to Georgia] I would become [head of a unit], but I did.

Several of the women noted that their migration experience had been central in bringing them to respect their own opinions and ideas. Others' judgments simply did not matter to them as much as they had before they left on the migration journey. Before, the women had tended to take into account how others would perceive their words or their actions. After, they have come to appreciate that their own opinions matter and that they determine actions by what they themselves consider "important" and "just" rather than simply in response to social expectations. As a 32-year-old who had spent time in Kazakhstan explained: "We were raised in a way that [it was important] what people would say. People never stop talking. They will always say something regardless of whether you do well or badly. You need to love yourself. Do not pay attention to what people say."

Changes in Values

The fact that emigration contributes to fundamental changes in the value systems of migrants is well documented in the scholarly literature (Remennick 2007; Lönnqvist, Jasinskaja-Lahti, and Verkasalo 2011). Our findings are consistent with what has been documented. Here, we note those values that were most often mentioned by respondents—specifically, the stress on non-material values over material ones.

Even as the women were motivated to emigrate for economic reasons and to contribute to the financial well-being of their families, they assert that a "search for happiness" was a most important value and not necessarily tied to achieving financial success. One returnee found herself urging family members to not value something simply because it is expensive. Another remarked that in contemporary Georgian society, people tend to pay "too much attention to possessing certain luxury items—for example, the latest model of an expensive cell phone or a car." She noted that in Georgia, "[w]hen you go out, everybody is really dressed up. At first when I came back [in 2014] I thought everybody was going to a wedding or something. Well, then I realized that it was like that before. In

Georgia it is always like that, 'I need to have that!'" In the view of these respondents, Georgians are more materialistic than the people they had observed abroad who they say live modestly, do not spend money on luxury items, and devote their resources to travel and education—values this cohort of women tended to appreciate.

Emotional and Social Development

Respondents reported that their emigration experience had contributed to their emotional development. Thinking about what they had been like before they emigrated, women used such descriptors as "weak," "overly trusting," "often betrayed and easily victimized," "quick to anger," and "emotionally repressed." They reported that their experiences living in other countries and establishing interactions with different people in various contexts, observing how relationships are formed and sustained, had substantially impacted on how they now deal with their emotions. For instance, returnees stressed that overall they are better able to understand the feelings of other people, and have better control over and are better able to express their own emotions. As one woman remarked, "I no longer keep myself in sadness, but say what needs to be said."

Returnees talked about being more at ease in expressing emotions, attributing this to the migration experience. Being separated from loved ones helped in this regard. Several women came to realize the importance of expressing their feelings to loved ones who lived far away. Communicating with family about how important they are in their lives helped sustain family ties at a distance. As one woman put it, living abroad enabled her "to better express the love that I have towards people whom I love."

Another factor that helped immigrant women develop strong social skills was the exposure they received living and working in a multicultural environment. "I learned how to navigate while interacting with people," one woman explained: "I discovered in myself a gift for communication. I opened up, became different—I became freer, better at communication. I met not only Greeks, but others as well—Ukrainians, Russians, Armenians, people of other nationalities. I got to know them, and I liked that. We became very good friends, and this was a very good moment."

Overall, the immigrant experience enabled the women to better understand people and to come to respect varying opinions and behaviors. They attributed their successful transition back into Georgian society to these newfound skills and abilities.

Gender Roles

The scholarly literature identifies links between migration and women's autonomy (Kandel and Massey 2002; Oishi 2005; Hofmann and Buckley 2013). Scholars note that women who are more autonomous are more inclined to emigrate in the first place, and that emigration, in turn, furthers migrant women's independence. Migration has been shown to facilitate awareness among women migrants about how gender roles are shaped and understood cross-culturally (Guendelman and Perez-Itriago 1987; Dannecker 2005). Some scholars hypothesize that as women migrate and participate in a workforce abroad, their experiences of independence and their reassessments of given gender roles lead to changes in how gender roles are perceived in their home country after they become returnees. Our study reveals that women returnees do feel they have become more independent and that their gender role attitudes have shifted. It is not clear what the long-term effects of their migration experience will be on their sense of self, their interpersonal relationships, or on Georgian gender ideology more generally.

A 2013 UNDP study in Georgia on public perceptions of gender equality with a specific focus on politics and business reveals that traditional attitudes toward gender roles is prevalent in Georgia (UNDP 2013: 4). The study found that in Georgian society, men are considered to be the heads of the household, the breadwinners, and the major decision makers, while women are considered to be subservient to men and their proper role is to be confined to household responsibilities, including child rearing and housekeeping (ibid.: 4–5). Respondents in our study claimed they held these culturally embedded views before they emigrated. They also claimed that mainstream approaches to child rearing contribute to the reproduction of existing gender norms and stereotypes. One said: "A girl here is an item—that's how it is in Georgia. A girl has to get married and has to have a baby. She should be a good mother and a good housekeeper—that's it. There are no prospects for girls in Georgia." Another noted that before emigrating to Greece, "I lived with my brothers and was very shy. I would ask permission to do everything—not that anybody required me to ask for permission, but I felt obliged to do so."

Since returning to Georgia, this same woman has seen things differently. Like others in the study, she attributes the change in her understanding of gender roles to be the result of her migration experience. "Since I came back," said the 28-year-old, "everything has changed in this respect. I am free now. I can express my opinion and my opinion is taken into account." For these women, "freedom" and "independence" are values they now hold dear. As one woman put it: "[Before] I thought differently—that a young girl should stay at home and that parents should watch her. Now I do not. You need to give space to a good person, a talented person, to achieve something, to fight for his/her life and future."

Some of the women managed to construct their lives in line with their changed views upon returning to Georgia. "I opened up there, and I returned here like this," one woman remarked. She went so far as to say that all people should have a migration experience, which she believes enables a journey toward self-realization: "Everybody should emigrate, spend time away from their parents, to understand if they can live alone." Still others said that they now speak up against the unequal distribution of gender power that plays out in Georgia, which they are no longer able to bear.

Social and Personal Transformation: Women's Perceptions and Attitudes

Castles proposes social transformation as a central conceptual framework for migration studies "in order to facilitate understanding of the complexity, interconnectedness, variability, contexuality and multi-level mediations of migratory processes in the context of rapid global change" (2010: 1565). Social scientists have long attempted to analyze fundamental changes in social relations and in social structures that can lead to individual and social transformation. Migration can be said to be a cause and an effect of social change at the level of the individual. As the women in our study have revealed, migration can result in important transformations in individual perceptions, attitudes, and identities. In the case of Georgian women migrants, the migration experience resulted in a shift in their value systems. They have reconsidered their gender identities, have claimed a role for women in the larger society, have come to appreciate their own independence, and have become more active in social life.

In their meta-analysis of cross-cultural research on gender and migration, Marta Tienda and Karen Booth identify "improvement," "erosion," and "restructured asymmetries" as three potential outcomes of female migration (Tienda and Booth 1991: 56, 68–69). "Improvement" refers to a positive move from an oppressive to a less oppressive social environment, enabling women more autonomy and access to material resources. "Erosion" refers to a regressive move in which women find they are unable to advance in terms of employment opportunities and/or in terms of retaining control over family decision making in situations where the women are separated from their families. "Restructured asymmetries" refers to structural changes in women's social position in a hierarchical social system and labor market, which Tienda and Booth argue has not been realized (ibid.: 70).

The women in our study have shown "improvement" in their material conditions, in the expansion of their social networks, and in terms of gaining new skills and experiences. This is true despite the fact that most of the women had limited employment opportunities, and worked mainly as domestics and babysitters.

Our findings are also consistent with those from Anna Secor's study of Turkish emigrant women on the positive effects of waged employment (Secor 2003). Secor argues that waged work positively influences women's self-positioning in their communities, outside the family or domestic sphere. Like Secor's respondents, the Georgian women in our study became "new themselves" or "different themselves" thanks to the fact of their employment and that they were earning their own wages. Our study contributes to discussions on how migration and labor force participation impacts on women's gender identities. We believe that the experience of working abroad is particularly important in terms of women's subjective self-assessments and, perhaps, in improving their social status in their country of origin.

Concluding Remarks

In sum, for this cohort of Georgian women, emigration proved overall to be a positive life-changing experience. It enabled the women to improve their own and their family's economic standing, including by paying off debts. Earnings contributed to improving their housing, education, and health statuses. More than that, the migration experience had a positive impact on the way they viewed themselves. They reported that they had been able to grow both emotionally and professionally, and that they had attained a newfound sense of independence and self-realization. For this reason, they tended to evaluate the whole of their emigration experience positively, even if they had had to face certain difficulties or hardships.

The women attributed the migration experience to their new ability to reflect critically on gender role expectations and traditions, now seeing these as culturally constructed, not inevitable. It also provided the women with an opportunity to conduct an assessment of their own values — to determine what they felt mattered rather than simply adopting values imposed by wider Georgian society. Overall, the women felt more fulfilled and more confident than they had before living and working abroad — a pattern that cut across all the women in the study, regardless of where they spent their years as immigrants. The women carried with them a new set of attitudes and beliefs upon returning to Georgia. It remains to be seen if and how they will be able to maintain this sense of self-efficacy.

Tamar Zurabishvili is director of Research and Development Foundation. She has PhD in sociology (from the Ilia State University, (Tbilisi, Georgia, 2008). She has served as a researcher/consultant for the International Center for Migration Policy Development, the International Organization for Migration, the Caucasian Institute for Peace, Democracy and Development, the European University Institute, the Europe Foundation (former Eurasia Partnership Foundation), and the Innovations and Reforms Center. She has received research scholarships from OSI, IIE, Carnegie Foundation, Caucasus Research Resource Center and the Böll Foundation.

Maia Mestvirishvili is an associate professor in the Faculty of Psychology and Educational Sciences at Tbilisi State University. Her major research interests are social identity, stigma and coping, moral judgment and religious attitudes. She has received international scholarships at Columbia University, NY; University of California, Berkeley; and Leuven University, Belgium. She was the principal investigator of research projects funded by the Academic Swiss Caucasus Network (ASCN) and the Norwegian Institute of International Affairs (NUPI).

Tinatin Zurabishvili is research director at the Caucasus Research Resource Center, Georgia, where she coordinates a number of empirical research projects, including the Caucasus Barometer survey. She received her PhD in the sociology of journalism from the Lomonosov State University in Moscow. Her major research interests are the sociology of migration, media studies, and social research methodology.

References

Castles, S. 2010. "Understanding Global Migration: A Social Transformation Perspective" *Journal of Ethnic and Migration Studies* 36(10): 1565–1586.
Dannecker, P. 2005. "Transnational Migration and the Transformation of Gender Relations: The Case of Bangladeshi Labour Migrants." *Current Sociology* 53(4): 655–74.
Guendelman, S., and A. Perez-Itriago. 1987. "Double Lives: The Changing Role of Women in Seasonal Migration." *Women's Studies* 13(3): 249–71.

Hofmann, E.T., and C.J. Buckley. 2013. "Global Changes and Gendered Responses: The Feminization of Migration From Georgia." *International Migration Review* 47(3): 508–38.

Kandel, W., and D.S. Massey. 2002. "The Culture of Mexican Migration: A Theoretical and Empirical Analysis." *Social Forces* 80(3): 981–1004.

Lönnqvist, J.-E., I. Jasinskaja-Lahti, and M. Verkasalo. 2011. "Personal Values Before and After Migration: A Longitudinal Case Study on Value Change in Ingrian–Finnish Migrants." *Social Psychological and Personality Science* 2(6): 584–91.

Oishi, N. 2005. *Women in Motion: Globalization, State Policies, and Labor Migration in Asia.* Stanford, CA: Stanford University Press.

Remennick, L. 2007. "'Being a Woman Is Different Here': Changing Perceptions of Femininity and Gender Relations among Former Soviet Women Living in Greater Boston." *Women's Studies International Forum* 30(4): 326–41.

Secor, A.J. 2003. "Belaboring Gender: The Spatial Practice of Work and the Politics of 'Making Do' in Istanbul." *Environment and Planning A* 35(12): 2209–27.

Tienda, M., and K. Booth. 1991. "Gender, Migration and Social Change." *International Sociology* 6(1): 51–72.

UNDP. 2013. *Public Perceptions on Gender Equality in Politics and Business.* Research Report. Retrieved on 18 April 2017. http://www.ge.undp.org/content/georgia/en/home/library/democratic_governance/public-perceptions-on-gender-equality-in-politics-and-business.html.

Van Tonder, C.L. 2013. "Migration as Personal Transition." *Procedia: Social and Behavioral Sciences* 82: 342–50.

Zurabishvili, T., and T. Zurabishvili. 2010. "The Feminization of Labor Migration from Georgia: The Case of Tianeti." *Laboratorium: Russian Review of Social Research* 2(1): 73–83.

Chapter 13

Being Transgender in Georgia

Natia Gvianishvili

Introduction

In post-Soviet Georgia, gender equality discourse often excludes transgender and gender variant persons. Despite women's rights NGOs starting up in Georgia in the 1990s, transgender issues remain relatively unaddressed, and discussion about gender variance is rare.

The emergence of LGBT organizations in Georgia since 2006 has not guaranteed inclusion of transgender persons or the specific issues of concern to them. Even though transgender persons (transgender women, to be precise) sometimes appear in the media, the depictions of them have tended to be sensationalist and exploitive. These depictions may boost ratings for the show, but they do nothing to facilitate understanding of transgender people or their experiences. Media images tend to perpetuate gender stereotypes and exclude those transgender identities that fall outside of the categories "male" and "female."

There is still a great deal of fragmentation among transgender people in Georgia; it would be difficult to consider that there is a transgender "community." Very recently, there has been some movement in organizing transgender activism by transgender persons who have begun to assert a transgender agenda for those organizations working on LGBT issues.

We now have some information on transgender persons living in Georgia as a result of two studies published in 2012 and 2015 by the Women's Initiatives Supporting Group (WISG), the first organization to start focusing specifically on the transgender community and on transgender issues

---

Notes for this chapter begin on page 204.

at the grassroots and advocacy levels (Gvianishvili 2012; Gvianishvili 2015). These needs assessment studies offer baseline data on the situation and problems faced by transgender persons living in Georgia. Results of the research show that transgender persons experience discrimination in nearly every aspect of their lives. According to the 2015 study, transgender persons (a) report having experienced physical violence because they are transgender; (b) feel constantly under psychological pressure; and (c) believe their labor rights are regularly violated (Gvianishvili 2015). This research shows that transgender persons feel that the obstacles they face and their particular concerns are not being adequately addressed by the state.

In the two year period between 2012 and 2014, important legislative changes took place in Georgia. The "Law on Elimination of All Forms of Discrimination" was adopted, as was the "National Human Rights Strategy and Action Plan." Moreover, homophobic and transphobic bias was covered as an "aggravating circumstance" in the Criminal Code of Georgia. However, there is weak implementation of these laws, and transgender people struggle to gain legal gender recognition. In addition, there is no official regulation of the process of transition, and medical expenses associated with transition are not included in the national healthcare plan.[1]

The situation leaves transgender persons with a painful dilemma when it comes to gender expression in public spaces. Those who choose to begin the transition are confronted with great financial and medical challenges. For example, there are great costs associated with hormone replacement and other procedures, and there is the risk of facing discrimination and physical violence, especially when transgender people produce their identification cards that show biological sex but not gender. On the other hand, those who refuse to undergo the transition, and who "appear" with a gender expression consistent with their biological sex, struggle with persistent psychological stress, which often has somatic consequences.

In this chapter, I summarize the experiences of transgender persons living in Georgia, which is based on in-depth interviews I conducted with nine people who self identify as transgender. My summary also references my earlier research, a study titled "Situation of Transgender Persons in Georgia" (Gvianishvili 2015). I also describe the public representation of transgender persons as depicted in several Georgian television shows. I argue that gender in Georgia is generally understood in biologically deterministic terms, which is reflected in the law and in societal attitudes. I analyze how determinist perceptions of gender, as well as violence and discrimination, work as restrictive mechanisms that affect the self-representation and self-perception of Georgian transgender persons. I also trace the relatively recent emergence of transgender persons in Georgian public space, and describe the transgender "community," which is marked by fragmentation, has limited access to information about gender and sexuality, and is subject to public humiliation by tabloid media. They are also subject to openly xenophobic politicians and other public figures who invoke fear-mongering images of transgender women to discredit political opponents or ideas, such as Georgian integration into the European Union. My chapter concludes with a description of how transgender activism is in the process of becoming a part of broader gender activist struggles.

The Situation of Transgender Persons in Georgia

Findings from the 2015 WISG study reveal that most of the interviewees (nine out of fourteen) claimed that they had experienced physical violence due to their gender identity and/or gender expression at least once in their life (Gvianishvili 2015). All respondents stated that they had regularly experienced psychological abuse from strangers, friends, and family members. This violence and abuse—expressed in various ways, from fairly subtle to the most extreme—seems to be rooted in the belief that the pressure will work to "correct" the transgender person's behavior, and lead them, for example, to wear clothes "appropriate" to their biological sex. The research suggests that the workplace is a particularly important setting for psychological abuse, with co-workers and/or employers overtly expressing homophobic and transphobic attitudes and beliefs. For the transgender respondents in the study, this has had profound effects on their emotional states. For the most part, respondents have experienced physical violence at the hands of strangers, and relatively rarely from friends and family members, who have been the main sources of their psychological stress. Even in cases where family members have not objected to their transgender children's coming out and have tried to support them, most have perceived the gender identity of their transgender child and/or family member as something abnormal. In the context of a society that consistently tries to place gender variant persons in either a "male" or "female" box, the level of stress experienced by transgender persons is very high, and it is nearly constant. According to the 2015 WISG study, the average index of depression in the group was 25, a rate that is higher than the acceptable index of 16.[2] The highest indexes (45 and 39) belonged to two respondents who had suffered clinical depression and were in treatment at the time of the research (Gvianishvili 2015).

As noted, the lack of a quick, transparent, and accessible procedure by which a transgender person can have their gender legally recognized is enormously challenging. Established practice in Georgia requires a person to provide proof of "full gender reassignment surgery" in order to have their gender changed on official documents.[3] The process is challenging. Another obstacle that transgender persons face as a group is access to medical services necessary for the transition, such as hormone therapy and different types of surgical operations, especially mastectomy or breast implants (Gvianishvili 2015). For transgender women willing to undergo breast implant surgery, the process is expensive but fairly straightforward. Those who have breast implant surgery go directly to a plastic surgeon for the procedure. The situation is more complicated for transgender men because a clear medical indication (e.g., a tumor) is required in order for a physician to perform a mastectomy. "Transitioning" is not recognized as a legitimate medical indicator for mastectomy. In addition, the Ministry of Labor, Health, and Social Affairs has no protocol or guidelines to enable a medical doctor to prescribe hormone therapy for a transgender person. As a result of these obstacles and the high costs associated with supervised hormone treatments, most transgender persons in Georgia who are in transition find other ways to acquire the hormones they need. As they are not under the supervision of medical professionals, they follow the advice of friends and fellow transgender activists from other countries in terms of the quantity and frequency of hormone medications.

Beyond mastectomies, other types of surgical and medical interventions associated with the transition are not prohibited by Georgian law, and nor are these procedures regulated. Thus, a decision about whether or not to provide these surgeries or other medical interventions is left to the discretion of individual doctors and clinics.

For gender reassignment surgery, plastic surgeons require a statement from a sexologist, which will serve as a basis for performing the operation. In Georgia, this statement is called the "true transsexual statement." In established practice, this means the document is issued by the sexologist after a minimum of a year of observation, and includes interviews with psychologists, psychiatrists, and sexologists. It also means undergoing various types of hormonal and chromosomal tests and ultrasonography examinations. Although insurance does not cover expenses accrued in order to obtain the certificate, and despite it requiring a long-term investment, most respondents in my study considered the process and the requirement of the medical statement as necessary and helpful in the development of their own self-confidence (Gvianishvili 2015).

As noted, neither the state nor private insurance cover any of the abovementioned procedures. Most transgender persons simply cannot afford the medical procedures that accompany the process of transition. Also, information about healthcare services specific to transgender people is sporadic; one cannot find good information from one central source. In part, this is due to the fact that transgender people's rights are often placed outside of the legal framework. Despite this, some transgender people living in Georgia manage to start the transition and bring their physical appearance more in harmony with their gender identity, although the transition is not necessarily complete. Partial transition brings them spiritual comfort, and affords them the chance to more easily integrate into society and to feel less vulnerable to transphobic attacks.

Transgender persons in Georgia live in a grey zone. Their identities are not recognized by society, and access to the services they need is limited. They are highly stigmatized, which puts them at risk of unemployment and poverty. In turn, poverty means access to the health services they need is less likely, and their chances of gaining legal recognition are slim. Since the idea of a spectrum of transgender identities is not acknowledged, people find themselves forced to choose between one sex or the other, which may lead to a hasty or unwise decision to undergo undesirable and/or unnecessary medical interventions, including sterilization. Transgender persons recognize that they face violence, abuse, and discrimination—forces that constitute a form of pressure that can lead them to act as cisgender men or women.

Media Representations of Transgender Persons

The media plays a key role in reproducing the idea of only two genders, and thus that transgender is abnormal. Since most schools do not cover the subject of gender and sexuality, the media becomes the only public source of information on these issues. As noted, the information provided by the media can be inaccurate, stigmatizing, and sensationalizing. Due to economic and cultural factors in Georgia, very few LGBT persons dare to come out. As a result, very few appear on television. Therefore, there is little positive visibility, and a great deal of negative association with lesbian, gay, bisexual, and transgender people and their lifestyles.

Among all LGBT persons, transgender women have appeared on Georgian television more than gay men or lesbians; no transgender men have appeared on television. The representations of transgender women on these shows tend to be voyeuristic, promising viewers a chance to see what "a man in a dress" looks and sounds like. Those who appear on these shows are given financial compensation by the networks.

The only two mechanisms available to provide networks with ethical guidelines on handling LGBT persons and issues are the Georgian Charter of Journalistic Ethics, which is not legally binding, and self-regulating policies developed by particular media organizations. Most journalists and talk-show hosts have learned that explicit use of homophobic and/or transphobic language will likely result in an official complaint to the network from human rights NGOs. The consequences for the network and for those responsible for the programming are minimal.

As noted by the activists I interviewed, the media in Georgia portray transgender persons in very problematic ways by focusing on stereotypes; they do not enable interviewees to meaningfully explain what it means to be transgender or to explain gender dysphoria. The media, they say, simply prey on scandal. In what follows are examples from three talk show programs in which transgender women appeared. As my description reveals, these programs, which purport to offer "balanced" perspectives by including transgender women, tend to reproduce dominant homophobic/transphobic discourse.

Sabi Beriani, a 20-year-old transgender woman, appeared on the talk show *Profili* in 2011. It was produced by Rustavi 2, one of the two mainstream television channels in Georgia. Throughout the show, the host continuously referenced Sabi's "real"—male—name and identity, contrasting it to her constructed femaleness—the way she "looks" as if she were a woman. The host asked Sabi to talk about her childhood. Who did she like to play with? Girls? When did she realize she "wanted to be a girl"? Sabi responded by talking about her "underlying innate femininity," and her heterosexuality. She did not refer to herself as a transgender woman. Instead, she talked about herself as a heterosexual woman, revealing what some may call a gender-traditional mindset and heteronormativity. For example, she stated that she could never offer sexual relations to a man before she became a "complete" woman, and described her personal interests and attributes as a mix of the qualities of the perfect housewife and the temptress. On the show, Sabi talked about enjoying housekeeping and cooking. The talk-show crew filmed her preparing *khachapuri*, a traditional Georgian dish, while Sabi told her interviewer that a woman should make her man understand that she will not be faithful unless he is strong enough to "hold" her. Even as she depicted herself in the most stereotypical ways, Sabi also came across as assertive and comfortable with her own decisions. For example, Sabi was firm in her decision to have children, explaining that she planned to adopt a child, and expected be a great mother. She also described how, when she began to undergo the transition, she did not hesitate to appear in public according to her gender identity (female), regardless of how she may have appeared to others. There were moments of poignant honesty, such as when Sabi spoke about her difficult relationship with her mother, and when her cisgender friend spoke about their friendship in the most open and accepting of ways.

The next example is from *100 Degrees Celsius,* a popular show on Imedi TV that is known for encouraging its guests to degrade themselves in front of the camera. In one episode, aired in 2012, Kesaria Abramidze, the first ever transgender woman to come out in Georgia, appeared with Sabi and with Leri Bekauri, a gay man. Kesaria is a model who had previously appeared on numerous other television shows, in photo shoots, and in newspapers and magazines; Leri had also appeared on several television shows. The show in which all three appeared together revolved around a "cat fight" between the two transgender women, set up to prove which of them was the more "authentic" woman—a dynamic that was crafted by the producers of the show. In between, Leri offered his own interjections: "[Sabi] might be a transvestite ... but is definitely not transgender." Likewise, Kesaria stated that Sabi is a "psychological" deviant who "looks like a man with jewelry." A segment on surrogacy followed the interview, which included the director of one of the largest fertility clinics in Georgia as one of the guests. It also featured Kesaria's journey to India to find a surrogate mother for her future child. Considering that, in Georgia, people tend to be reactionary when it comes to LGBT issues and surrogacy as a means of providing same-sex couples with "babies they will inevitably corrupt," it is not surprising that this episode did a great deal to push back LGBT issues in general, and transgender issues in particular.

In 2015, an equally "scandal-oriented" show featured a transgender woman. The show *Skhva Rakursi* (also on Imedi TV), featured Bianka Shigurova, a frequent guest on Georgian television. In the studio and in her native village, Bianka told her story, including how neighbors had physically assaulted her, forcing her to leave the village. The show's host constructed a narrative of dysfunction and misfortune, explaining Bianka's "condition" as a result of her experiences of neglect and abuse, including that she had been raped by a male neighbor at the age of eight, and that as a teenager she was "forced" to do domestic (woman's) work. The underlying message of the narrative was that Bianka is "really" a man whose gender identity had been derailed by a miserable, unhappy life. In contesting the host's narrative, Bianka insisted that she has a very "traditional" mindset when it comes to women's and men's roles; she even made a homophobic remark to emphasize the point. The most humanistic moment in the show was a short interview with Bianka's grandmother, the only family member who had not rejected her.

In November, 2014, Sabi was murdered. Various media outlets, including online and mainstream television news, picked up the story. The first broadcasts described the murder of "a young man, who allegedly belonged to the LGBT community." Later, when it became clear that the victim was a 23-year-old transgender woman who had appeared on television several times, reporters referred to the victim by her male name, or as "a young man." Only a very few outlets referred to the victim as "Sabi," her preferred name, or bothered to interview activists involved in LGBT issues, and linked the murder to the problems faced by transgender persons, including their dehumanization by those who fear difference. For example, the *Kurieri PS* news program, on the network Rustavi, humanized Sabi in their reports. "Another woman was murdered in Tbilisi," they reported, acknowledging Sabi's gender identity and attributing her murder to "raging femicide" that had taken the lives of thirty-three Georgian women in 2014. They also interviewed activists and a professional expert who spoke about problems and obstacles that transgender people face in Georgia.

In 2014–15, Identoba, a human rights organization in Georgia, made two short films that provided alternative representations of LGBT persons. One was a documentary of Bianka's story, done in a sensitive way—not degrading or stigmatizing. Another was a short feature titled *Red Dress* that tells the moving story of a mother who comes to support her transgender daughter. These productions were following an important shift in policy by producers of *Profili,* mentioned earlier, and one of the most famous, mainstream Georgian talk shows. In 2015, *Profili* began to focus on social issues and to shy away from the tabloid format.

Thus, while the visibility of the transgender community is important, the way it is presented and portrayed generally does not advance understanding, and results in more misinformation. At best, this results in hostility, and at worst, in injury and even death. Talk show hosts and journalists are themselves ignorant about gender identity and the problems that transgender persons face in their daily lives. When interviewing transgender women, talk show hosts tend to take on the aura of a person who is afraid to catch a disease, and also tend to adopt a tone of pity.

Is There a Transgender Community? Envisioning a Movement

The general hostility towards transgender persons—which includes symbolic and real violence; failing to understand the social and economic difficulties they face; stigmatizing media representations; and the lack of accurate information about sexuality, gender construction, and gender identity—contributes significantly to the isolation of transgender persons in Georgia. It is noteworthy that in the past, very few transgender persons had access to nongovernmental organizations working on LGBT issues, such as the Inclusive Foundation (established in 2006) and the Women's Initiatives Supporting Group (WISG). More recently, new organizations have emerged that focus on outreach and on creating and distributing original and translated information on transgender issues. As a result, something like a transgender community has begun to emerge. In June 2015, WISG offered work space and other resources to a small group of transgender activists looking to mobilize and build what they hoped would be a transgender community. Since that time, the group has been meeting regularly, working on awareness raising, exchanging experiences, choosing people to represent Georgian transgender at various international events, and planning activities, such as collecting a set of transgender narratives (written stories and essays), and creating an exhibit dedicated to them.

The nine transgender activists I interviewed offered their perceptions of the current status of the transgender community, and their visions of what transgender activism in Georgia should look like. Five respondents believe there is a "community," which they describe as a "family" and as constituting "a different world" where people understand each other, accept each other, and where they can stand together in their difference. For one transgender man, the community is a "safe space" that offers a sense of solidarity among its members. For another, the community constitutes a group of people who have specific goals. One respondent noted that the community is made up of members of a "family," who share the common experience of "being trapped in the wrong body," of feeling a certain "hatred" for this body, and of knowing the stigma that results (20-year-old Genderqueer respondent).

Two activists believed that the notion of a transgender "community" has its pitfalls. As one respondent noted, "There should be no such thing as transgender community" (or any other community) because creating separate communities is divisive, and enhances segregation from the rest of the society.

Whether or not the group constitutes a cohesive "community," there is consensus among the nine activists that well-informed and trained transgender persons can best represent transgender issues. There is also agreement that transgender activism should focus on the following issues: psychological and legal empowerment of transgender people, increasing positive visibility, combating violence, and informing wider society about transgender issues, including providing accurate information on the phenomenon of transsexuality.

Only one respondent mentioned that activism should also use more "atypical" tools such as "fun and cross-dressing." Another respondent mentioned that transgender activists should not employ propaganda but should focus on "behaving like normal people." Overall, there is an understanding among transgender persons that they need to take their time to shape the specific agenda for transgender activism. There is consensus on the importance of continuing to use the resources offered by WISG, while remaining primary decision makers about the structure of the group, the topics to address, and the activities to carry out.

Conclusion

In this chapter I have described the situation for transgender persons, and traced the origins of transgender activism, which is at an early stage. A clear political transgender agenda has yet to be put forth in Georgia. It is difficult to talk in terms of a transgender "community," which at best might be described as fragmented. In the Georgian context, it is not surprising that there is no cohesive transgender community, given the high level of violence and discrimination that transgender persons in Georgia experience. On the level of the individual, these social conditions lead to suppression in everyday representations of gender self-perception, which is more intense for transgender women than for transgender men. In turn, suppression and silencing constitute an obstacle to transgender political organizing.

Georgian society's general lack of knowledge about the issues of gender and sexuality is nurtured by the exclusion of these topics in the educational system and by highly biased representations in the media. In the context of this hostile environment, the seeds for future transgender activism are being planted. This is best represented in the emergence of a transgender group that has been meeting on a regular basis since June 2015. Their first effort has been to build solidarity among transgender persons, and to claim agency in representing itself rather than allowing cisgender activists to address transgender issues. Even so, these transgender activists recognize the importance of alliance and solidarity, as transgender issues are tied to a broader gender rights agenda in the country, an agenda that is gaining traction. It is likely that the coming years will see more favorable ground for empowered transgender activists to demand a transgender-sensitive agenda alongside other social and civil rights movements in Georgia.

Natia Gvianishvili is a lesbian feminist activist and researcher from Georgia. She is director of the Women's Initiatives Supporting Group (WISG), a feminist organization working on LGBT issues, with special focus on lesbian, bisexual women and transgender persons. In 2012 she received a Master's degree in gender studies from Tbilisi State University. She is author of "Transgender Persons in Georgia," a chapter in the WISG report,

Situation of LGBT Persons in Georgia (2012), and of the WISG study, "The Situation of Transgender Persons in Georgia" (2015).

Notes

1. The process of bringing an individual's physical appearance and social role in conformity with his/her/their gender may or may not include a range of medical procedures, voluntarily chosen by the individual. In terms of medical intervention, the process may include only a small-scale intervention, therapy, as well as a gender reassignment surgery.
2. Center for Epidemiologic Studies Depression Scale (CES-D), NIMH; http://www.chcr.brown.edu/pcoc/cesdscale.pdf.
3. The name change is available for everyone and there are no gender specific restrictions, which is considered to be a relief by transgender persons.

References

Gvianishvili, N. 2012. "Transgender Persons in Georgia." In *Situation of LGBT Persons in Georgia*, 67–72. Tbilisi: Women's Initiatives Supporting Group. Retrieved on 16 May 2016. http://women.ge/data/docs/publications/WISG_situation-of-lgbt-persons-in-Georgia_ENG-www.pdf.

———. 2015. "Situation of Transgender Persons in Georgia." Tbilisi: Women's Initiatives Supporting Group. Retrieved on 16 May 2016. http://women.ge/en/publications/40/Situation%20of%20transgender%20people%20in%20Georgia.

Chapter 14

Tracing the LGBT Movement in the Republic of Georgia
Stories of Activists

Anna Rekhviashvili

Introduction

In early fall of 2010, David asked me to attend a strategic planning meeting in the small town of Signagi in eastern Georgia. We had met at a social event hosted by Inclusive Foundation, the first and only LGBT organization in Georgia at that time.[1] David was a freshly minted social work graduate, enthusiastic and full of ideas. He was looking for similar-minded people to start planning the future of LGBT work, since Inclusive Foundation was about to dissolve. He thought my familiarity with gender and sexuality issues might be useful, and so I agreed to participate.

Signagi is a quiet town. The day we visited, it was fairly empty. There I was, strolling through the parks and sitting in a cafe with a small group of people I hardly knew, our aim to imagine a new grassroots organization for Georgia, one that would tackle the entrenched homophobia pervasive in the country. We talked, planned, and strategized. Most of us had academic backgrounds in the social sciences, gender studies or social work. Our conversation tended towards the abstract and theoretical. We discussed intersectionality, the importance of considering multiple layers of oppression and inequality, and of class and ethnicity. We talked about developing an inclusive politics. But how? What strategies would reduce homophobia? How could we create safe spaces for queer communities in

---

Notes for this chapter begin on page 219.

Georgia? What I knew of these topics was what I had read in books. I did not believe that any of this was possible. I did not believe that one day it would be possible to hear or give a lecture on sexual diversity at Tbilisi State University (TSU) without being rejected, ridiculed, or even physically attacked.

I was wrong. Well, I was partially wrong. Writing this chapter six years after that first meeting, I am confident that one would be hard pressed to find anyone in Georgia who has not heard of Identoba, the Georgian LGBT rights and gender equality NGO that was born at that meeting, and in which I have been active since its inception.[2] It would also be difficult to find anyone in Georgia today who does not have an opinion on LGBT issues.

Over the course of six years (2010–16), LGBT activists in Georgia have celebrated great victories and mourned terrible losses. We have organized festive street actions and large national LGBT conferences. We have been featured on the most popular Georgian television talk shows to speak about LGBT discrimination. We have opened community centers in two large cities outside of Tbilisi, have advocated in the courts, and have even heard Bidzina Ivanishvili, former prime minister of Georgia, speak favorably about LGBT rights ("PM Comments on Planned Gay Rights Rally" 2013). The topics of gender and sexuality have made it onto the syllabi of university courses, including those at TSU where I have taught for several years.[3]

On the darker side, we have experienced harassment, rejection, and violence. Every Georgian activist has received death threats, sometimes on a daily basis. Activists have been beaten up, followed in the street, blackmailed, and some even disowned by their families. There is the tragic case of Sabi Beriani, one of a very few visible transgender women in Georgia, who was stabbed to death in her own home and set on fire.[4] Press reports covering the controversy about the ban on homosexuals donating blood include hostile quotes about "Georgians drinking homosexual blood on their festive tables." And then there was the 2013 incident in which a few dozen activists holding a street rally barely escaped a hostile attack by thousands of homophobic Georgians. The more visible LGBT activists become, the more they are seen as the frightening "other"—the main threat to the Georgian nation-state.

The story of the emergence and establishment of LGBT rights activism in Georgia has not yet been told in any comprehensive way. I take the opportunity in this chapter to narrate the history of LGBT activism in Georgia. I base this narrative on in-depth and semi-structured interviews I conducted with activists in 2015, as well as on my perspective as a participant-observer who is an activist and a gender scholar.

In what follows, I reconstruct the inception and development of LGBT rights activism in post-Soviet Georgia, situating it in relation to the wider Georgian political and social scene. My ethnographic account reveals the silence that surrounded the topic of sexuality during the first years of the post-Soviet period during the 1990s, and how the issue of LGBT rights has become a main battleground in contemporary Georgian social life and politics.

In tracing the path of LGBT rights activism in Georgia, I have come to understand that specific activities initiated by individuals played an important role in the development of what we call LGBT rights activism in Georgia today. At the same time, local or transnational influences in the context of a changing social and political climate enabled these initiatives to be shaped and carried out, and influenced the reactions of the public to them. In order to have a more comprehensive picture and a better understanding of how a tiny group of LGBT activists managed to bring the issue of sexuality into the light of day, and simultaneously to put themselves in the political spotlight, it is essential to consider the importance of changing local and transnational politics, as well as the role of individual actors and initiatives.

Methodological and Theoretical Challenges

Clare Hemmings famously noted that feminist writers tend to be aware of the political nature of history, and that, by telling stories, they let certain narratives and voices dominate over others; she writes: "All history takes place in the present ... as we make and remake stories about the past to enable a particular present to gain legitimacy" (Hemmings 2005: 118). These observations reflect the methodological challenge I faced as I confronted the task of researching and writing this piece of Georgian history. As I approached this project, I posed these questions for myself: Whose knowledge and experiences do I privilege in choosing whose versions of events I gather, and whose not? What story do I want to tell? Are there others who may tell a different story? How do I determine which events matter and which do not, and how do I recognize significant milestones? How can I write a history that has never been written?

These concerns shaped the direction of the project. I began by asking open-ended questions of activists in my circle to capture their versions of events, what they considered the main stages and key episodes in this history, and even how they defined activism and whom they would consider to be an activist. This led me to identify particular "stages" in the history of LGBT activism in Georgia, and to land on a list of eight potential interviewees who had been actively involved in LGBT work at key points in time.

All respondents were individuals who spearheaded key actions and events that shaped the Georgian LGBT scene. They are or have been affiliated with particular organizations in Georgia; thus, theirs may be considered a form of "organizational activism." The stories of the "armies" of activists—those who have participated in activities and made many of the activist events possible—are not included in this project. Their perspectives may differ from those of the "insiders" in the organizations whose versions of events are at the center of this chapter. It would be worthwhile to expand this documentary history to include a wider range of activist voices.

This project also brought to the surface my need to confront and problematize the fact that these activist organizations were supported by Western development aid projects that would frame goals and activities of the organization and of the activists themselves. The organizations would adopt a Western model of human rights that included applying the discourse of human rights and LGBT identity categories to Georgian non-heterosexual or non-gender-conforming people and communities. As critical race and postcolonial scholars have noted, the protection of universalized LGBT subjects has become central to imperial projects that position the West as the signifier of progress in contrast to non-Western states that are cast as "not democratic" or "not modern enough." Thus, the imperial West is vested with the power to define the terms of sexual citizenship, the construction of racial superiority and racial subordination (Grewal and Kaplan 2001; Bacchetta and Haritaworn 2011; Agathangelow 2013; Puar 2013; Sabsay 2013). Some scholars have also critiqued the way subaltern queers identify with Western identity categories, depicting theirs as a patron–client relationship resulting in a form of "coercive mimeticism" (Bowman 2010; Bacchetta and Haritaworn 2011).

Such a critique and the charge that subaltern queers are subject to "coercive mimeticism" left me uneasy as an activist and as a scholar. How would I be able to discern agency in such an imperial context? Considering Georgia has a long history as a Russian colony and continues to face a constant military threat from Russia, I find it difficult to find my right place within the simplistic binary of the (imperial) West versus the rest.

Philosopher Madina Tlostanova offers an alternative decolonial analysis. She argues for complicating the map and conceptualizing post-Soviet spaces as double colonies—colonies of a Russian empire, which in turn is subaltern to Europe and the United States (Tlostanova 2015). She shows the ways a double colony of a secondary empire does not fit intelligibly into a West versus the rest framework. Moreover, sociologist Amina Jamal argues for moving beyond essentialist and universalist frameworks, examining the specificities and nuances of particular movements rather than depicting activists as merely passive victims of Western colonialism and imperialism (Jamal 2005). As Jamal shows in the case of a women's movement in Pakistan, the rhetoric of human rights and democracy can be effective tools for mobilizing against the repressive state, and can still be counterhegemonic, as these discourses travel, are taken up, appropriated, modified, and often put into effect by activist groups. My commitment to telling activist history through the voices of the activists themselves, and my effort to give context to the story, is informed by these debates and scholarly challenges.

Post-Soviet Georgia and Non-Normative Sexualities: The 1990s

Queer activism in Georgia must be understood in the context of the country's geopolitical history. I begin by summarizing the unstable political and economic situation in Georgia in the immediate aftermath of the collapse of the Soviet Union, which was accompanied by the revival of intense nationalism and a series of civil wars.

The Soviet legacy of criminalizing homosexuality remained law in Georgia in the 1990s. That fact as well as the great stigma surrounding non-normative sexualities inhibited any kind of queer mobilizing. During this period, there was a hidden and male-dominated queer scene, which did not transform into political activism. The activists I interviewed were largely unfamiliar with the queer scene during that period.

Political instability and economic hardship marked the early days of Georgian independence from the Soviet Union (Tsikhistavi 2003: 13). Ethnic nationalism filled the political vacuum in the immediate aftermath of the Soviet collapse, which led to several civil wars and an ever-weakening state. More than 13,000 people died in the war with Abkhazia, an estimated 250,000 to 300,000 people were internally displaced, and self-organized military forces overthrew the government (Zurcher 2007: 116; UNHCR 2009). This difficult and intense political and economic situation was not compatible with the emergence and sustenance of human rights–oriented groups. The few nongovernmental organizations that appeared in 1992 were minimally active (Nodia 2005a). The situation changed in the late 1990s when there was a surge in the number of NGOs closely linked with Western (United States and European Union) interest in supporting post-Soviet countries that had contributed to the dissolution of the Soviet Union. Western funding sources defined the mandates of these NGOs, which centered on supporting the development of what can be called a

Western standard of liberal democracy. This period saw the emergence of a number of women's organizations, though there was a resounding silence in terms of queer rights and sexuality.

There was a general consensus among my respondents that this silence may be attributed to the economic and political situation in Georgia at the time. Nika, one of the earliest gay activists among my interviewees and whose name is associated with the inception of the LGBT movement in Georgia, explained: "Should I talk about the 'dark 90s'? There was no Internet then. I did not go anywhere other than school. These were terrible years of hunger, of war. The armies were wandering around Tbilisi. Nothing was happening."

The year 2006 was a turning point in terms of LGBT activism. That was the year of the founding of the Inclusive Foundation, the first queer activist organization in Georgia, which will be discussed in the next section. Marika, a feminist, community mobilizer, and LGBT activist, described the political uncertainty that had plagued Georgia before that:

> The 1990s was the period when physical survival was a priority. Nobody was thinking about building a human rights–oriented state. It took years for the violent and bloody conflicts to calm down. If anyone talked about LGBT rights in that period, it would only result in laughter. The Rose Revolution brought stability, and the first gay organization appeared at the same time.

There is a dearth of information on queer life in Georgia during the 1990s. I have located only one scholarly text on the topic: Shorena Gabunia's article on homosexual subcultures in Tbilisi (Gabunia 2009). Based on interviews with men who have sex with men, Gabunia describes the underground social scene in parks, bathhouses, and closed elite parties that were sites for gathering and socializing. These spaces were highly secretive, exclusively male, and did not transcend into political engagement. Kakha, who identified as a woman in the early 1990s before his transition, and who is now one of the most prominent leaders in the transgender and queer movements, recalled no sign of any LGBT community life before the 2000s. He remarks:

> You know, I am old. I am 44. There was nothing like that [community gathering] in my day. There was no education in this field. I did not know who I was. I thought I was a lesbian, because I liked women. I had not even heard of the concept of transgender then. There was nothing really. There was no sex in the Soviet Union. How would an LGBT community exist?

Kakha's comment reveals the lack of sexual labels and identity categories available for queers at the time. In her research, Gabunia also struggled to define the sexual orientation of the men she interviewed, some of whom identified as heterosexual, and were married. She resolved the dilemma by referring to them as "bisexual," even if such a label may have been as foreign to these men as the term "transgender" was to Kakha. It was only later, with the advent of political stability and the Internet, that identity categories became available, a mobilizing axis for the movement.

Transformations

The activists in my study consider the 2000s as a transformative period. In the immediate aftermath of the Rose Revolution in 2003 and the rise to power of the United National Movement (UNM) opposition party, Georgia transitioned from a poor and infamously corrupt post-Soviet state to what some consider a model of democratization (Dobbins 2014). New modernization projects were introduced, including the implementation of anticorruption policies, education and police reforms, investments in building, and the restructuring of state institutions (Nodia 2005b). The Rose Revolution did create the feeling of stability and improved the quality of life for some among the population, even though UNM's neoliberal economic policies generated a significant rise in poverty and inequality (Gugushvili 2014), and resulted in the centralization of power and entrenchment of authoritarian rule (Dobbins 2014).

The early 2000s in Georgia brought increased political stability, an explicit Western orientation in state ideology and institutions (including the decriminalization of homosexuality), the emergence of a middle class in urban areas, and access to the Internet—all of this enabled the opening up of queer scenes (that had previously been underground) and the establishment of groups by a young generation of queers.[5] Individuals within them openly identified these groups as "gay," and in 2006 established the Inclusive Foundation, the first formal LGBT rights organization in Georgia. The framework of Western LGBT human rights shaped the groups and the organization, and financial support was provided by funds from European "development" sources, including COC Netherlands, the first LGBT organization in the world. This framework and the financial support enabled the Inclusive Foundation to engage in advocacy activities in a country hostile to such activities (Quinn 2007).

In recounting the factors that enabled the establishment of the Inclusive Foundation, Nika recalled it as "the period when a new generation of queers were getting access to the Internet. It enabled them to learn something about themselves. This was happening with the rapid development of technology during that time. These changes were part of our very intimate lives. As trivial as it sounds, the Internet gave people the opportunity to get to know each other and meet more freely." The technology provided the tool, and individuals embraced the opportunity to generate a more public space for the gay community in Georgia.

Nika recounted participating in creating the first online gay forum named "Gay Tbilisi." For Nika, access through the Internet meant accessing Western-originated information, including the identity categories of gay, lesbian, bisexual, and transgender. The very act of naming the forum "Gay Tbilisi" was an act of claiming the identity category and an attempt to unite a group of men under it. These naming and identity claims constituted an important political act in the early days of organizing and activism.

In terms of the emergence of a Georgian middle class as it relates to queers in Georgia, Nika ironically referred to this process as "the gentrification of gays." This gentrification is indicated by the increased involvement of gay men in the flourishing nightclub culture in Tbilisi at that time, and their role in facilitating daytime socializing in open, public spaces. A handful of centrally located cafes in Tbilisi became the main sites for gay socializing in early 2000s, with "Success Bar" the most famous among them. As Nika explained, communities among gay men that were connected through shared socializing practices began to take shape. He also described these as class-stratified communities that struggled to find commonality amid class difference. As an activist, Nika believed a first step in bringing together these disparate groups and mobilizing them for political action was to unite them under the gay label in a physical space, not simply a virtual one. Nika recalled the early days: "I was furious because these people had such a false feeling of freedom and happiness when together on online spaces ... But they would not even say hello to one another elsewhere [in real-life settings]. He continued:

> I decided that I had to do something. So I printed invitations. For one full week I sat in Success Bar handing out invitations to anyone who came in who I knew was possibly my target audience. I was telling them that there was an official gay party at "Success" on Saturday, and they were invited.

Thus, the first "official gay party" in Tbilisi was held on 2 April 2005. According to my respondents, this date represents the launch of LGBT community activism. For the rest of that year, social parties were organized and held at Success Bar. At the same time, Nika began working with feminist activists and human rights organizations looking to engage more systematically on queer rights in Georgia. Once these early activists had established networks with regional and Western queer groups, they formed the Inclusive Foundation on 19 March 2006 and began publishing the first Georgian LGBT magazine, *ME*. Their initiatives were largely supported through existing LGBT / human rights networks, such as ILGA Europe, and with funding primarily from COC Netherlands. The Inclusive Foundation shared office space in Tbilisi with the Women's Initiatives Supporting Group (WISG), the first space for queer women to gather, socialize, and get involved in activist work. The Inclusive Foundation operated for three years between 2006 and 2009, when it was shut down in a police raid.

In late December 2009, police attacked the office of Inclusive Foundation and arrested Paata Sabelashvili, who served as its director, for possession of marijuana (ILGA Europe n.d.). It remains unclear if this was a legitimate drug raid or if it was a purposeful attack on an LGBT organization. Activists involved in the organization at that time are convinced that the timing and location of the arrest was motivated by homophobia. The police entered the office during a meeting of the WISG's women's club. Tamuna, who worked at Inclusive Foundation and remained involved in LGBT and feminist movements for just a few years after Inclusive Foundation closed, reports what happened:

> The girls were locked in the room for seven hours. Their phones were taken away and they could not call their families. The policemen were shouting at them, shouting nasty stuff like "Look at how ugly they are. I'm starting to hate women." They took photographs and threatened to send these photographs to their families. They strip-searched them.

For weeks afterwards, the staff of the Inclusive Foundation were under police surveillance. Tamuna reports that she had been chased by random men when walking down the street, that undercover police had listened to conversations she had with colleagues and friends in cafes, and that people had checked through her garbage.

Looking back on the Inclusive Foundation and its operation over the three years of its life, respondents identified it as an important space for establishing the feeling of community and for providing much needed information about gender and sexuality, where none had been before. "This was a space for me to rest," Kakha remembers. "I could probably compare it with heaven. Everyone was welcome. No one was gossiping behind your back, whether you were a girl or a boy."

Even as they acknowledged the organization's contributions, respondents also acknowledged its elitist tendencies, its male-centrism and its inability to engage the wider public. Maka, an openly lesbian feminist and queer activist who is today among the most visible leaders of the movement, observed: "I rarely saw anyone in Inclusive who was not an average, statistical, fashionable gay. I am not saying this as a negative thing. But it is true. These were people who were friends with designers, models, photographers. They also had money." Marika also offered a comment that reflects a sense that the organization was not entirely inclusive: "From what I know, their work was mostly social. Parties for gay men? I know that they were very hidden." Likewise, activists at once appreciate and recognize the limitations of the Foundation's magazine *ME*. David, an activist who became actively involved in LGBT rights after the dissolution of the Inclusive Foundation, and who today is among the most prominent gay activists, remarked that *ME* "was a specific cultural publication. It was sent to specific targets by mail. It was not really available to the wider public. It did not create any scandal."

The Inclusive Foundation could not regain its legs after the raid, even though activists involved in the organization had informed diplomatic missions stationed in Georgia and international human rights groups about the incident (ILGA Europe n.d.). WISG continued its work but the Inclusive Foundation dissolved. Out of its ashes emerged Identoba (originally named the Diversity Research and Community Activism Association), which inherited the Inclusive Foundation's historical documents and material possessions (Identoba 2013). Together with feminist and other queer activists, Identoba's founding members helped shape and continue to shape the LGBT activist scene in Georgia.

Creating Noise

The years 2010 to 2012 marked a turning point in Georgian LGBT activism, which became louder and more visible. The time was right for the activists to leverage the moment. Georgian politics was again in upheaval. The United National Movement (UNM) political party was in crisis, becoming more authoritarian even as it continued to orient itself toward the West. As opposition to the dominant political party began to grow in 2009, the government began arresting political enemies, and increased state surveillance of citizens (Sosnowski 2012: 79). For the most part, LGBTs and their organizations were ignored, in part because UNM's outspoken Western orientation made it politically difficult to target LGBTs and because LGBT activism had not yet scaled up to be unavoidably noticed. That would soon change.

The police raid on the Inclusive Foundation would come back as a political specter to haunt UNM. The raid received wide international press coverage, and UNM's reputation as a beacon of democracy was being called into question. Activists recall this as being an opportune time to act. "For me, this was the hottest period of activism," said Lika, who had gotten involved in the LGBT movement at the time Identoba was established, and has since been at the forefront of queer activism, even when not formally affiliated with any organization.

The activist community became larger and the activities became more diverse. Identoba launched the online magazine, *IDMag,* which moved away from *ME*'s norm of writing in academic prose in order to write in accessible language about LGBT relationships, sex, politics, and religion. Identoba and WISG together have been central to creating new ways of speaking about gender and sexuality, as well as creating and disseminating knowledge in Georgia about the lived experiences of LGBT people and their communities.

For the activists I interviewed, these critical years of radical politics involved the disruption of comfort zones and the creation of noise. According to Marika, "this was the time when people began to say, 'This is who we are, and we are not hiding. We will talk about sexuality.' That was a radical act." For David, interrupting the norm was a form activism that revealed the status quo as no longer acceptable. "There were gay men who were themselves public figures," David explained. "They believed discrimination was simply the norm. Before we declared that Georgian gays existed, they believed that nobody would ever know about their private sexual preferences. Disrupting the comfort zones of people who had become conformist to the system was key to our activism."

That period in Georgian LGBT activism was also marked by an unprecedented intensification in knowledge generation and information dissemination. "We were translating lots of material," Maka explained, "[because] there was very little information about anything. Even though much more local knowledge is being produced today ... the frame of LGBT rights discourse was created then." We hear in Maka's words the influence of the West. Information was literally being translated from European and US sources into Georgian, and the "frame of discourse" was rooted in Western LGBT experiences as well as in theories of gender and sexuality. Considering the silences in the Georgian context, these resources were invaluable toward the liberation of LGBT politics in this post-Soviet state. For example, Irma, an attorney who has been involved in LGBT work for over four years, recalled her personal history of domestic abuse and late coming out. She reflected on how much her involvement in knowledge creation about gender and sexuality had impacted her personal struggles:

> For the first time, I began hearing about concepts such as patriarchy, discrimination based on one's gender, and cultures of violence. It was important to me. I had never thought about this before. I knew I didn't feel good but I could only articulate these feelings with general phrases such as "Every man treats women badly," and "All men are the same." But I could not go any further. I only knew I did not like it.

Formal legal and advocacy work became central to the activist agenda during this time. For example, activists initiated and won a constitutional court case against homophobic regulations prohibiting gay men from donating blood that is codified in Georgian law.[6] Activists also advocated for and achieved the inclusion of sexual orientation and gender identity as an aggravating circumstance for a hate crime in 2012. The media and the wider public largely ignored these activities and successes.

LGBT activism also went public by means of demonstrations in the street. In the two-year period between 2010 and 2012, a series of street actions were organized. Kakha is a founder of LGBT Georgia, another LGBT rights–oriented civil organization currently operating a community center in Tbilisi. In 2011, Kakha organized activists in a public candlelight vigil against homophobia and transphobia celebrated annually on 17 May.[7] In addition, in March 2012, Transgender Visibility Day was celebrated on Rustaveli Avenue, the most central street in Tbilisi. Lika participated in these street actions. Like the other activists who reflected on the first street actions, she said, "we were walking in the dark," not realizing the consequences that would result from these public actions: "For Transgender Visibility Day we were happily marching down Rustaveli with cakes and flags. No one knew what we were doing. We were happy and naïve. But our activities drew more interest in us, with unfortunate results. Before that, it was a great, uplifting period."

The noise generated by the street actions led to the mobilization of extremist right-wing religious groups and later of the official Georgian Orthodox Church against LGBT rights. This led to unprecedented violence against LGBT activists in May 2013.

The Backlash: 17 May and the Politicization of LGBT Issues

The first organized attack on LGBT activists occurred on 17 May 2012. For the first time, activists had given public notice of the street protest, which would be a demonstration in honor of the International Day against Homophobia and Transphobia. Prior to the 2012 event, all other events had appeared to the public as spontaneous. Given the advance notice, several Orthodox priests known for their aggressive nationalist rhetoric and the Orthodox Parent's Union, a radical religious group, attacked the demonstration and the demonstrators. Numbering around fifty, the counter-protesters physically attacked several of the activists. The police did not intervene to protect the LGBT activists—instead, they arrested some of them.[8]

As Maka asserted, 17 May (2012) is a significant date in Georgian LGBT history; indeed, it is an important date in Georgian history. For the activists, it marked a collective "coming out." As Maka put it:

[On this day], it became clear that we had not been working for nothing. Many people who previously would not have dared to come to the street came to the demonstration. They were afraid, but they still came. Some were covering their faces from the cameras, but they came out and stood with us. When the attack started they did not run away. They did not back up. They could [have], but they did not. For me, this was very important.

That day was also the first time the mainstream media paid attention and talked about LGBT issues. The day triggered widespread debate in the media about human rights, traditional values, the importance of claiming public space, and the "dangers" of the gay pride parade. The activists were encouraged, and called for a continuation of what they called "loud" politics. They began planning for the next year, another pre-announced and organized public event to be held on 17 May 2013. The plan was to hold a rally in a square in front of the old parliament building in Tbilisi.

Alerted to the rally, the Orthodox Church made plans of its own. Priests gave sermons to congregants warning people of the dangers of the impending homosexual scourge. The Georgian patriarch, Ilia II, publicly condemned the rally and homosexuality ("Georgian Orthodox Church Leader Calls for Gay-Rights Rally Ban" 2013). Tensions escalated in the days leading up to the event. Georgia's prime minister issued a statement asserting the rights of sexual minorities, and promised to protect LGBT demonstrators ("Georgian Prime Minister Says Sexual Minorities Have Equal Rights" 2013).

Activists were not sure what to expect. The day had arrived. The fifty or so LGBT demonstrators had begun to congregate downtown. I was one among them, as were the eight people interviewed for this history. Antigay demonstrators had filled the space in front of the parliament building. This prompted the activists to move the demonstration to Freedom Square, where they hoped to mark International Day against Homophobia and Transphobia. However, thousands of homophobes—mostly men, and led by priests—descended on the square and the demonstrators.[9]

There was a violent clash. LGBT demonstrators were attacked physically and verbally. The police were slow to respond but finally managed to shepherd the activists into buses that had been driven into the center of the chaos. The antigay protesters did not give up easily. They threw objects at the buses, breaking windows. Their bodies, pushed up against the vehicles, rocked the buses as they made their way out of the angry crowd into safety. The LGBT protesters rightfully feared for their lives, and were glad to have gotten away with injuries that would heal.

The spectacle of 17 May reflects the articulation of at least three forces operating in larger Georgian politics. One force was LGBT activism itself, which had "come out of the closet" to be on public display as a statement indicating the growing strength of the movement. A second force was the stated interest by Georgia's political leadership to ally itself with the West. Two years earlier, Georgia's president, Mikheil Saakashvili, had reaffirmed the country's interest in joining the European Union (EU), which it had been attempting to do since its independence. At the time of the May 2013 event, the government was in the final negotiations for the Georgia–EU Association Agreement that would be an important step in the process (signed in June 2014). Among the conditions of the legal agreement was the protection of the rights of sexual minorities. A third force was the Georgian Orthodox church, which has strong ties with the Russian Orthodox Church that during this same time identified opposition to LGBT rights as its main political goal (Vacharadze 2015).

These dynamics reveal that the heated discussion over LGBT rights in Georgia is situated in political rhetoric and contestation over Western versus "traditional" values. On the one hand, sexual citizenship became a signal for Georgia's qualification to enter the European Union, as it had been for other East European countries (Kulpa 2014; Moss 2014; Kahlina 2015). On the other hand, appeals to nationalist and traditionalist sentiments by means of the Russian–Georgian Orthodox Church alliance reflects Russia's "traditionalism" as strategic to its imperial project to reclaim power over former Soviet colonies (Polyakova 2014; Riabov and Riabova 2014; Laruelle 2015; Persson 2015).

Post-2013

For LGBT activists, the events of May 2013 resulted in increased concerns over security, a lessening of confrontational politics, and fewer public and street actions. All three Georgian LGBT organizations continued working with a new focus on building alliances with other human rights actors in the country, organizing workshops and conferences, and cooperating with the state to draft new human rights policies and anti-discrimination legislation. There was no rally planned for May 2014, though a disembodied protest was held in the form of an installation. Titled "Protest on Behalf of the Invisible and Against Invisibility," the installation featured one hundred pairs of shoes to honor International Day against Homophobia and Transphobia, and to mark the one-year anniversary of the violence in Freedom Square.

While some activists have embraced the new approach and appreciate legislative and others gains that are being made, others caution about activists getting too comfortable working alongside the state. As Irma noted, this work may be good but not necessarily "good enough"—it is important to ensure some distance, leaving room to "confront the state." That space may be taken up by a new generation of LGBT activists in Georgia. For example, the Georgian Young Greens have taken up the cause ("Greens against Homophobia" 2015), and a loose coalition of queer youth political groups has emerged. It remains to be seen what their politics and their activities will look like, and whether or not they will conform to an LGBT rights framework.[10]

As indicated by this short history of the LGBT movement, gender, sex, and sexuality constitute a burning political issue involving global geopolitics, the Georgian Orthodox Church, homophobia, rights, nationalism, and public opinion in Georgia (see Rener and Ule 1998 on these issues in post-Soviet spaces more generally). In tracing the silences—and the reasons for it—that surrounded the topics of sexuality and gender in the 1990s as well as the reverberations of the movement over time, I have revealed how and why the issue of LGBT rights has become a main battleground in Georgian social life and politics. This history reveals the contributions that individual activists and activism itself make in bringing an issue out of the shadows and into public discussion, resulting in meaningful social change. It also reveals how a set of larger forces can shape the trajectory of activism in ways that may advance or thwart goals, sometimes at the same time. The particular form of future LGBT activism is uncertain. Even so, as the novelist Daphne du Maurier once wrote, "We can never go back again, that much is certain" (du Maurier 2006: 5).

Anna Rekhviashvili is a doctoral student in gender, feminist and women's studies at York University, Toronto, Canada. In 2012–15 she taught undergraduate and graduate students in the Department of Gender Studies at Tbilisi State University and was a returning scholar of the Academic Development Program, Open Society Foundations. She has also been actively involved in the LGBTQ rights movement in Georgia. Her dissertation research focuses on analyzing the work of LGBT rights movements in Eastern Europe in relation to regional as well as transnational geopolitics of sexuality.

Notes

1. To protect individual identities, names of interviewees in this chapter are pseudonyms.
2. As indicated on its website, "Identoba is one of Georgia's premier multi-issue LGBT & general human rights NGOs committed to social change, community organization, education, and policy reform. Founded in 2010, Identoba seeks to end discrimination and

systemic oppression of Georgia's marginalized communities, particularly LGBT persons, women, disabled, disadvantaged youth, and Roma communities. Identoba envisions a common good that acknowledges the intrinsic diversity of Georgian civil society, promoting the active integration of the marginalized into public life. Through our research publications, journalism, community organization, and policy work, Identoba aims to center the narratives of minority voices in the entirety of our work—advancing their visibility in the public consciousness and national dialogue" (http://identoba.ge/).
3. Despite this progress, there continue to be major setbacks. For example, in February 2016, Identoba had planned to hold a sexualities conference at Tbilisi State University (TSU). In response to protests by self-proclaimed "traditionalists" affiliated with the Young National Alliance and *Erovnulebi* (Nationals), TSU refused to accommodate the conference, which was then held in Identoba's offices ("Protesters Succeed in Preventing LGBT Conference at TSU" 2016).
4. The court originally acquitted Levan Kochlashvili of the murder but convicted him of arson. Two years and several appeals later, in 2016 he was convicted of the murder and sentenced to ten years in prison.
5. Georgia's membership in the Council of Europe in 1999 signaled its ideological orientation toward Europeanization. Membership in the council led to the decriminalization of homosexuality in 2000. The legal change was not widely publicized, did not enter public discourse, and did not spark widespread debates about sexuality. During this period, the topic of sexuality was not on the public agenda.
6. The case was decided upon in 2014. As of January 2016, the Ministry of Health, responsible for implementing the changes according to the ruling, has not yet done so.
7. May 17th marks International Day against Homophobia and Transphobia (IDAHOT).
8. Activists initiated a European Court of Human Rights (ECHR) case against Georgia because of the illegal actions by the police on 17 May 2012. The activists won the case. The ruling of the court was announced on 12 May 2015.
9. The exact number of anti-gay protesters is not known. Some activists claim there were more than forty thousand; news reports note there were "thousands."
10. The research for this chapter was finalized in December 2015. In February 2016, major changes took place at Identoba. A few employees accused its administrators of fraud, which resulted in a public scandal and a complete change in Identoba's administration. Other employees left the organization as a sign of protest over unexpected changes. The investigation about the allegations has not yet been concluded. However, these events led to Identoba's evaporation as a public actor in the Georgian LGBT scene just before International Day against Homophobia and Transphobia 2016, as well as before the October elections. Soon after the events, the Georgian Parliament began discussing a constitutional change to define marriage as a union between a man and a woman (the current Georgian constitution defines marriage between two people; heteronormativity of marriage was only institutionalized by civil law), which many consider to be an effort by the government to gain the votes of a majority of the population. In this chapter, I have relied primarily on data from the interviews to reconstruct the history; thus, these latest developments in the Georgian LGBT scene are not part of this chapter. These events, however, reveal that the story and the history continue to unfold.

References

Agathangelou, A.M. 2013. "Neoliberal Geopolitical Order and Value: Queerness as a Speculative Economy and Anti-Blackness as Terror." *International Feminist Journal of Politics* 15(4): 453–76.

Bacchetta, P., and J. Haritaworn. 2011. "There are Many Transatlantics: Homonationalism, Homotransnationalism." In *Transatlantic Conversations: Feminism As Travelling Theory*, ed. K. Davis and M. Evans, 127–44. Aldershot: Ashgate Publishing.
Bowman, P. 2010. "Introduction: Rey Chow and Postcolonial Social Semiotics." *Social Semiotics* 20(4): 329–41.
Dobbins, M. 2014. "The Post-Rose Revolution Reforms as a Case of Misguided Policy Transfer and Accidental Democratisation?" *Europe–Asia Studies* 66(5): 759–74.
du Maurier, D. 2006. *Rebecca*. New York: William Morrow Paperbacks.
Gabunia, Sh. 2009. "Homosexuality in Tbilisi Urban Culture." Tbilisi: Heinrich Böll Foundation, South Caucasus. Retrieved 10 January 2016 from https://ge.boell.org/sites/default/files/downloads/Shorena_Gabunia_2009.pdf.
"Georgian Orthodox Church Leader Calls for Gay-Rights Rally Ban." 2013. *Radio Free Europe*, 13 May. Retrieved 3 May 2016 from http://www.rferl.org/content/georgia-patriarch-gay-rights/24988151.html.
"Georgian Prime Minister Says Sexual Minorities Have Equal Rights." 2013. *Radio Free Europe*, 15 May. Retrieved 3 May 2016 from http://www.rferl.org/content/georgia-lgbt-equal-rights/24986492.html
"Greens against Homophobia." 2015. *Georgian Young Greens*, 2 March. Retrieved 2 May 2016 from http://younggreens.ge/greens-against-homophobia/.
Grewal, I., and C. Kaplan. 2001. "Global Identities: Theorizing Transnational Studies of Sexuality." *GLQ: A Journal of Lesbian and Gay Studies* 7(4): 663–79.
Gugushvili, D. 2014. "Do the Benefits of Growth Trickle Down to Georgia's Poor? A Case for a Strong Welfare System." PhD dissertation. University of Kent.
Hemmings, C. 2005. "Telling Feminist Stories." *Feminist Theory* 6(2): 115–39.
Identoba. 2013. "Violations of the Rights of Lesbian, Gay, Bisexual, and Transgender People in Georgia." Retrieved 2 May 2016 from http://tbinternet.ohchr.org/Treaties/CCPR/Shared%20Documents/GEO/INT_CCPR_NGO_GEO_15206_E.pdf.
ILGA Europe. n.d. "The Status of Lesbian, Gay, Bisexual and Transgender Rights in Georgia." Retrieved 2 May 2016 from http://lib.ohchr.org/HRBodies/UPR/Documents/Session10/GE/JS3_JointSubmission3-eng.pdf.
Jamal, A. 2005. "Transnational Feminism as Critical Practice: A Reading of Feminist Discourses in Pakistan." *Meridians: Feminism, Race, Transnationalism* 5(2): 57–82.
Kahlina, K. 2015. "Local Histories, European LGBT Designs: Sexual Citizenship, Nationalism, and 'Europeanisation' in Post-Yugoslav Croatia and Serbia." *Women's Studies International Forum* 49: 73–83.
Kulpa, R. 2014. "Western Leveraged Pedagogy of Central and Eastern Europe: Discourses of Homophobia, Tolerance, and Nationhood." *Gender, Place & Culture* 21(4): 431–48.
Laruelle, M. 2015. "The 'Russian World': Russia's Soft Power and Geopolitical Imagination." Center on Global Interests. Retrived 10 January 2016 from http://globalinterests.org/wp-content/uploads/2015/05/FINAL-CGI_Russian-World_Marlene-Laruelle.pdf.
Moss, K. 2014. "Split Europe: Homonationalism and Homophobia in Croatia." In *LGBT Activism and the Making of Europe: A Rainbow Europe?*, ed. P.M. Ayoub and D. Paternotte, 212–232. Basingstoke: Palgrave Macmillan.
Nodia, G. 2005a. "Civil Society Development in Georgia: Achievements and Challenges." Policy paper. Tbilisi: Caucasus Institute for Peace, Democracy and Development.
———. 2005b. "Dimensions of Insecurity." In *Statehood and Security: Georgia after the Rose Revolution*, ed. B. Coppieters and R. Legvold, 248–76. Cambridge, MA: The MIT Press.
Persson, E. 2015. "Banning 'Homosexual Propaganda': Belonging and Visibility in Contemporary Russian Media." *Sexuality & Culture* 19(2): 256–74.
"PM Comments on Planned Gay Rights Rally." 2013. *Civil Georgia*, 13 May. Retrieved 2 May 2016 from http://civil.ge/eng/article.php?id=26055.

Polyakova, A. 2014. "Strange Bedfellows: Putin and Europe's Far Right." *World Affairs*, September/October. Retrieved 10 January 2016 from http://www.worldaffairsjournal.org/article/strange-bedfellows-putin-and-europe%E2%80%99s-far-right.

"Protesters Succeed in Preventing LGBT Conference at TSU." 2016. *Democracy and Freedom Watch*, 22 February. Retrieved 2 May 2016 from http://dfwatch.net/protesters-succeed-in-preventing-lgbt-conference-at-tbilisi-state-university-40360\.

Puar, J. 2013. "Homonationalism as Assemblage: Viral Travels, Affective Sexualities." *Jindal Global Law Review* 4(2): 23–43.

Quinn, S. 2007. "Forced Out: LGBT People in Georgia." Report on ILGA-Europe / COC Fact-finding Mission. Retrieved 3 May 2016 from http://www.ilga-europe.org/sites/default/files/Attachments/forces_out_lgbt_people_in_georgia_august_2007.pdf.

Rener, T., and M. Ule. 1998. "Back to the Future: Nationalism and Gender in Post-socialist Societies." In *Women, Ethnicity and Nationalism: The Politics of Transition*, ed. R.E. Miler and R. Wilford, 104–114. London: Routledge.

Riabov, O., and T. Riabova. 2014. "The Remasculinization of Russia: Gender, Nationalism, and the Legitimation of Power under Vladimir Putin." *Problems of Post-Communism* 61(2): 23–35.

Sabsay, L. 2013. "Queering the Politics of Global Sexual Rights?" *Studies in Ethnicity and Nationalism* 13(1): 80–90.

Sosnowski, A. 2012. *The Georgia Syndrome*, trans. M. Turner. Rottenburg: Mauer Verlag Wilfried Kriese.

Tlostanova, M. 2015. "Between the Russian/Soviet Dependencies, Neoliberal Delusions, Dewesternizing Options, and Decolonial Drives." *Cultural Dynamics* 27(2): 267–83.

Tsikhistavi, T. 2003. "Georgia after the Collapse of the Soviet Union: A Case Study in Conflict Analysis – Period from the Independence of Georgia till the End of Internal Conflicts – 1991–1994." MAS Dissertation. European University Center for Peace Studies.

UNHCR. 2009. "Protection of Internally Displaced Persons in Georgia: A Gap Analysis." Retrieved 10 January 2016 from http://www.unhcr.org/4ad827f59.pdf.

Vacharadze, I. 2015. "The End of the Georgian Orthodox Christian Church, As We Know It." In *Traditional Religion and Political Power: Examining the Role of the Church in Georgia, Armenia, Ukraine and Moldova*, ed. A. Hug, 53–56 . The Foreign Policy Centre (FPC). Retrieved 10 January 2016 from http://fpc.org.uk/fsblob/1707.pdf

Zurcher, C. 2007. *The Post-Soviet Wars: Rebellion, Ethnic Conflict, and Nationhood in the Caucasus*. New York: NYU Press.

Afterword

Elizabeth Cullen Dunn

When the feminist movement was revived in United States in the 1970s, one of the key tenets of the movement was that "the personal is political." In the Republic of Georgia, however, the personal is deeply, innately "geopolitical," thanks to Georgia's geographical position as the crumple zone between expanding empires. Each of the chapters in this collection is, whether implicitly or explicitly, set in the context of a high-stakes political conflict between a neoimperialist Russia and a Euro-American alliance, which is, however ambivalently, expansionist. The conflict between these two empires has been fought on many grounds, including trade (for example, during Russia's 2006 ban on Georgian imports) and ethnicity (as when the United States backed an ethnic Georgian government of the breakaway province of South Ossetia, while Russia backed the Ossetians). The conflict has been, and continues to be, fought militarily: the Russian 58th Army has created an entire system of bases along the administrative boundary line between Georgia and South Ossetia, while the United States arms and trains the Georgian Army. But the battle has been no more fiercely engaged than on the terrain of gender. Women's bodies, labor, emotions, and sexualities have become the grounds for a geopolitical conflict expressed in terms of morality and values. While Western NGOs continue to use pre-packaged programs to promote "gender mainstreaming" and to advance an agenda of women's equality, the Putin government has declared itself the guardian of so-called "traditional values," especially ones around gender and sexuality, and has convinced the Georgian Orthodox Church, the most powerful institution in Georgian society, to follow along.

To even raise the topic of gender, then, always means talking about more than gender identity or sexual orientation. In ways that are more or less coded, talking about gender means exploring the effects of Georgia's geopolitical predicament on these embodied habituses, both historically and in the present, and seeking to understand how men's and women's performances of gender in their everyday lives factor into regional and global politics. Many of the chapters in this book take a descriptive approach—they claim only to describe attitudes and practices, not to mandate them. In adopting the framework of Western feminism and LGBT rights, many of them also assume a yardstick of idealized Western values, such as gender equality and tolerance of diversity. That, in contemporary Georgia, is a bold approach: as Tskhadadze (this volume) points out, the notion that gender roles might be mutable or that the burden of domestic work could be divided differently is very far away from being common sense. To oppose gender essentialism is to constantly refer to values that are new, politically marked, fragile, and bitterly contested in the regional battle for "spheres of influence." It also, as Tskhadadze further points out, places Georgia in the uncomfortable position of being somehow underdeveloped or behind, and rules out the possibility of developing some sort of uniquely Georgian gender politics, rather than being forced to choose between two models introduced from abroad.

Collectively, then, the works in this volume also implicitly question unstated notions of desire in Georgia. Are calls for a more equal division of household labor, or gay rights, or government opposition to domestic violence, really only about one's personal or domestic life? Or are they about the desire for Europe and the desire to be "European," whatever that means? On the flip side, is the constitution of the exaggerated heteronormative femininity now common across the country really only about demanding that women evoke sexual desire in men? Or is it also about evoking a desire in men for social dominance, even in a context where their roles have been weakened by unemployment, wage decline, and the transformation of the economy? Could the "traditional desire for a 'Big Other,'" in Zizek's sense, be embodied here by an attraction to a resurgent (and idealized) Russia? Or is this all simply nostalgic, about some desire for some imagined stability in the past, before the turmoil caused by the collapse of the USSR, when people ostensibly "knew their places" in terms of gender, ethnicity, occupation, and other categories? As the contributors to this volume have shown, it is not always clear what, exactly, people in Georgia are talking about, or what they want when they talk about gender. But controversies about gender are always about political, social, and economic formations that go far beyond gender itself.

The Soviet Period

The mythologized past, when men were men and women were women and everyone knew their place, is of course a nostalgic fantasy. The chapters in this volume demonstrate how the turbulent geopolitics of Sovietization and the construction of a deeply gendered *homo Sovieticus* led to equally turbulent gender relations. This was not all due to the dreams of Bolshevik revolutionaries like Aleksandra Kollontai (indeed, as Gaprindashvili's chapter shows, Bolshevism both quashed the nascent feminist movement in Georgia and promoted it). Nor was it all due to the USSR's ideological commitment to the transformation of gender roles, even though, as both Barkaia and Tsopurashvili (this volume) show, the Soviets used talk about the equality of women to demonstrate the progressive nature of their regime. In the end, the centrally planned economy, which made labor a commodity as much in shortage as any other, demanded that women be swept into the workforce, and this was profoundly transformative both for women's sense of self, their activities in the public sphere, and their domestic relations (see Grabowska, this volume). Whether or not they subscribed to "feminism" as an ideological or political project, the very fact that women were in the workforce and in the Communist Party apparatus opened up new possibilities for action. True, much of this action was reactive or adaptive rather than creative: it was aimed at finding a way to "get by" in a politically and economically challenging situation that was still very much dominated by men. But there were also new rights and new possibilities for creation. Social supports such as legal abortion and childcare services freed up women's labor; mandated quotas for women in politics gave them opportunities to participate in governance; and state subsidies for art, music, literature, scientific research, and other creative endeavors opened up avenues for women to participate in the intellectual life of the nation.

As Grabowska also shows, the argument that feminism was somehow quashed during the Soviet period and only revived after the fall of the USSR is to misunderstand the complex and ambivalent historical transformation of what it meant to be a woman (or a man) during that era, and what the incorporation of gendered and ethnicized bodies meant to the Soviet project, and thus to misunderstand the ways that the forms the Soviet project took shaped both everyday life and the geopolitics of the postsocialist period. Although gender discrimination was still rampant in the Soviet period, and women indeed faced a "double burden" of employment and housework, many women in fact did get important, high-ranking jobs—an experience that stood them in good stead during the postsocialist period. Grabowska's research demonstrates how women's experiences in the Communist Party gave them skills that they transformed in the two decades after the end of socialism in order to become researchers, NGO leaders, politicians, and so on.

But Georgian women did not have an uncomplicated view of the role of feminism in either Soviet ideology or the Soviet economy. As in other state socialist countries, because feminism was so ideologically tied to the state, opposition to the state often entailed opposition to feminism. To be in favor of "traditional" gender roles was to create a domestic space ostensibly free from the state, to deny the state the right to define familial relations, and even to oppose the incorporation of diverse national groups into a "Soviet" polity or identity. This, too, would become consequential in the post-Soviet period. Like national identity, gender is a language and a metaphor through which other political and geopolitical issues—including the form and meaning of "the nation," and the question of national independence—can be discussed.

The 1990s

The collapse of the USSR, which severed many but not all of the economic and political connections between Georgia and Russia, had profound effects on gendered power and gendered labor. Georgia experienced a massive economic collapse in 1991, and began to experience economic involution. As the country lost many of its exports to and imports from other former Soviet republics and also the Warsaw Pact countries, the economy began to divert resources from production to exchange and consumption. This meant the Georgian economy was eating away at its own foundations (Burawoy 1999). Factories, the products of Soviet industrialization, closed and were looted for scrap metal. The country's infrastructure decayed: electricity was only randomly available, and many urban areas no longer had a reliable supply of running water.

Most importantly, involution meant that the Soviet food production, processing, and distribution system collapsed. This meant that many families, both rural and urban, had to fall back on small-scale subsistence farming (Dunn 2008). Cities, once the proud results of Soviet industrialization and urbanization, took on the attributes of villages: people raised chickens and pigs in urban apartment buildings, and cattle roamed the streets even in large cities such as Kutaisi. Most of the tasks associated with the subsistence economy fell to women: raising chickens or milking cattle, for example, were deemed tasks for women, as was canning fruits and vegetables to ensure a food supply in winter. Women's domestic chores became essential to family survival in the 1990s; given the absence of waged jobs, their labor was often the difference between starving and not. Meanwhile, men's economic activity often became oriented towards the gray market: smuggling fruits and vegetables, buying and selling gasoline at venues unregulated by the state, and trafficking cigarettes, guns and drugs—all became viable means of earning a living (see Kukhianidze, Kupatadze, and Gotsiridze 2004).

Economic and political involution gave neotraditionalist gender roles a value they might otherwise not have had. Ideas about gendered labor, which had once been challenged by the Soviet drive to get women in the workplace, were reorganized along essentialist lines. Because Georgia had no functioning state to regulate foreign trade or conduct foreign affairs, and because Russia, its largest trading partner, was in political and economic disarray, the country turned inwards, both politically and economically. Linking women to the domestic sphere and the household economy was thus part of both economic involution and an isolationist geopolitical orientation.

Yet, isolation was never really possible. During the 1990s, the military conflicts with both Abkhazia and South Ossetia, which claimed to want to be independent states, were deeply premised on their relationships with the Russian government. Ademon Nykhas, the South Ossetian popular front, openly declared that it wanted to have South Ossetia join the Russian Federation (Kaufman 2001). Abkhazia did not openly lobby to join the Russian Federation, but nonetheless became intensely dependent on Russian financial and military aid after it split from Georgia in 1993. As Kabachnik, Grabowska, and Regulska (2013) argue, although the resulting expulsion of nearly a quarter of a million people from the territory of Abkhazia was framed in ethno-national terms, its lived effects were mostly experienced in gendered terms. The loss of men's occupational status and economic power, coupled with women's rising economic importance, led both men and women to experience displacement as first and foremost a violation of hegemonic gender norms, and thus a violation of the normal order of things, rather than purely a question of national identity or territorial loss.

The Rose Revolution

With Mikheil Saakashvili's Rose Revolution in 2003, Georgia's geopolitical orientation changed—and so, too, did the ways that geopolitics shaped gender identities and gender relations. The reformers of Saakashvili's United National Movement promised to transform the Georgian economy along the same neoliberal lines that Poland, the Czech Republic, and Hungary had deployed in the 1990s. By encouraging foreign investment, reducing or eliminating unregulated economic activity, and relentlessly commodifying labor, the United National Movement hoped to break the trend toward involution, and reorient the Georgian economy to trade outside the country's own borders. An externally facing politics was part and parcel of these reforms. Deploying a strategy long-used in Georgian geopolitics, Saakashvili sought to play one empire against another, and in doing so, carve out space for Georgian political and economic independence. Where Georgia was once limited to traffic with geographically contiguous empires, the twenty-first century offered the possibility of involving empires that were not geographically proximate. The Euro-American alliance, embodied in NATO and, partially, the European Union, had expanded dramatically in the early 2000s. The dream of joining them—or at least using that possibility to hold an equally expansionist Russia back—seemed feasible. And so Saakashvili began holding out membership of NATO and the European Union as political goals.

Proving Georgia's essential Europeanness was a major part of the campaign to join NATO and the EU. But Europeanness was, and is, a murky quality, one that hinges not only on political institutions and legal frameworks, but on the performance of an ineffable cultural quality, one aligned more to the rhetoric of the EU than to the actual acts of any European country. A commitment to gender equity, as well as to other human rights, has been a cornerstone of EU policy, and was widely regarded as an indicator of readiness to join the community of European nations. To drive that message home, the EU funded studies on gender relations in Georgia, and funded a wide array of projects designed to "empower" and "mobilize" women. Additionally, the EU made "gender mainstreaming," or the deliberate inclusion of women, a required part of many of its humanitarian aid and development projects. The message was clear: to be European, one had to support the equality of women and men. This was not lost on the Georgian government, which rushed to pass a State Concept on Gender Equality (2006), a Gender Equality Law (2010), and a series of Gender Equality Action Plans (2007–2009 and 2011–2013).

Yet, just as forced migration and the shift from men to women as family breadwinners did not change hegemonic gender norms for displaced Georgians, the social changes wrought by European intervention and the drive towards Europeanization did not often change "traditional" gender norms, but reinforced them. Despite all the rhetoric around gender equality, for example, little was done to improve women's place in the labor market or their representation in government (see Chkheidze, this volume). As Sumbadze (this volume) shows, stereotypes about women's intelligence and suitability for different jobs continued to handicap them in education, in the workforce, and in civic participation. The division of household labor that was hardened during the involution of the 1990s continued to place enormous burdens on women that de facto kept them from career advancement and greater participation in the public sphere (see Duban 2010). As late as 2012, 88.5 percent of the Georgian population believed that "a woman's main duty is to take care of the family" (Jumpstart Georgia 2013).

Although the commodification of labor under neoliberalism created new opportunities for women in the labor market, both in the domain of waged labor, as small businesses began opening at a greater rate, and in the sphere of unofficial trading (Duban 2010), the commodification of women's labor too often resulted in the commodification of women. The blend of the Soviet-era valorization of physical appearance combined with "Westernization" and commercialization too often led to a strange hyperfemininity, in which women became products for the (male-dominated) market. Georgian women were simultaneously held to a rigid standard of physical attractiveness while, at least in the minds of 77 percent of the population, being expected to be a virgin at the time of marriage (Lomsadze 2010). As one of Lomsadze's interviewees complained, "Sex is something you do in Ukraine, Russia or some other place where people are grown-up about this, while here you just get married." Men, not held to the same standard of premarital sexual purity or marital fidelity, drove a rise in the sex trade, where women not only from Georgia but from Turkey, Bosnia, and Central Asia literally became commodities. But other women, too, faced attempts to commodify them: Western-style advertising and hypersexualized images of women in the media all promoted extremely conservative ideals for gendered performance, including the idea that a woman's value is only defined as a consumable object of male desire.

The tension that these two, very often opposing, pressures create, not only for women but for the polity as a whole, can be extremely intense. On the one hand women are expected to be "modern," "European," sexualized objects of desire; on the other hand, they are expected to be "traditional," "Georgian," sexually restrained keepers of the family honor and the domestic sphere. These opposing values are, not surprisingly, also mapped onto Georgian national-level politics as well as onto international geopolitics. At national-level politics, there is acute tension between those (including members of the UNM and others) who want to declare Georgia to be "modern" and "European," and to make NATO and/or EU accession a top priority. On the other hand, there are those who believe the country should stick to its "traditional" orientation.

This tension has, in recent years, been brought into the realm of geopolitical conflict. After the 2008 war in Georgia, which pitted Russia against the Euro-American alliance, much of the continuing conflict between the two superpowers has been fought in the domain of culture. In deliberate opposition to the progressive vision of the European Union, the Putin administration has advanced a vision of Russia as the guardian of so-called traditional values—which, of course, rest heavily on the regulation of gender identity and sexuality. Laws such as Russia's "anti-homopropaganda" laws, which had a severe chilling effect on the expression of or discussion about alternative gender identities or forms of sexual orientation, attempted to legally enforce heteronormative ideas of gender and sexuality (see Wilkinson 2014). This new form of morality politics, as Sharafutdinova (2014) shows, aims to forge a new basis of political legitimacy for the Putin administration, which was badly shaken by the Pussy Riot incident and other forms of protest in 2010–11 (see also Gessen 2014). These "traditional values" are, of course, thoroughly modern in their engagement with politically progressive and neoliberal politics: they are deliberately put forward as an alternative to Western cosmopolitanism, multiculturalism, feminism, and tolerance of sexual difference (see Kirchick 2014).

The political logic of this call for a return to conservative values has not been limited to Russia. Similar ideas have been put forward in Georgia by the Georgian Orthodox Church, which has strong ties to the Russian Orthodox Church (which in turn has strong ties to the Kremlin). The 2013 attack on members of a gay rights organization, discussed by Rekhviashvili (this volume), was led by Orthodox priests and condoned by Patriarch Ilia II, who referred to the nearly lethal attack as merely "impolite." The attack was also covertly condoned by the Georgian government, led by Irakli Garibashvili of the anti-Saakashvili Georgian Dream Party. The government took more than four days to arrest the priests who led the attack, and then released them after they had paid a $60 fine (Antelava 2013). The notion that "traditional values" are under attack by the West has diffused throughout Georgian society: in May 2016, the Kiwi Cafe, a vegan restaurant known to have English-speaking foreign workers and gay and lesbian patrons, was attacked by far-right nationalist extremists (Synovitz 2016). While the headlines were funny—"Sausage-Wielding Extremists Attack Vegan Cafe"—the underlying political message was not: for Georgian nationalists, the entire complex of foreign/vegan/feminist/homosexual was a threat to Georgian national identity. In a larger sense, for nationalists and conservatives, the rejection of heteronormative gender identities, sexual orientations, or gender roles in any shape threatens to unravel the fabric of the nation, which they see as essentially bound up with ideas of gender and kinship. This view, which is becoming more widespread in Georgia, plays into Russian political aims. By encouraging Georgians to reject cultural and social integration into the West, the notion of "traditional values" also encourages them to reject political and economic integration, and thus mitigates against the idea of Georgia becoming a member of NATO or the EU—a specter that the Putin administration finds intolerable.

Conclusion

It is easy to miss both the bravery and the importance of the chapters in this volume. To a Western reader, they often echo ideas that might seem common sense. But these ideas are in no way common sense in the Republic of Georgia: they are, in fact, views that run deeply against the grain of contemporary nationalism, religious revival, and politics. To advocate for simple notions like equality in the workplace, a more just division of household labor, and the rights of gay and transgendered people is to openly contest the current, highly gendered, political and social order, to criticize the government, and to challenge the church.

A feminist approach to the study of Georgia is thus about putting forward a view of the country's future that is in no way assured. The neoliberal vision put forward by the Saakashvili government implied a teleology—a one-way developmental path in which Georgia would follow the same historical development that Western Europe faced, complete with the growth of Western-style human rights. But that vision, which also implied a set of geopolitical alliances that would bring Georgia ever closer to the West, is in fact no way assured: it is one vision of the country's future competing with many others. The ambivalent political situation that Georgia faces in the post-Saakashvili era shows how deeply Western notions of rights, which are attached to individuals, conflict with other ideas of rights rooted in the Russian imperial and Soviet periods, which prioritize the rights and identities of collectivities, particularly nations, over the rights of individuals. That conflict, though, opens the door to other ideas about what the Georgian polity and Georgian society could be— visions that go beyond the simple dichotomy between "modern" (read: neoliberal) and "traditional" values. The chapters in this volume offer windows onto a vision of Georgian society that could be something other than the hyper-individualist, hyper-marketized vision that the neoliberals put forward, which did not take into account the complex attachments of kinship, community, and belonging that matter so deeply in Georgia. But so, too, do they offer the possibility of a future in which women, gay people, transgendered people and others can live outside the narrow confines of the roles to which they have heretofore been assigned. These chapters talk very much about the ways that those marginalized by their gender or orientation can assume a new kind of citizenship, one that does not leave them merely as rights-bearing individuals but ensures them a central role in the polity.

The words in this volume, then, are fraught by their very nature, and will enter into a political battleground the moment they are published. They are an intrinsic part of the wider conversation about what Georgia, still engaged in massive social transformation, could become. They are also part of a wider conversation about Georgia's geopolitical alliances: to talk about futures other than the ones laid out by the Europeans, the Americans, and the Russians is also, inherently, to rethink Georgia's political role and to imagine the country as an independent political entity that can carve its own path, rather than merely following the policies laid down by one or another empire. This breadth of imagination makes the chapters in this volume all the more significant, not just for what they contribute to the larger study of gender and sexuality, but for what they contribute to the future of the country they analyze.

Elizabeth Cullen Dunn is associate professor of geography and international studies, Indiana University, Bloomington. She is author of *No Path Home: Humanitarian Camps and the Grief of Displacement* (Cornell University Press, 2017), based on fieldwork in IDP settlements in the Republic of Georgia she has been conducting since 2009. Professor Dunn publishes widely on displacement, humanitarianism, and the effects of large bureaucratic systems during periods of cataclysmic social change, including most recently on refugee camps for *The Boston Review* (28 September 2015) and *Slate* (1 October 2015).

References

Antelava, N. 2013. "What Was Behind Georgia's Anti-Gay Rally?" *New Yorker*, 23 May. Retrieved 16 August 2016 from http://www.newyorker.com/news/news-desk/what-was-behind-georgias-anti-gay-rallypa.

Burawoy, M. 1999. "The Great Involution: Russia's Response to the Market." Unpublished ms. http://burawoy.berkeley.edu/Russia/involution.pdf.

Duban, E. 2010. "Gender Assessment: USAID Georgia." http://pdf.usaid.gov/pdf_docs/Pnads884.pdf.

Dunn, E.C. 2008. "Postsocialist Spores: Disease, Bodies and the State in the Republic of Georgia." *American Ethnologist* 35 (2): 243–258.

Gessen, M. 2014. *Words Will Break Cement: The Passion of Pussy Riot*. New York: Riverhead Books.

Jumpstart Georgia. 2013. "Men and Women's Roles in a Family in Georgia" (infographic). https://feradi.info/en/visualizations/ojakhshi-saqmis-ganatsileba-qalebsa-da-katsebs-shoris.
Kabachnik, P., M. Grabowska, and J. Regulska. 2013. "Traumatic Masculinities: The Gendered Geographies of Georgian IDPs from Abkhazia." *Gender, Place and Culture* 20(6): 773–93.
Kaufman, S.J. 2001. *Modern Hatreds: The Symbolic Politics of Ethnic War.* Ithaca, NY: Cornell University Press.
Kirchick, J. 2014. "Why Putin's Defense of 'Traditional Values' is Really a War on Freedom." *Foreign Affairs,* 3 January. http://foreignpolicy.com/2014/01/03/why-putins-defense-of-traditional-values-is-really-a-war-on-freedom/.
Kukhianidze, A., A. Kupatadze, and R. Gotsiridze. 2004. "Smuggling through Abkhazia and Tskhinvali Region of Georgia." Working paper. Washington, DC: Transnational Crime and Corruption Center, American University. http://traccc.gmu.edu/pdfs/publications/Georgia_Publications/Kukhianidze_Kupatadze_Smuggling_Georgia_Eng._2004.pdf.
Lomsadze, G. 2010. "The Virginity Institute: Sex and the Georgian Woman." http://www.eurasianet.org/node/61048.
Sharafutdinova, G. 2014. "The Pussy Riot Affair and Putin's Demarche from Sovereign Democracy to Sovereign Morality." *Nationalities Papers* 42(4): 615–21.
Synovitz, R. 2016. "Sausage-Wielding Extremists Attack Vegan Cafe in Tbilisi." *RFERL,* 30 May. http://www.rferl.org/content/georgia-nationalists-attack-vegan-cafe-with-sausages/27766236.html.
Wilkinson, C. 2014. "Putting 'Traditional Values' into Practice: The Rise and Contestation of Anti-Homopropaganda Laws." *Journal of Human Rights* 3: 363–79.

Index

A
Abkhazia, 14, 68, 125, 127–133, 140–142, 145, 148–149, 151n3, 209, 227
abortion, 43, 66–67, 75, 96, 100, 225
accident, 3, 5
activism, 25, 27, 29, 80, 101, 212
    LGBT activism, 206–207, 210, 214–217, 219
    queer activism, 209
    transgender activism, 194, 196, 202–203
    women's activism, 10, 12, 22, 30, 61–65, 67, 71, 73
advocacy, 10, 89–90, 211, 215
agency, 9, 14–15, 62, 67, 72–73, 75, 138–140, 142–146, 149–150, 157, 161, 167, 169–170, 203, 208
Akhnazarov, Artem, 28
Andronikashvili, Zaal, 53–54
anti-discrimination legislation, 218
Anti-Domestic Violence Law of Georgia, 111, 113, 115
anti-Western propaganda, 48
    anti-Western sentiments, 6, 52
Armand, Inessa, 63, 65
armed conflict, 14, 125–126, 129. *See also* war
    ethnic conflict, 79

B
backwardness, 34–35, 49–52
Beria, Lavrentyi, 131
Beriani, Sabi, 199, 206
Berishvili, Zakaria, 158–159
Bolsheviks, 11, 29–30, 65, 100, 102, 166
Böröcz, József, 49–50, 53
breadwinner, 14, 79, 117, 141, 143, 147, 150, 173, 178, 189, 228
bribe, 133–134
Brooks, Abigail, 127
Bulgakowa, Oksana, 157

C
catching up, 51–52, 54
Caucasus, 9, 157, 162
Chakrabarty, Dipesh, 35, 48–49, 58
Chatterjee, Partha, 58
Chiaureli, Mikheil, 165
Chveni Gza, 11, 33–34, 37, 98, 103
class,
    class enemy, 165–166
    ruling class, 156
    upper class, 161
    working class, 165
    working class family, 128
    working class women, 133, 167
colonial difference, 52
colonialism, 47, 49, 58, 209
coming out, 196, 198, 215–216
Committee for Household Economics, 62, 69
Comrade Courts, 103–104
Convention on the Elimination of all Forms of Discrimination Against Women (CEDAW), 56, 86, 89

D
decolonization, 8
decriminalization
    abortion, 43
    of homosexuality, 211, 220
development, 4, 49–50, 63, 71–74, 129, 173, 208, 228, 231
    development of LGBT rights activism, 207
    emotional development, 188

discrimination, 40, 70, 74, 88, 195, 198, 203, 206, 215, 225
discursive politics, 7, 14, 34, 42, 49, 51–52, 56, 64, 74–75, 85, 194, 199, 208–209, 215
displaced women, 14, 79, 125, 127, 136, 138–139, 142, 149
displacement, 13–14, 125–128, 136, 138–140, 142, 147–149, 227
domestic violence, 13, 53, 86, 95–98, 100–106, 110–121, 134, 166–167, 224
double burden, 68, 70, 75, 101, 143, 225
double oppression, 34
double shift, 67, 97
Duluth model, 111

E
Eisenstein, Sergei, 158
election system, 88, 90
Eliso, 162–165, 170
emigration, 181–182, 185–189, 191
    Reasons, 182–183
employment, 9, 40, 67, 80–81, 141, 175–176, 179, 181, 185–186, 225
    employment opportunities, 190–191
enfranchisement of women, 26
equal opportunities, 73, 174
equal rights, 27, 55–56, 86, 96–97, 99, 173
Eristavi-Jorjadze, Barbare, 10, 22–25, 30
Europe, 8, 40, 48–53, 57, 72, 208, 224
European Union (EU), 13, 218, 228

F
Fairbanks, Charles, 57–58
family, 34, 36, 42–43, 66–67, 98–105, 117–118, 130, 135, 141–145, 148, 150, 176, 188, 191
feminist scholars, 7, 65, 72, 127
feminist standpoint, 64, 127
Fernandez, Dominique, 158
Frederiksen, Martin Demant, 4–5

G
gender equality, 12, 21–22, 51– 56, 63, 71–72, 75, 85–89, 95–98, 100, 113, 120, 172–179, 228
gender roles, 7, 100, 113, 117, 138, 141, 150, 172, 189, 224–226
gender studies, 2–3, 7
Georgian films
    Georgian cinema, 155, 157
    Georgian futurists, 157

Georgian Orthodox Church, 2, 5–7, 16, 120, 216–219, 223, 230
Georgian State Cinema Production, 157
governance, 140, 148, 225
Gray, Richard, 164
Gvianishvili, Natia, 55

H
hegemony, 8–9, 47
herstories, 10, 22, 30
heterosexuality, 199
    heterosexual woman, 199
homophobia, 15, 58, 205, 213, 216–219
homosexuality, 209, 211, 217
housework, 37, 42, 101, 225
human rights, 12, 29, 48, 95, 172, 177, 208–209, 211, 217, 231
    human rights discourse, 52

I
identity, 6, 99, 139–140, 150, 184, 208, 210, 212, 226
    European identity, 51
    gender identity, 146–147, 196, 198–201, 216, 223, 230
    LGBT identity, 208
    masculine identity, 40
    nationalist identity, 6, 227
ideology, 54, 82, 98, 100, 211
    ideology and gender, 10, 33
IDMag, 215
Ignatova, Tamara, 156
Inclusive Foundation, 201, 205, 210–214
internally displaced, 14, 79, 125–127, 136, 138, 209
International Day against Homophobia and Transphobia, 15, 216–218. *See also* May 17
International Nongovernmental Organizations, 7–9, 111. *See also* Nongovernmental Organizations
intimate ethnography, 14, 127
Istanbul Convention, 114, 120
imperialism, 11, 47, 75, 209

K
Kabachnik, Peter, 126, 147
Kachkachishvili, Iago, 53
Kazbegi, Alexandre, 162
Kezeli, David, 28
Kolkhoz, 130–131
Kollontai, Alexandra, 36, 63, 65, 71

Kurdadze, Paata, 54

L
Ladaria, Konstantine, 6–7
lagging behind, 49, 51–52, 54
Law on Elimination of All Forms of Discrimination, 195. *See also* anti-discrimination legislation
League of Polish Women, 67
Lenin, 11, 34, 36–37, 42, 165
LGBT
    LGBT activist, 206, 210, 216, 218 (*see also* activism)
    LGBT community, 210
    LGBT Georgia, 216
    LGBT issues, 48, 194, 200–201, 206, 216
    LGBT movement, 15, 210
    LGBT organizations, 194, 205, 211, 213, 218
    LGBT persons, 198, 201,
    LGBT rights, 55, 57, 206–207, 214–216, 218–219, 224
liberal subjects, 5, 9
life story, 127, 129

M
Makashvili, Maro, 30
Manning, Paul, 3–5
Marx, Karl, 36, 40, 98–99
May 17, 15, 57, 216–217
Mayne, Judith, 159
ME, LGBT Magazine, 212, 214
media, 23, 34, 39, 52, 110, 120, 194, 196, 198–201, 216–217
migrants, 15, 172, 181–185, 187, 189, 190
migration experience, 182, 184, 186–191
Mikeladze, Kato, 10, 22, 28–30
Mill, John, Stuart, 26
modernization, 4, 6, 9, 48, 72, 211
Morozov, Pavlik, 159
mother, 26, 30, 43, 66, 119, 127–128, 131, 138, 144, 150, 157–161, 174–175, 186, 189, 199–201
    phallic mother, 159–160
    rejected mother, 160
motherhood, 33, 40, 42–43, 69–70
multiculturalism, 69, 133, 230
myth-making, 129

N
Nakashidze-Bolkvadze, Elisabed, 29
National Action Plan, 85–87, 113–114
national identity, 6, 226
nationalism, 6, 75, 79, 165, 209, 231
National Referral Mechanism, 113
NATO, 6, 47, 228, 231
neoliberalism, 229
    neoliberal development, 4
    neoliberal capitalist political economy, 9
    neoliberal economic policies, 211
    neoliberal enthusiasm, 5
    neoliberal lines, 227
    neoliberal modernity, 12
    neoliberal politics, 230
    neoliberal vision, 231
New Soviet Man, 156, 165
New Soviet Woman, 35, 39, 42, 155–157, 165, 167, 169–170
Nongovernmental Organizations (NGOs), 9, 51, 85–87, 102, 111, 113–116, 121, 140–141, 148, 194, 199, 209, 223

O
oedipal conflicts, 158–159. *See also* revolt against the father
Open Society Foundation, 8–9, 15
Open Society Institute, 8
oppression, 34, 73, 105, 167, 205
orientalized East, 157

P
Pankhurst, Emmeline, 29
Patriarch Ilia II, 217, 230
patriarchy, 9, 215
    patriarchal structures, 139
Peneff, Jean, 129
political parties, 13, 78, 80–85, 88–89
positionality, 11, 72, 75
Post-Soviet Georgia, 6, 11–12, 21, 48, 81, 194, 207, 209
power, 6, 8–10, 54, 73, 79, 81, 83, 99, 113, 138–139, 149, 163, 167, 170, 175–176, 211, 226
    power relations, 8, 110, 140
private
    realm, 99, 166, 172, 177
    sphere, 58, 102, 173, 173
prison cell, 158–161, 170
progress, 12–14, 35, 48, 50–51, 63, 71–72, 208
Proletarian men, 40

Proletarian women, 11, 34–35, 37, 39, 41, 134
Protective order, 112. *See also* restrictive order
public
    good, 157
    realm, 166–167, 169, 175
    sphere, 22, 36–38, 40, 42–43, 80, 99, 103, 141, 159, 167, 225, 229
Pudovkin, Vsevolod, 159

R
religious nationalism, 6
representations of women in film, 15, 155
restrictive order, 112
revolt against the father, 158–159. *See also* oedipal conflict
revolution, 42, 65, 67, 155, 158–159, 161
    Bolshevik revolution, 97
    cultural revolution, 165–166
    Rose Revolution, 4, 8, 79, 82, 210–211, 227
    Russian revolution, 63, 73
Russia, 8–10, 14, 22, 103, 130, 134, 157, 223, 230
    migration to Russia, 181, 183–184
    Russian empire, 22, 26, 51, 54–55, 208
Rylko–Bauer, Barbara, 127–128

S
Saakashvili, Mikheil, 4, 6, 218, 227–228
Saba, 165–170
Salukvadze Joseph, 5
Samegrelo, 130–131
Sangster, Joan, 133
Saqartvelos Qali, 100
sexual minorities, 48, 217–218
sexuality, 9, 15, 49, 57, 96, 170, 196, 201, 206–207, 210, 215, 219, 230
sexual orientation, 54, 210, 216, 230
Sherouse, Perry, 5
Shevardnadze, Eduard, 47
social networks, 141, 144, 149, 191
Sokhumi, 130, 135
Sologhashvili, Ana, 29
South Ossetia, 14, 125, 140–141, 223, 227
Soviet Union, 2, 8, 10, 34, 36–38, 41, 43, 50–51, 54–56, 65, 67, 70, 73, 78, 95–97, 100–102, 105, 141, 156–157, 181, 209
    Communist Party of the Soviet Union (CPSU), 41

Stalin, 39, 43, 97, 100, 165
    Stalinism, 11, 42
state, 6, 70, 80, 89, 97, 101, 103, 105, 148, 172, 208, 218, 226
    post–Soviet state, 7, 211, 215
    repressive state, 209
    socialist state, 34–35, 39, 41, 43
    Soviet state, 34, 38–39, 41, 43, 95, 97
    state socialism, 62–67, 70–76
    state violence, 14
Success Bar, 212
suffragists, 29
Svaneti, 130–131

T
Tabukashvili, Olgha, 163
Tarkhnishvili-Gabashvili, Ekaterine, 10, 26–27
Tbilisi (city), 2, 4–5, 10, 15, 25, 27, 57, 67–68, 110, 115, 165, 210, 212–213, 216–217
Tbilisi State University, 2–3, 7, 13, 61, 206
Terfarsegova-Makhviladze, Eleonora, 29
Toroshelidze, Minadora, 30
transgender
    activism, 196, 202
    community, 196, 201–202
    issues, 194, 200, 202–203
    men, 197, 203
    persons, 15, 194–195, 197–199, 202
    women, 196–200, 203, 206
Transgender Visibility Day, 216
transition, 7–8, 48–50, 79–80, 140, 146, 195, 197
trauma, 140, 147
    traumatic masculinities, 126
Tretyiakov, Sergei, 157, 162
Tsiskari, 23, 25

U
unemployment, 121, 126, 141, 172, 179, 198, 224
United Nations Conference,
    in Nairobi, 62
    in Beijing, 73
urban planning, 5

V
Vachnadze, Nato, 156
value(s), 51, 78, 102, 144, 178, 182, 184, 187–191, 218, 223–224
    traditional values, 217–218, 224, 230–231

Vashakidze, Ekvtime, 28
victim, 113, 115, 120, 200–201
violence, 13–15, 55, 57, 80, 86, 96, 98, 110, 112, 118, 148, 167–168, 195–196, 201, 218. *See* also domestic violence
   economic violence, 110
   emotional violence, 110
   gender–based violence, 55, 110, 114
   physical violence, 15, 110, 120, 195–196
   sexual violence, 76, 80, 110

W

war, 14, 71, 79, 97, 126, 129–130, 132, 135–136, 142, 145, 209–210, 229
   World War II, 66, 69
   War in Iraq, 47
Waterston, Alisse, 127–128
West, 2, 7, 10–12, 47–52, 54–58, 63, 71–72, 75, 208, 215, 218, 230
   as a norm, 49
Western orientation, 55, 57–58, 211, 214
woman question, 96–97

women's access to education, 25
women's Councils, 103
Women's Initiatives Supporting Group (WISG), 194, 196, 201–203, 213–215
Women's International Democratic Federation, 74
women's movement, 12, 29, 62–63, 71, 75
   postsocialist women's movement, 63
   transnational women's movement, 63, 75
women's political participation, 29, 84, 87, 90n2
women's political representation, 12, 82, 85, 88
women's rights, 9, 22, 51, 53, 55–56, 63–64, 72–75, 85, 95–96, 102–103, 105

Z

Zedania, Giga, 6, 51
Zhenotdel, 34, 38, 65, 102–103, 107n9
Zhensovety, 66

www.ingramcontent.com/pod-product-compliance
Lightning Source LLC
Chambersburg PA
CBHW070920030426
42336CB00014BA/2470